Companies Act (U.K.)

Recht-Wirtschaft-Steuern
www.salzwasserverlag.de

Bibliographische Information:
Die Deutsche Bibliothek verzeichnet diesen Titel in der Deutschen Nationalbibliografie. Bibliografische Daten sind unter http://dnb.ddb.de verfügbar.

Companies Act (U.K.)

Mit einer Einführung von Klaus Degenhardt

1. Auflage 2006

ISBN: 3-937686-49-5

Band 4 der Schriftenreihe: „Die Limited in Deutschland"

Band 1: Klaus Degenhardt, Die Limited in Deutschland (3-937686-43-6)
Band 2: John Cleary, Bilanzen und Steuern der Limited in Deutschland (3-937686-27-4)
Band 3: Janet Lührsen, GmbH oder Limited? (3-937686-35-5)

Druck und Herstellung: Hohnholt Reprografischer Betrieb GmbH, Bremen (www.hohnholt.com)

Dieser Titel unterliegt dem Gesetz zur Regelung der Preisbindung von Verlagserzeugnissen (BGBl. I Nr. 63 vom 5. September 2002)

Einführung

Die „Limited", oder, mit vollem Namen „private company limited by shares", ist in aller Munde. Seit der Europäische Gerichtshof in der „Inspire Art" - Entscheidung den Weg der Limited aus ihrem Heimatland hinein ins (gesellschaftsrechtlich) rückständige Kontinentaleuropa geebnet hat, erlebt diese Rechtsform auf dem Kontinent ihren Durchbruch. Leicht und schnell zu gründen, ohne Stammkapital, dennoch volle Haftungsbeschränkung gewährend - was soll man da noch mit einer altmodischen und teuren GmbH? Die Limited braucht - außer einem Briefkasten - auch keinen Sitz mehr im England zu unterhalten, was sie vollends als ein Schnäppchen erscheinen lässt.

Die Anzeigenteile der einschlägigen Journale sind denn auch voll mit Offerten von Dienstleistern, die eine Limited für wenige hundert Euro, fertig vorgegründet und innerhalb weniger Tage wunschgemäß verfügbar, anbieten. Die „England-GmbH", wie sie auch gerne (aber unzutreffend) genannt wird, biete nicht nur den gleichen Schutz wie die einheimische GmbH, sondern sei darüber hinaus auch wesentlich unkomplizierter in der täglichen Handhabung.

Dies ist, wenn überhaupt, nur die halbe Wahrheit. Sie suggeriert, die Limited werde nach ihrem Umzug nach Deutschland wie eine einheimische Gesellschaft geführt. Dem ist mitnichten so. Die Limited ist und bleibt eine englische Gesellschaft, deren innere Verfassung sich immer und überall auf der Welt zwingend ausschließlich nach englischem Recht richtet. Diese banale - und gänzlich unumstrittene - Erkenntnis wird freilich gerne verschwiegen. Denn ihre Konsequenzen sind weitreichend. Fragen zur Durchgriffshaftung, zu Geschäftsführerpflichten- und Rechten, zu Gewinnentnahmen, aber auch zu gerne verdrängten Dingen wie dem Insolvenzrecht richten sich nach englischem Recht und weichen zum Teil erheblich von dem ab, was wir in Deutschland kennen und worauf wir im täglichen Geschäftsleben zu achten trainiert sind.[1]

Und dass eine Limited immer auch zwingend in England nach englischem Recht bilanzieren und Steuererklärungen abzugeben hat, ist ein Umstand, der die auf den ersten Blick so preiswerte Limited rasch aufwendig erscheinen lässt, nämlich spätestens dann, wenn man für die regelmäßige Beauftragung des englischen Steuerberaters so hohe laufende Aufwendungen zu verbuchen hat, dass man eines Tages vielleicht neidvoll auf den Wettbewerber nebenan schaut, der den traditionellen Weg gegangen ist.

Doch es gibt auch Konstellationen, in denen sich der Einsatz einer Limited auf dem Kontinent lohnt. Frei nach dem Motto: zehntausende Geschäftsleute können sich nicht irren.... Und es gibt sie tatsächlich, die Fälle, in denen der Einsatz einer Limited sinnvoll ist. Zwar sind es nur wenige (ich schätze etwas boshaft, von den vielen gemeldeten Gründungen haben 95 % den Charakter von Eintagsfliegen), aber es gibt sie, und sie sind wirtschaftlich bedeutend. Etwa als Ersatz der ungeliebten Arbeitsgemeinschaft z.B. bei großen Bauvorhaben, für wirtschaftlich bedeutsame Projekte mit absehbarer Lebensdauer, für die Abwicklung von Geschäften mit überwiegendem Auslandsbezug.

Wer eine Limited nutzt, muss viel über sie wissen. Die Grundmuster, die wir im deutschen Geschäftsleben von der GmbH kennen, gelten nur zum Teil. Es gibt in wichtigen Punkten wesentliche Abweichungen. Ohne genaue Kenntnis der rechtlichen Rahmenbedingungen läuft man Gefahr, eine auf den ersten Blick zwar preiswerte, letztlich aber doch teure Lösung zu schaffen, wenn sich herausstellt, dass man etwa weniger als hierzulande möglich aus dem Unternehmen

---

[1] Grundlegend und ausführlich hierzu: Degenhardt, Die Limited in Deutschland, 4. Auflage, ISBN: 3-937686-43-6

entnehmen darf oder die Rechte der anderen Beteiligten ungewohnt groß sind.

Die innere Verfassung der Limited richtet sich im Wesentlichen nach dem Companies Act, der - vergleichbar mit dem deutschen GmbH-Gesetz - die Grundbedingungen regelt, unter denen die Limited gegründet und tätig werden kann. Daneben ist die Satzung der Limited, das sog. „Memorandum of Articles", von ausschlaggebender Bedeutung für die Regelung des Rechtsrahmens der Gesellschaft.[2]

Der Companies Act gliedert sich in 10 Teile und hat darüber hinaus 24 Anlagen.[3] Es handelt sich um ein Rahmengesetz, das wiederum eine Reihe anderer namentlich genannter Gesetze ändert, gleichwohl aber aus sich heraus im Zusammenhang verständlich ist.

Der *Teil 1* regelt die Buchführungsvorschriften für die Limited und ist damit von zentraler Bedeutung. Diese Vorschriften sind nicht abdingbar und gelten auch in vollem Umfang für die Limited in Deutschland. Die Buchführung muss dem Grundsatz der Wahrheit und Klarheit entsprechen, alle relevanten Unterlagen sind immer - auch nach dem Umzug der Gesellschaft nach Deutschland - in England aufzubewahren. Dazu bedient man sich in der Regel eines Domizilierungsservices, der freilich auch immer Kosten verursacht. Dort ist in der Regel auch der Companies Secretary angesiedelt, für dessen Stellung ebenfalls Kosten anfallen. Die Personalunion von Geschäftsführer und Companies Secretary ist unzulässig.

Teil 2 enthält Vorschriften für die Buch- und Rechnungsprüfung, deren Stringenz sich auch nach der Größe des Unternehmens richtet. Kleine Unternehmen (Definition: sec. 247 CA, verkürzt: Umsatz

---

[2] Erläutertes ausführliches Muster bei: Degenhardt, Die Limited in Deutschland (3-937686-43-6)

[3] Die Anlagen sind hier aus Platzgründen nicht abgedruckt und unter http://www.uk-companies-act-1989.co.uk verfügbar

bis 2 Mio. £ und bis zu 60 Arbeitnehmer) sind von etlichen Verpflichtungen befreit. Sondervorschriften gelten für die im Auslandsgeschäft wichtigen Mantelgesellschaften (sec. 250 CA).

London, im Januar 2006

Klaus Degenhardt

Companies Act U.K.

Part I: Company Accounts   14
    1.   Introduction   14

Provisions applying to companies generally   15
    2.   Accounting records   15
    3.   A company's financial year and accounting reference periods   17
    4.   Individual company accounts   19
    5.   Group accounts   20
    6.   Additional disclosure required in notes to accounts   24
    7.   Approval and signing of accounts   27
    8.   Directors' report   27
    9.   Auditors' report   29
    10.   Publication of accounts and reports   31
    11.   Laying and delivering of accounts and reports   33
    12.   Remedies for failure to comply with accounting requirements   37

Exemptions and special provisions   41
    13.   Small and medium-sized companies and groups   41
    14.   Dormant companies   45
    15.   Public listed companies: provision of summary financial statement   47
    16.   Private companies: election to dispense with laying of accounts and reports before general meeting   48
    17.   Unlimited companies: exemption from requirement to deliver accounts and reports   50
    18.   Banking and insurance companies and groups: special provisions   51

Supplementary provisions   54
    19.   Accounting standards   54
    20.   Power to alter accounting requirements   54
    21.   Parent and subsidiary undertakings   55
    22.   Other interpretation provisions   57

Consequential amendments   62
    23.   Consequential amendments   62

Part II: Eligibility for Appointment as Company Auditor   62
    24.   Introduction   62
    25.   Eligibility for appointment   63
    26.   Effect of appointment of partnership   63
    27.   Ineligibility on ground of lack of independence   63
    28.   Effect of ineligibility   64
    29.   Power of Secretary of State to require second audit   65

Recognition of supervisory bodies and professional qualifications   65
    30.   Supervisory bodies   65
    31.   Meaning of "appropriate qualification"   66
    32.   Qualifying bodies and recognised professional qualifications   67
    33.   Approval of overseas qualifications   68
    34.   Eligibility of individuals retaining only 1967 Act authorisation   69

Duties of recognised bodies   69
    35.   The register of auditors   69
    36.   Information about firms to be available to public   70
    37.   Matters to be notified to the Secretary of State   71
    38.   Power to call for information   71
    39.   Compliance orders   72

40.	Directions to comply with international obligations	72

Offences   **73**

41.	False and misleading statements	73
42.	Offences by bodies corporate, partnerships and unincorporated associations	73
43.	Time limits for prosecution of offences	74
44.	Jurisdiction and procedure in respect of offences	74

Supplementary provisions   **75**

45.	Fees	75
46.	Delegation of functions of Secretary of State	75
47.	Restrictive practices	76
48.	Exemption from liability for damages	77
49.	Service of notices	78
50.	Power to make consequential amendments	78
51.	Power to make provisions in consequence of changes affecting accountancy bodies	79
52.	Meaning of "associate"	80
53.	Minor definitions	80
54.	Index of defined expressions	81

Part III: Investigations and Powers to Obtain Information   **82**

55.	Investigations by inspectors not leading to published report	83
56.	Production of documents and evidence to inspectors	83
57.	Duty of inspectors to report	84
58.	Power to bring civil proceedings on the company's behalf	84
59.	Expenses of investigating a company's affairs	84
60.	Power of Secretary of State to present winding-up petition	85
61.	Inspectors' reports as evidence	86
62.	Investigation of company ownership	86
63.	Secretary of State's power to require production of documents	87
64.	Entry and search of premises	87
65.	Provision for security of information obtained	90
66.	Punishment for destroying, mutilating, &c. company documents	92
67.	Punishment for furnishing false information	93
68.	Disclosure of information by Secretary of State or inspector	93
69.	Protection of banking information	94
70.	Investigation of oversea companies	95
71.	Investigation of unregistered companies	95

Amendments of the Financial Services Act 1986   **95**

72.	Investigations into collective investment schemes	95
73.	Investigations into affairs of persons carrying on investment business	97
74.	Investigations into insider dealing	98
75.	Restrictions on disclosure of information	99
76.	Entry and search of premises	100

Amendments of other enactments   **102**

77.	Amendments of the Insurance Companies Act 1982	102
78.	Amendment of the Insolvency Act 1986	104
79.	Amendment of the Company Directors Disqualification Act 1986	104
80.	Amendment of the Building Societies Act 1986	104
81.	Amendments of the Banking Act 1987	104

Powers exercisable to assist overseas regulatory authorities   **105**

82.	Request for assistance by overseas regulatory authorities	105
83.	Power to require information, documents or other assistance	107
84.	Exercise of powers by officer, &c	107

85.	Penalty for failure to comply with requirement, &c	108
86.	Restrictions on disclosure of information	109
87.	Exceptions from restrictions on disclosure	109
88.	Exercise of powers in relation to Northern Ireland	112
89.	Prosecutions	113
90.	Offences by bodies corporate, partnerships and unincorporated associations	113
91.	Jurisdiction and procedure in respect of offences	114

Part IV: Registration of Company Charges   **114**

92.	Introduction	114

Registration in the companies charges register   **115**

93.	Charges requiring registration	115
94.	The companies charges register	117
95.	Delivery of particulars for registration	118
96.	Delivery of further particulars	120
97.	Effect of omissions and errors in registered particulars	120
98.	Memorandum of charge ceasing to affect company's property	121
99.	"Further provisions with respect to voidness of charges	122
100.	"Additional information to be registered	124

Copies of instruments and register to be kept by company   **126**

101.	Copies of instruments and register to be kept by company	126

Supplementary provisions   **127**

102.	Power to make further provision by regulations	127
103.	Other supplementary provisions	128
104.	Interpretation, &c	130
105.	Charges on property of oversea company	132
106.	Application of provisions to unregistered companies	132
107.	Consequential amendments	133

Part V: Other amendments of Company Law   **133**

108.	A company's capacity and the power of the directors to bind it	133
109.	Invalidity of certain transactions involving directors	136
110.	Statement of company's objects	138
111.	Charitable companies	138
112.	Charitable companies (Scotland)	141

De-regulation of private companies   **142**

113.	Written resolutions of private companies	142
114.	Written resolutions: supplementary provisions	145
115.	Election by private company to dispense with certain requirements	148
116.	Elective Resolution of private company	149
117.	Power to make further provision by regulations	151

Appointment and removal of auditors and related matters   **151**

118.	Introduction	151
119.	Appointment of auditors	151
120.	Rights of auditors	155
121.	Remuneration of auditors	158
122.	Removal, resignation, &c. of auditors	159
123.	Statement by person ceasing to hold office as auditor	163
124.	Auditors of trade unions and employers' associations	166
125.	Delivery of documents to the registrar	166
126.	Keeping and inspection of company records	168
127.	Supplementary provisions as to company records and related matters	170

Miscellaneous   **171**

128.	Form of articles for partnership company	171
129.	Membership of holding company	171
130.	Company contracts and execution of documents by companies	173
131.	Members' rights to damages, &c	176
132.	Financial assistance for purposes of employees' share scheme	176
133.	Issue of redeemable shares	176
134.	Disclosure of interests in shares	177
135.	Orders imposing restrictions on shares	179
136.	A company's registered office	179
137.	Effecting of insurance for officers and auditors of company	180
138.	Increase of limits on certain exemptions	181
139.	Annual returns	181
140.	Floating charges (Scotland)	186
141.	Application to declare dissolution of company void	187
142.	Abolition of doctrine of deemed notice	188
143.	Rights of inspection and related matters	188
144.	"Subsidiary", "holding company" and "wholly-owned subsidiary"	191
145.	Minor amendments	194

Part VI: Mergers and Related Matters   194

146.	Restriction on references where prior notice given	194
147.	Undertakings as alternative to merger reference	200
148.	Enforcement of undertakings	203
149.	Temporary restrictions on share dealings	204
150.	Obtaining control by stages	206
151.	False or misleading information	207
152.	Fees	208
153.	Other amendments about mergers and related matters	210

Part VII: Financial Markets and Insolvency   210

154.	Introduction	210

Recognised investment exchanges and clearing houses   211

155.	Market contracts	211
156.	Additional requirements for recognition: default rules, &c	211
157.	Changes in default rules	212
158.	Modifications of the law of insolvency	212
159.	Proceedings of exchange or clearing house take precedence over insolvency procedures	213
160.	Duty to give assistance for purposes of default proceedings	214
161.	Supplementary provisions as to default proceedings	215
162.	Duty to report on completion of default proceedings	215
163.	Net sum payable on completion of default proceedings	216
164.	Disclaimer of property, rescission of contracts, &c	217
165.	Adjustment of prior transactions	218
166.	Powers of Secretary of State to give directions	219
167.	Application to determine whether default proceedings to be taken	220
168.	Delegation of functions to designated agency	221
169.	Supplementary provisions	222

Other exchanges and clearing houses   222

170.	Certain overseas exchanges and clearing houses	222
171.	Certain money market institutions	223
172.	Settlement arrangements provided by the Bank of England	224

Market charges   225

173.	Market charges	225
174.	Modifications of the law of insolvency	225

175.	Administration orders, &c	226
176.	Power to make provision about certain other charges	227

Market property — **228**

177.	Application of margin not affected by certain other interests	228
178.	Priority of floating market charge over subsequent charges	228
179.	Priority of market charge over unpaid vendor's lien	229
180.	Proceedings against market property by unsecured creditors	229
181.	Power to apply provisions to other cases	229

Supplementary provisions — **230**

182.	Powers of court in relation to certain proceedings begun before commencement	230
183.	Insolvency proceedings in other jurisdictions	231
184.	Indemnity for certain acts, &c	232
185.	Power to make further provision by regulations	233
186.	Supplementary provisions as to regulations	233
187.	Construction of references to parties to market contracts	233
188.	Meaning of "default rules" and related expressions	233
189.	Meaning of "relevant office-holder"	234
190.	Minor definitions	234
191.	Index of defined expressions	235

Part VIII: Amendments of the Financial Services Act 1986 — **237**

192.	Statements of principle	237
193.	Restriction of right to bring action for contravention of rules, regulations, &c.	239
194.	Application of designated rules and regulations to members of self-regulating organisations	239
195.	Codes of practice	241
196.	Relations with other regulatory authorities	242
197.	Construction of references to incurring civil liability	244
198.	Offers of unlisted securities	245
199.	Offers of securities by private companies and old public companies	246
200.	Jurisdiction of High Court and Court of Session	247
201.	Directions to secure compliance with international obligations	247
202.	Offers of short-dated debentures	248
203.	Standard of protection for investors	249
204.	Costs of compliance	249
205.	Requirements for recognition of investment exchange	251
206.	Consequential amendments and delegation of functions on commencement	251

Part IX: Transfer of Securities — **252**

207.	Transfer of Securities	252

Part X: Miscellaneous and General Provisions — **254**

Miscellaneous — **254**

208.	Summary proceedings in Scotland for offences in connection with disqualification of directors	254
209.	Prosecutions in connection with insider dealing	254
210.	Restriction of duty to supply statements of premium income	254
211.	Building societies: miscellaneous amendments	255

General Provisions — **256**

212.	Repeals	256
213.	Provisions extending to Northern Ireland	256
214.	Making of corresponding provision for Northern Ireland	257
215.	Commencement and transitional provisions	258
216.	Short title	258

Companies Act[4]

Act to amend the law relating to company accounts; to make new provision with respect to the persons eligible for appointment as company auditors; to amend the Companies Act 1985 and certain other enactments with respect to investigations and powers to obtain information and to confer new powers exercisable to assist overseas regulatory authorities; to make new provision with respect to the registration of company charges and otherwise to amend the law relating to companies; to amend the Fair Trading Act 1973; to enable provision to be made for the payment of fees in connection with the exercise by the Secretary of State, the Director General of Fair Trading and the Monopolies and Mergers Commission of their functions under Part V of that Act; to make provision for safeguarding the operation of certain financial markets; to amend the Financial Services Act 1986; to enable provision to be made for the recording and transfer of title to securities without a written instrument; to amend the Company Directors Disqualification Act 1986, the Company Securities (Insider Dealing) Act 1985, the Policyholders Protection Act 1975 and the law relating to building societies; and for connected purposes.

[16th November 1989]

BE IT ENACTED by the Queen's most Excellent Majesty, by and with the advice and consent of the Lords Spiritual and Temporal, and Commons, in this present Parliament assembled, and by the authority of the same, as follows:—

Part I: Company Accounts

1. **Introduction**

   1. The provisions of this Part amend Part VII of the [1985 c. 6.] Companies Act 1985 (accounts and audit) by—

   (a) inserting new provisions in place of sections 221 to 262 of that Act, and

   (b) amending or replacing Schedules 4 to 10 to that Act and inserting new Schedules.

---

[4] crown copyright 1989

Provisions applying to companies generally

2. Accounting records

The following sections are inserted in Part VII of the [1985 c. 6.] Companies Act 1985 at the beginning of Chapter I (provisions applying to companies generally)—

"Accounting records

Duty to keep accounting records.

221.—(1) Every company shall keep accounting records which are sufficient to show and explain the company's transactions and are such as to—

    (a) disclose with reasonable accuracy, at any time, the financial position of the company at that time, and

    (b) enable the directors to ensure that any balance sheet and profit and loss account prepared under this Part complies with the requirements of this Act.

(2) The accounting records shall in particular contain—

    (a) entries from day to day of all sums of money received and expended by the company, and the matters in respect of which the receipt and expenditure takes place, and

    (b) a record of the assets and liabilities of the company.

(3) If the company's business involves dealing in goods, the accounting records shall contain—

    (a) statements of stock held by the company at the end of each financial year of the company,

    (b) all statements of stocktakings from which any such statement of stock as is mentioned in paragraph (a) has been or is to be prepared, and

    (c) except in the case of goods sold by way of ordinary retail trade, statements of all goods sold and purchased, showing the goods and the buyers and sellers in sufficient detail to enable all these to be identified.

(4) A parent company which has a subsidiary undertaking in relation to which the above requirements do not apply shall take reasonable steps to secure that the undertaking keeps such accounting records as to enable the directors of the parent company to ensure that any balance sheet and profit and loss account prepared under this Part complies with the requirements of this Act.

(5) If a company fails to comply with any provision of this section, every officer of the company who is in default is guilty of an offence unless he shows that he acted honestly and that in the circumstances in which the company's business was carried on the default was excusable.

(6) A person guilty of an offence under this section is liable to imprisonment or a fine, or both.

Where and for how long records to be kept.

222.—(1) A company's accounting records shall be kept at its registered office or such other place as the directors think fit, and shall at all times be open to inspection by the company's officers.

(2) If accounting records are kept at a place outside Great Britain, accounts and returns with respect to the business dealt with in the accounting records so kept shall be sent to, and kept at, a place in Great Britain, and shall at all times be open to such inspection.

(3) The accounts and returns to be sent to Great Britain shall be such as to—

    (a) disclose with reasonable accuracy the financial position of the business in question at intervals of not more than six months, and

    (b) enable the directors to ensure that the company's balance sheet and profit and loss account comply with the requirements of this Act.

(4) If a company fails to comply with any provision of subsections (1) to (3), every officer of the company who is in default is guilty of an offence, and liable to imprisonment or a fine or both, unless he shows that he acted honestly and that in the circumstances in which the company's business was carried on the default was excusable.

(5) Accounting records which a company is required by section 221 to keep shall be preserved by it—

    (a) in the case of a private company, for three years from the date on which they are made, and

    (b) in the case of a public company, for six years from the date on which they are made.

This is subject to any provision contained in rules made under section 411 of the Insolvency Act 1986 (company insolvency rules).

(6) An officer of a company is guilty of an offence, and liable to imprisonment or a fine or both, if he fails to take all reasonable steps for securing compliance by the company with subsection (5) or intentionally causes any default by the company under that subsection."

3. **A company's financial year and accounting reference periods**

The following sections are inserted in Part VII of the [1985 c. 66.] Companies Act 1985—

"A company's financial year and accounting reference periodsA company's financial year.

A company's financial year and accounting reference periods

223.—(1) A company's "financial year" is determined as follows.

(2) Its first financial year begins with the first day of its first accounting reference period and ends with the last day of that period or such other date, not more than seven days before or after the end of that period, as the directors may determine.

(3) Subsequent financial years begin with the day immediately following the end of the company's previous financial year and end with the last day of its next accounting reference period or such other date, not more than seven days before or after the end of that period, as the directors may determine.

(4) In relation to an undertaking which is not a company, references in this Act to its financial year are to any period in respect of which a profit and loss account of the undertaking is required to be made up (by its constitution or by the law under which it is established), whether that period is a year or not.

(5) The directors of a parent company shall secure that, except where in their opinion there are good reasons against it, the financial year of each of its subsidiary undertakings coincides with the company's own financial year.

Accounting reference periods and accounting reference date.

224.—(1) A company's accounting reference periods are determined according to its accounting reference date.

(2) A company may, at any time before the end of the period of nine months beginning with the date of its incorporation, by notice in the prescribed form given to the registrar specify its accounting reference date, that is, the date on which its accounting reference period ends in each calendar year.

(3) Failing such notice, a company's accounting reference date is—

(a) in the case of a company incorporated before the commencement of section 3 of the Companies Act 1989, 31st March;

(b) in the case of a company incorporated after the commencement of that section, the last day of the month in which the anniversary of its incorporation falls.

(4) A company's first accounting reference period is the period of more than six months, but not more than 18 months, beginning with the date of its incorporation and ending with its accounting reference date.

(5) Its subsequent accounting reference periods are successive periods of twelve months beginning immediately after the end of the previous accounting reference period and ending with its accounting reference date.

(6) This section has effect subject to the provisions of section 225 relating to the alteration of accounting reference dates and the consequences of such alteration.

Alteration of accounting reference date.

225.—(1) A company may by notice in the prescribed form given to the registrar specify a new accounting reference date having effect in relation to the company's current accounting reference period and subsequent periods.

(2) A company may by notice in the prescribed form given to the registrar specify a new accounting reference date having effect in relation to the company's previous accounting reference period and subsequent periods if—

> (a) the company is a subsidiary undertaking or parent undertaking of another company and the new accounting reference date coincides with the accounting reference date of that other company, or
>
> (b) an administration order under Part II of the Insolvency Act 1986 is in force.

A company's "previous accounting reference period" means that immediately preceding its current accounting reference period.

(3) The notice shall state whether the current or previous accounting reference period—

> (a) is to be shortened, so as to come to an end on the first occasion on which the new accounting reference date falls or fell after the beginning of the period, or
>
> (b) is to be extended, so as to come to an end on the second occasion on which that date falls or fell after the beginning of the period.

(4) A notice under subsection (1) stating that the current accounting reference period is to be extended is ineffective, except as mentioned below, if given less than five years after the end of an earlier accounting reference period of the company which was extended by virtue of this section.

This subsection does not apply—

> (a) to a notice given by a company which is a subsidiary undertaking or parent undertaking of another company and the new accounting reference date coincides with that of the other company, or

> (b) where an administration order is in force under Part II of the Insolvency Act 1986,

or where the Secretary of State directs that it should not apply, which he may do with respect to a notice which has been given or which may be given.

(5) A notice under subsection (2)(a) may not be given if the period allowed for laying and delivering accounts and reports in relation to the previous accounting reference period has already expired.

(6) An accounting reference period may not in any case, unless an administration order is in force under Part II of the Insolvency Act 1986, be extended so as to exceed 18 months and a notice under this section is ineffective if the current or previous accounting reference period as extended in accordance with the notice would exceed that limit."

4. Individual company accounts

—(1) The following section is inserted in Part VII of the [1985 c. 6.] Companies Act 1985—

Individual company accounts.

„Annual accounts

Duty to prepare individual company accounts.

226.—(1) The directors of every company shall prepare for each financial year of the company—

> (a) a balance sheet as at the last day of the year, and

> (b) a profit and loss account.

> Those accounts are referred to in this Part as the company's "individual accounts".

(2) The balance sheet shall give a true and fair view of the state of affairs of the company as at the end of the financial year; and the profit and loss account shall give a true and fair view of the profit or loss of the company for the financial year.

(3) A company's individual accounts shall comply with the provisions of Schedule 4 as to the form and content of the balance sheet and profit and loss account and additional information to be provided by way of notes to the

accounts.

(4) Where compliance with the provisions of that Schedule, and the other provisions of this Act as to the matters to be included in a company's individual accounts or in notes to those accounts, would not be sufficient to give a true and fair view, the necessary additional information shall be given in the accounts or in a note to them.

(5) If in special circumstances compliance with any of those provisions is inconsistent with the requirement to give a true and fair view, the directors shall depart from that provision to the extent necessary to give a true and fair view.

Particulars of any such departure, the reasons for it and its effect shall be given in a note to the accounts.
"

(2) Schedule 4 to the [1978 c. 30.] Companies Act 1985 (form and content of company accounts) is amended in accordance with Schedule 1 to this Act.

5. Group accounts

—(1) The following section is inserted in Part VII of the [1986 c. 45.] Companies Act 1985—

"Duty to prepare group accounts.

Group accounts

227.—(1) If at the end of a financial year a company is a parent company the directors shall, as well as preparing individual accounts for the year, prepare group accounts.

(2) Group accounts shall be consolidated accounts comprising—

(a) a consolidated balance sheet dealing with the state of affairs of the parent company and its subsidiary undertakings, and

(b) a consolidated profit and loss account dealing with the profit or loss of the parent company and its subsidiary undertakings.

(3) The accounts shall give a true and fair view of the state of affairs as at the end of the financial year, and the profit or loss for the financial year, of the undertakings included in the consolidation as a whole, so far as concerns members of the company.

(4) A company's group accounts shall comply with the provisions of Schedule 4A as to the form and content of the consolidated balance sheet and consolidated profit and loss account and additional information to be provided by way of notes to the accounts.

(5) Where compliance with the provisions of that Schedule, and the other provisions of this Act, as to the matters to be included in a company's group accounts or in notes to those accounts, would not be sufficient to give a true and fair view, the necessary additional information shall be given in the accounts or in a note to them.

(6) If in special circumstances compliance with any of those provisions is inconsistent with the requirement to give a true and fair view, the directors shall depart from that provision to the extent necessary to give a true and fair view.

Particulars of any such departure, the reasons for it and its effect shall be given in a note to the accounts.

(2) Schedule 2 to this Act (form and content of group accounts) is inserted after Schedule 4 to the [1985 c. 6.] Companies Act 1985, as Schedule 4A.

(3) The following sections are inserted in Part VII of the [1985 c. 6.] Companies Act 1985—

"Exemption for parent companies included in accounts of larger group.

228.—(1) A company is exempt from the requirement to prepare group accounts if it is itself a subsidiary undertaking and its immediate parent undertaking is established under the law of a member State of the European Economic Community, in the following cases—

    (a) where the company is a wholly-owned subsidiary of that parent undertaking;

    (b) where that parent undertaking holds more than 50 per cent. of the shares in the company and notice requesting the preparation of group accounts has not been served on the company by shareholders holding in aggregate—

        (i) more than half of the remaining shares in the company, or

        (ii) 5 per cent. of the total shares in the company.

Such notice must be served not later than six months after the end of the financial year before that to which it relates.

(2) Exemption is conditional upon compliance with all of the following conditions—

    (a) that the company is included in consolidated accounts for a larger group drawn up to the same date, or to an earlier date in the same financial year, by a parent undertaking established under the law of a member State of the European Economic Community;

(b) that those accounts are drawn up and audited, and that parent undertaking's annual report is drawn up, according to that law, in accordance with the provisions of the Seventh Directive (83/349/EEC);

(c) that the company discloses in its individual accounts that it is exempt from the obligation to prepare and deliver group accounts;

(d) that the company states in its individual accounts the name of the parent undertaking which draws up the group accounts referred to above and—

(i) if it is incorporated outside Great Britain, the country in which it is incorporated,

(ii) if it is incorporated in Great Britain, whether it is registered in England and Wales or in Scotland, and

(iii) if it is unincorporated, the address of its principal place of business;

(e) that the company delivers to the registrar, within the period allowed for delivering its individual accounts, copies of those group accounts and of the parent undertaking's annual report, together with the auditors' report on them; and

(f) that if any document comprised in accounts and reports delivered in accordance with paragraph (e) is in a language other than English, there is annexed to the copy of that document delivered a translation of it into English, certified in the prescribed manner to be a correct translation.

(3) The exemption does not apply to a company any of whose securities are listed on a stock exchange in any member State of the European Economic Community.

(4) Shares held by directors of a company for the purpose of complying with any share qualification requirement shall be disregarded in determining for the purposes of subsection (1)(a) whether the company is a wholly-owned subsidiary.

(5) For the purposes of subsection (1)(b) shares held by a wholly-owned subsidiary of the parent undertaking, or held on behalf of the parent undertaking or a wholly-owned subsidiary, shall be attributed to the parent undertaking.

(6) In subsection (3) "securities" includes—

(a) shares and stock,

(b) debentures, including debenture stock, loan stock, bonds, certificates of deposit and other instruments creating or acknowledging indebtedness,

(c) warrants or other instruments entitling the holder to subscribe for securities falling within paragraph (a) or (b), and

(d) certificates or other instruments which confer—

    (i) property rights in respect of a security falling within paragraph (a), (b) or (c),

    (ii) any right to acquire, dispose of, underwrite or convert a security, being a right to which the holder would be entitled if he held any such security to which the certificate or other instrument relates, or

    (iii) a contractual right (other than an option) to acquire any such security otherwise than by subscription.

Subsidiary undertakings included in the consolidation.

229.—(1) Subject to the exceptions authorised or required by this section, all the subsidiary undertakings of the parent company shall be included in the consolidation.

(2) A subsidiary undertaking may be excluded from consolidation if its inclusion is not material for the purpose of giving a true and fair view; but two or more undertakings may be excluded only if they are not material taken together.

(3) In addition, a subsidiary undertaking may be excluded from consolidation where—

(a) severe long-term restrictions substantially hinder the exercise of the rights of the parent company over the assets or management of that undertaking, or

(b) the information necessary for the preparation of group accounts cannot be obtained without disproportionate expense or undue delay, or

(c) the interest of the parent company is held exclusively with a view to subsequent resale and the undertaking has not previously been included in consolidated group accounts prepared by the parent company.

The reference in paragraph (a) to the rights of the parent company and the reference in paragraph (c) to the interest of the parent company are, respectively, to rights and interests held by or attributed to the company for the purposes of section 258 (definition of "parent undertaking") in the absence of which it would not be the parent company.

(4) Where the activities of one or more subsidiary undertakings are so different from those of other undertakings to be included in the consolidation that their inclusion would be incompatible with the obligation to give a true and fair view, those undertakings shall be excluded from consolidation.

This subsection does not apply merely because some of the undertakings are industrial, some commercial and some provide services, or because they carry on industrial or commercial activities involving different products or provide different services.

(5) Where all the subsidiary undertakings of a parent company fall within the above exclusions, no group accounts are required."

(4) The following section is inserted in Part VII of the [1985 c. 6.] Companies Act 1985—

"Treatment of individual profit and loss account where group accounts prepared.

230.—(1) The following provisions apply with respect to the individual profit and loss account of a parent company where—

(a) the company is required to prepare and does prepare group accounts in accordance with this Act, and

(b) the notes to the company's individual balance sheet show the company's profit or loss for the financial year determined in accordance with this Act.

(2) The profit and loss account need not contain the information specified in paragraphs 52 to 57 of Schedule 4 (information supplementing the profit and loss account).

(3) The profit and loss account must be approved in accordance with section 233(1) (approval by board of directors) but may be omitted from the company's annual accounts for the purposes of the other provisions below in this Chapter.

(4) The exemption conferred by this section is conditional upon its being disclosed in the company's annual accounts that the exemption applies."

6. Additional disclosure required in notes to accounts

—(1) The following section is inserted in Part VII of the [1985 c. 6.] Companies Act 1985—

"Disclosure required in

Additional disclosure required in notes to accounts

notes to accounts: related undertakings.

231.—(1) The information specified in Schedule 5 shall be given in notes to a company's annual accounts.

(2) Where the company is not required to prepare group accounts, the information specified in Part I of that Schedule shall be given; and where the company is required to prepare group accounts, the information specified in Part II of that Schedule shall be given.

(3) The information required by Schedule 5 need not be disclosed with respect to an undertaking which—

> (a) is established under the law of a country outside the United Kingdom, or
>
> (b) carries on business outside the United Kingdom,

if in the opinion of the directors of the company the disclosure would be seriously prejudicial to the business of that undertaking, or to the business of the company or any of its subsidiary undertakings, and the Secretary of State agrees that the information need not be disclosed.

This subsection does not apply in relation to the information required under paragraph 5(2), 6 or 20 of that Schedule.

(4) Where advantage is taken of subsection (3), that fact shall be stated in a note to the company's annual accounts.

(5) If the directors of the company are of the opinion that the number of undertakings in respect of which the company is required to disclose information under any provision of Schedule 5 to this Act is such that compliance with that provision would result in information of excessive length being given, the information need only be given in respect of—

> (a) the undertakings whose results or financial position, in the opinion of the directors, principally affected the figures shown in the company's annual accounts, and
>
> (b) undertakings excluded from consolidation under section 229(3) or (4).

This subsection does not apply in relation to the information required under paragraph 10 or 29 of that Schedule.

(6) If advantage is taken of subsection (5)—

> (a) there shall be included in the notes to the company's annual accounts a statement that the information is given only with respect to

such undertakings as are mentioned in that subsection, and

(b) the full information (both that which is disclosed in the notes to the accounts and that which is not) shall be annexed to the company's next annual return.

For this purpose the "next annual return" means that next delivered to the registrar after the accounts in question have been approved under section 233.

(7) If a company fails to comply with subsection (6)(b), the company and every officer of it who is in default is liable to a fine and, for continued contravention, to a daily default fine."

(2) Schedule 3 to this Act (disclosure of information: related undertakings) is substituted for Schedule 5 to the [1985 c. 6.] Companies Act 1985.

(3) The following section is inserted in Part VII of the [1985 c. 6.] Companies Act 1985—

"Disclosure required in notes to accounts: emoluments and other benefits of directors and others.

232.—(1) The information specified in Schedule 6 shall be given in notes to a company's annual accounts.

(2) In that Schedule—

Part I relates to the emoluments of directors (including emoluments waived), pensions of directors and past directors, compensation for loss of office to directors and past directors and sums paid to third parties in respect of directors' services,

Part II relates to loans, quasi-loans and other dealings in favour of directors and connected persons, and

Part III relates to transactions, arrangements and agreements made by the company or a subsidiary undertaking for officers of the company other than directors.

(3) It is the duty of any director of a company, and any person who is or has at any time in the preceding five years been an officer of the company, to give notice to the company of such matters relating to himself as may be necessary for the purposes of Part I of Schedule 6.

(4) A person who makes default in complying with subsection (3) commits an offence and is liable to a fine."

(4) Schedule 6 to the [1985 c. 6.] Companies Act 1985 is amended in accordance with Schedule 4 to this Act.

7. Approval and signing of accounts

The following section is inserted in Part VII of the [1985 c. 6.] Companies Act 1985—

"Approval and signing of accounts

Approval and signing of accounts.

233.—(1) A company's annual accounts shall be approved by the board of directors and signed on behalf of the board by a director of the company.

(2) The signature shall be on the company's balance sheet.

(3) Every copy of the balance sheet which is laid before the company in general meeting, or which is otherwise circulated, published or issued, shall state the name of the person who signed the balance sheet on behalf of the board.

(4) The copy of the company's balance sheet which is delivered to the registrar shall be signed on behalf of the board by a director of the company.

(5) If annual accounts are approved which do not comply with the requirements of this Act, every director of the company who is party to their approval and who knows that they do not comply or is reckless as to whether they comply is guilty of an offence and liable to a fine.

For this purpose every director of the company at the time the accounts are approved shall be taken to be a party to their approval unless he shows that he took all reasonable steps to prevent their being approved.

(6) If a copy of the balance sheet—

(a) is laid before the company, or otherwise circulated, published or issued, without the balance sheet having been signed as required by this section or without the required statement of the signatory's name being included, or

(b) is delivered to the registrar without being signed as required by this section,

the company and every officer of it who is in default is guilty of an offence and liable to a fine."

8. Directors' report

—(1) The following sections are inserted in Part VII of the [1985 c. 6.] Companies Act 1985—

"Directors' report

Duty to prepare

234.—(1) The directors of a company shall for each financial year prepare a directors' report. report—

(a) containing a fair review of the development of the business of the company and its subsidiary undertakings during the financial year and of their position at the end of it, and

(b) stating the amount (if any) which they recommend should be paid as dividend and the amount (if any) which they propose to carry to reserves.

(2) The report shall state the names of the persons who, at any time during the financial year, were directors of the company, and the principal activities of the company and its subsidiary undertakings in the course of the year and any significant change in those activities in the year.

(3) The report shall also comply with Schedule 7 as regards the disclosure of the matters mentioned there.

(4) In Schedule 7—

Part I relates to matters of a general nature, including changes in asset values, directors' shareholdings and other interests and contributions for political and charitable purposes,

Part II relates to the acquisition by a company of its own shares or a charge on them,

Part III relates to the employment, training and advancement of disabled persons,

Part IV relates to the health, safety and welfare at work of the company's employees, and

Part V relates to the involvement of employees in the affairs, policy and performance of the company.

(5) In the case of any failure to comply with the provisions of this Part as to the preparation of a directors' report and the contents of the report, every person who was a director of the company immediately before the end of the period for laying and delivering accounts and reports for the financial year in question is guilty of an offence and liable to a fine.

(6) In proceedings against a person for an offence under this section it is a defence for him to prove that he took all reasonable steps for securing compliance with the requirements in question.

Approval and signing of directors' report.

234A.—(1) The directors' report shall be approved by the board of directors and signed on behalf of the board by a director or the secretary of the company.

(2) Every copy of the directors' report which is laid before the company in general meeting, or which is otherwise circulated, published or issued, shall state the name of the person who signed it on behalf of the board.

(3) The copy of the directors' report which is delivered to the registrar shall be signed on behalf of the board by a director or the secretary of the company.

(4) If a copy of the directors' report—

    (a) is laid before the company, or otherwise circulated, published or issued, without the report having been signed as required by this section or without the required statement of the signatory's name being included, or

    (b) is delivered to the registrar without being signed as required by this section,

the company and every officer of it who is in default is guilty of an offence and liable to a fine."

(2) Schedule 7 to the [1985 c. 6.] Companies Act 1985 (matters to be included in directors' report) is amended in accordance with Schedule 5 to this Act.

9. Auditors' report

The following sections are inserted in Part VII of the [1985 c. 6.] Companies Act 1985—

"Auditors' report

Auditors' report. **235.**—(1) A company's auditors shall make a report to the company's members on all annual accounts of the company of which copies are to be laid before the company in general meeting during their tenure of office.

(2) The auditors' report shall state whether in the auditors' opinion the annual accounts have been properly prepared in accordance with this Act, and in particular whether a true and fair view is given—

    (a) in the case of an individual balance sheet, of the state of affairs of the company as at the end of the financial year,

    (b) in the case of an individual profit and loss account, of the profit or loss of the company for the financial year,

    (c) in the case of group accounts, of the state of affairs as at the end of the financial year, and the profit or loss for the financial year, of the undertakings included in the consolidation as a whole, so far as concerns members of the company.

(3) The auditors shall consider whether the information given in the directors' report for the financial year for which the annual accounts are prepared is consistent with those accounts; and if they are of opinion that it is not they shall state that fact in their report.

Signature of auditors' report.	**236.**—(1) The auditors' report shall state the names of the auditors and be signed by them.

(2) Every copy of the auditors' report which is laid before the company in general meeting, or which is otherwise circulated, published or issued, shall state the names of the auditors.

(3) The copy of the auditors' report which is delivered to the registrar shall state the names of the auditors and be signed by them.

(4) If a copy of the auditors' report—

(a) is laid before the company, or otherwise circulated, published or issued, without the required statement of the auditors' names, or

(b) is delivered to the registrar without the required statement of the auditors' names or without being signed as required by this section,

the company and every officer of it who is in default is guilty of an offence and liable to a fine.

(5) References in this section to signature by the auditors are, where the office of auditor is held by a body corporate or partnership, to signature in the name of the body corporate or partnership by a person authorised to sign on its behalf.

Duties of auditors.	**237.**—(1) A company's auditors shall, in preparing their report, carry out such investigations as will enable them to form an opinion as to—

(a) whether proper accounting records have been kept by the company and proper returns adequate for their audit have been received from branches not visited by them, and

(b) whether the company's individual accounts are in agreement with the accounting records and returns.

(2) If the auditors are of opinion that proper accounting records have not been kept, or that proper returns adequate for their audit have not been received from branches not visited by them, or if the company's individual accounts are not in agreement with the accounting records and returns, the auditors shall state that fact in their report.

(3) If the auditors fail to obtain all the information and explanations which, to the best of their knowledge and belief, are necessary for the purposes of their audit, they shall state that fact in their report.

(4) If the requirements of Schedule 6 (disclosure of information: emoluments and other benefits of directors and others) are not complied with in the annual accounts, the auditors shall include in their report, so far as they are reasonably able to do so, a statement giving the required particulars."

10. Publication of accounts and reports

The following sections are inserted in Part VII of the [1985 c. 6.] Companies Act 1985—

Publication of accounts and reports

"Publication of accounts and reportsPersons entitled to receive copies of accounts and reports.

238.—(1) A copy of the company's annual accounts, together with a copy of the directors' report for that financial year and of the auditors' report on those accounts, shall be sent to—

(a) every member of the company,

(b) every holder of the company's debentures, and

(c) every person who is entitled to receive notice of general meetings,

not less than 21 days before the date of the meeting at which copies of those documents are to be laid in accordance with section 241.

(2) Copies need not be sent—

(a) to a person who is not entitled to receive notices of general meetings and of whose address the company is unaware, or

(b) to more than one of the joint holders of shares or debentures none of whom is entitled to receive such notices, or

(c) in the case of joint holders of shares or debentures some of whom are, and some not, entitled to receive such notices, to those who are not so entitled.

(3) In the case of a company not having a share capital, copies need not be sent to anyone who is not entitled to receive notices of general meetings of the company.

(4) If copies are sent less than 21 days before the date of the meeting, they shall, notwithstanding that fact, be deemed to have been duly sent if it is so

agreed by all the members entitled to attend and vote at the meeting.

(5) If default is made in complying with this section, the company and every officer of it who is in default is guilty of an offence and liable to a fine.

(6) Where copies are sent out under this section over a period of days, references elsewhere in this Act to the day on which copies are sent out shall be construed as references to the last day of that period.

Right to demand copies of accounts and reports.

239.–(1) Any member of a company and any holder of a company's debentures is entitled to be furnished, on demand and without charge, with a copy of the company's last annual accounts and directors' report and a copy of the auditors' report on those accounts.

(2) The entitlement under this section is to a single copy of those documents, but that is in addition to any copy to which a person may be entitled under section 238.

(3) If a demand under this section is not complied with within seven days, the company and every officer of it who is in default is guilty of an offence and liable to a fine and, for continued contravention, to a daily default fine.

(4) If in proceedings for such an offence the issue arises whether a person had already been furnished with a copy of the relevant document under this section, it is for the defendant to prove that he had.

Requirements in connection with publication of accounts.

240.–(1) If a company publishes any of its statutory accounts, they must be accompanied by the relevant auditors' report under section 235.

(2) A company which is required to prepare group accounts for a financial year shall not publish its statutory individual accounts for that year without also publishing with them its statutory group accounts.

(3) If a company publishes non-statutory accounts, it shall publish with them a statement indicating–

(a) that they are not the company's statutory accounts,

(b) whether statutory accounts dealing with any financial year with which the non-statutory accounts purport to deal have been delivered to the registrar,

(c) whether the company's auditors have made a report under section 235 on the statutory accounts for any such financial year, and

(d) whether any report so made was qualified or contained a statement under section 237(2) or (3) (accounting records or returns inadequate, accounts not agreeing with records and returns or failure to obtain necessary information and explanations);

and it shall not publish with the non-statutory accounts any auditors' report under section 235.

(4) For the purposes of this section a company shall be regarded as publishing a document if it publishes, issues or circulates it or otherwise makes it available for public inspection in a manner calculated to invite members of the public generally, or any class of members of the public, to read it.

(5) References in this section to a company's statutory accounts are to its individual or group accounts for a financial year as required to be delivered to the registrar under section 242; and references to the publication by a company of "non-statutory accounts" are to the publication of—

(a) any balance sheet or profit and loss account relating to, or purporting to deal with, a financial year of the company, or

(b) an account in any form purporting to be a balance sheet or profit and loss account for the group consisting of the company and its subsidiary undertakings relating to, or purporting to deal with, a financial year of the company,

otherwise than as part of the company's statutory accounts.

(6) A company which contravenes any provision of this section, and any officer of it who is in default, is guilty of an offence and liable to a fine."

11. Laying and delivering of accounts and reports

The following sections are inserted in Part VII of the [1985 c. 6.] Companies Act 1985—

"Laying and delivering of accounts and reports

Accounts and reports to be laid before company in general meeting.

241.—(1) The directors of a company shall in respect of each financial year lay before the company in general meeting copies of the company's annual accounts, the directors' report and the auditors' report on those accounts.

(2) If the requirements of subsection (1) are not complied with before the end of the period allowed for laying and delivering accounts and reports, every person who immediately before the end of that period was a director of the company is guilty of an offence and liable to a fine and, for continued contravention, to a daily default fine.

(3) It is a defence for a person charged with such an offence to prove that he took all reasonable steps for securing that those requirements would be complied with before the end of that period.

(4) It is not a defence to prove that the documents in question were not in fact prepared as required by this Part.

Accounts and

242.—(1) The directors of a company shall in respect of each financial year

| reports to be delivered to the registrar. | deliver to the registrar a copy of the company's annual accounts together with a copy of the directors' report for that year and a copy of the auditors' report on those accounts.

If any document comprised in those accounts or reports is in a language other than English, the directors shall annex to the copy of that document delivered a translation of it into English, certified in the prescribed manner to be a correct translation.

(2) If the requirements of subsection (1) are not complied with before the end of the period allowed for laying and delivering accounts and reports, every person who immediately before the end of that period was a director of the company is guilty of an offence and liable to a fine and, for continued contravention, to a daily default fine.

(3) Further, if the directors of the company fail to make good the default within 14 days after the service of a notice on them requiring compliance, the court may on the application of any member or creditor of the company or of the registrar, make an order directing the directors (or any of them) to make good the default within such time as may be specified in the order.

The court's order may provide that all costs of and incidental to the application shall be borne by the directors.

(4) It is a defence for a person charged with an offence under this section to prove that he took all reasonable steps for securing that the requirements of subsection (1) would be complied with before the end of the period allowed for laying and delivering accounts and reports.

(5) It is not a defence in any proceedings under this section to prove that the documents in question were not in fact prepared as required by this Part.

Civil penalty for failure to deliver accounts.

242A.—(1) Where the requirements of section 242(1) are not complied with before the end of the period allowed for laying and delivering accounts and reports, the company is liable to a civil penalty.

This is in addition to any liability of the directors under section 242.

(2) The amount of the penalty is determined by reference to the length of the period between the end of the period allowed for laying and delivering accounts and reports and the day on which the requirements are complied with, and whether the company is a public or private company, as follows:—

Length of period	*Public company*	*Private company*
Not more than 3 months.	£500	£100
More than 3 months but not more than 6 months.	£1,000	£250

More than 6 months but not more than 12 months.	£2,000	£500
More than 12 months.	£5,000	£1,000

(3) The penalty may be recovered by the registrar and shall be paid by him into the Consolidated Fund.

(4) It is not a defence in proceedings under this section to prove that the documents in question were not in fact prepared as required by this Part.

Accounts of subsidiary undertakings to be appended in certain cases.

243.—(1) The following provisions apply where at the end of the financial year a parent company has as a subsidiary undertaking—

    (a) a body corporate incorporated outside Great Britain which does not have an established place of business in Great Britain, or

    (b) an unincorporated undertaking,

which is excluded from consolidation in accordance with section 229(4) (undertaking with activities different from the undertakings included in the consolidation).

(2) There shall be appended to the copy of the company's annual accounts delivered to the registrar in accordance with section 242 a copy of the undertaking's latest individual accounts and, if it is a parent undertaking, its latest group accounts.

If the accounts appended are required by law to be audited, a copy of the auditors' report shall also be appended.

(3) The accounts must be for a period ending not more than twelve months before the end of the financial year for which the parent company's accounts are made up.

(4) If any document required to be appended is in a language other than English, the directors shall annex to the copy of that document delivered a translation of it into English, certified in the prescribed manner to be a correct translation.

(5) The above requirements are subject to the following qualifications—

    (a) an undertaking is not required to prepare for the purposes of this section accounts which would not otherwise be prepared, and if no accounts satisfying the above requirements are prepared none need be appended;

    (b) a document need not be appended if it would not otherwise be required to be published, or made available for public inspection, anywhere in the world, but in that case the reason for not appending it shall be stated in a note to the company's accounts;

(c) where an undertaking and all its subsidiary undertakings are excluded from consolidation in accordance with section 229(4), the accounts of such of the subsidiary undertakings of that undertaking as are included in its consolidated group accounts need not be appended.

(6) Subsections (2) to (4) of section 242 (penalties, &c. in case of default) apply in relation to the requirements of this section as they apply in relation to the requirements of subsection (1) of that section.

Period allowed for laying and delivering accounts and reports.

244.–(1) The period allowed for laying and delivering accounts and reports is—

    (a) for a private company, 10 months after the end of the relevant accounting reference period, and

    (b) for a public company, 7 months after the end of that period.

This is subject to the following provisions of this section.

(2) If the relevant accounting reference period is the company's first and is a period of more than 12 months, the period allowed is—

    (a) 10 months or 7 months, as the case may be, from the first anniversary of the incorporation of the company, or

    (b) 3 months from the end of the accounting reference period,

whichever last expires.

(3) Where a company carries on business, or has interests, outside the United Kingdom, the Channel Islands and the Isle of Man, the directors may, in respect of any financial year, give to the registrar before the end of the period allowed by subsection (1) or (2) a notice in the prescribed form—

    (a) stating that the company so carries on business or has such interests, and

    (b) claiming a 3 month extension of the period allowed for laying and delivering accounts and reports;

and upon such a notice being given the period is extended accordingly.

(4) If the relevant accounting period is treated as shortened by virtue of a

notice given by the company under section 225 (alteration of accounting reference date), the period allowed for laying and delivering accounts is that applicable in accordance with the above provisions or 3 months from the date of the notice under that section, whichever last expires.

(5) If for any special reason the Secretary of State thinks fit he may, on an application made before the expiry of the period otherwise allowed, by notice in writing to a company extend that period by such further period as may be specified in the notice.

(6) In this section "the relevant accounting reference period" means the accounting reference period by reference to which the financial year for the accounts in question was determined."

12. Remedies for failure to comply with accounting requirements

The following sections are inserted in Part VII of the [1985 c. 6.] Companies Act 1985—

Remedies for failure to comply with accounting requirements

"Revision of defective accounts and reports

Voluntary revision of annual accounts or directors' report.

245.—(1) If it appears to the directors of a company that any annual accounts of the company, or any directors' report, did not comply with the requirements of this Act, they may prepare revised accounts or a revised report.

(2) Where copies of the previous accounts or report have been laid before the company in general meeting or delivered to the registrar, the revisions shall be confined to—

(a) the correction of those respects in which the previous accounts or report did not comply with the requirements of this Act, and

(b) the making of any necessary consequential alterations.

(3) The Secretary of State may make provision by regulations as to the application of the provisions of this Act in relation to revised annual accounts or a revised directors' report.

(4) The regulations may, in particular—

(a) make different provision according to whether the previous accounts or report are replaced or are supplemented by a document indicating the corrections to be made;

(b) make provision with respect to the functions of the company's auditors in relation to the revised accounts or report;

(c) require the directors to take such steps as may be specified in the regulations where the previous accounts or report have been—

> (i) sent out to members and others under section 238(1),
>
> (ii) laid before the company in general meeting, or
>
> (iii) delivered to the registrar,

or where a summary financial statement based on the previous accounts or report has been sent to members under section 251;

(d) apply the provisions of this Act (including those creating criminal offences) subject to such additions, exceptions and modifications as are specified in the regulations.

(5) Regulations under this section shall be made by statutory instrument which shall be subject to annulment in pursuance of a resolution of either House of Parliament.

Secretary of State's notice in respect of annual accounts.

245A.—(1) Where copies of a company's annual accounts have been sent out under section 238, or a copy of a company's annual accounts has been laid before the company in general meeting or delivered to the registrar, and it appears to the Secretary of State that there is, or may be, a question whether the accounts comply with the requirements of this Act, he may give notice to the directors of the company indicating the respects in which it appears to him that such a question arises, or may arise.

(2) The notice shall specify a period of not less than one month for the directors to give him an explanation of the accounts or prepare revised accounts.

(3) If at the end of the specified period, or such longer period as he may allow, it appears to the Secretary of State that no satisfactory explanation of the accounts has been given and that the accounts have not been revised so as to comply with the requirements of this Act, he may if he thinks fit apply to the court.

(4) The provisions of this section apply equally to revised annual accounts, in which case the references to revised accounts shall be read as references to further revised accounts.

Application to court in respect of defective accounts.

245B.—(1) An application may be made to the court—

> (a) by the Secretary of State, after having complied with section 245A, or
>
> (b) by a person authorised by the Secretary of State for the pur-

poses of this section,

for a declaration or declarator that the annual accounts of a company do not comply with the requirements of this Act and for an order requiring the directors of the company to prepare revised accounts.

(2) Notice of the application, together with a general statement of the matters at issue in the proceedings, shall be given by the applicant to the registrar for registration.

(3) If the court orders the preparation of revised accounts, it may give directions with respect to—

> (a) the auditing of the accounts,
>
> (b) the revision of any directors' report or summary financial statement, and
>
> (c) the taking of steps by the directors to bring the making of the order to the notice of persons likely to rely on the previous accounts,

and such other matters as the court thinks fit.

(4) If the court finds that the accounts did not comply with the requirements of this Act it may order that all or part of—

> (a) the costs (or in Scotland expenses) of and incidental to the application, and
>
> (b) any reasonable expenses incurred by the company in connection with or in consequence of the preparation of revised accounts,

shall be borne by such of the directors as were party to the approval of the defective accounts.

For this purpose every director of the company at the time the accounts were approved shall be taken to have been a party to their approval unless he shows that he took all reasonable steps to prevent their being approved.

(5) Where the court makes an order under subsection (4) it shall have regard to whether the directors party to the approval of the defective accounts knew or ought to have known that the accounts did not comply with the requirements of this Act, and it may exclude one or more directors from the order or order the payment of different amounts by different directors.

(6) On the conclusion of proceedings on an application under this section, the applicant shall give to the registrar for registration an office copy of the

court order or, as the case may be, notice that the application has failed or been withdrawn.

(7) The provisions of this section apply equally to revised annual accounts, in which case the references to revised accounts shall be read as references to further revised accounts.

Other persons authorised to apply to court.

245C.—(1) The Secretary of State may authorise for the purposes of section 245B any person appearing to him—

(a) to have an interest in, and to have satisfactory procedures directed to securing, compliance by companies with the accounting requirements of this Act,

(b) to have satisfactory procedures for receiving and investigating complaints about the annual accounts of companies, and

(c) otherwise to be a fit and proper person to be authorised.

(2) A person may be authorised generally or in respect of particular classes of case, and different persons may be authorised in respect of different classes of case.

(3) The Secretary of State may refuse to authorise a person if he considers that his authorisation is unnecessary having regard to the fact that there are one or more other persons who have been or are likely to be authorised.

(4) Authorisation shall be by order made by statutory instrument which shall be subject to annulment in pursuance of a resolution of either House of Parliament.

(5) Where authorisation is revoked, the revoking order may make such provision as the Secretary of State thinks fit with respect to pending proceedings.

(6) Neither a person authorised under this section, nor any officer, servant or member of the governing body of such a person, shall be liable in damages for anything done or purporting to be done for the purposes of or in connection with—

(a) the taking of steps to discover whether there are grounds for an application to the court,

(b) the determination whether or not to make such an application, or

(c) the publication of its reasons for any such decision,

unless the act or omission is shown to have been in bad faith."

Exemptions and special provisions

13.   Small and medium-sized companies and groups

—(1) The following sections are inserted in Part VII of the [1985 c. 6.] Companies Act 1985, as the beginning of a Chapter II—

Small and medium-sized companies and groups

Exemptions for small and medium-sized companies.

246.—(1) A company which qualifies as a small or medium-sized company in relation to a financial year—

(a) is exempt from the requirements of paragraph 36A of Schedule 4 (disclosure with respect to compliance with accounting standards), and

(b) is entitled to the exemptions provided by Schedule 8 with respect to the delivery to the registrar under section 242 of individual accounts and other documents for that financial year.

(2) In that Schedule—

Part I relates to small companies,

Part II relates to medium-sized companies, and

Part III contains supplementary provisions.

(3) A company is not entitled to the exemptions mentioned in subsection (1) if it is, or was at any time within the financial year to which the accounts relate—

(a) a public company,

(b) a banking or insurance company, or

(c) an authorised person under the Financial Services Act 1986,

or if it is or was at any time during that year a member of an ineligible group.

(4) A group is ineligible if any of its members is—

(a) a public company or a body corporate which (not being a company) has power under its constitution to offer its shares or debentures to the public and may lawfully exercise that power,

(b) an authorised institution under the Banking Act 1987,

(c) an insurance company to which Part II of the Insurance Companies Act 1982 applies, or

(d) an authorised person under the Financial Services Act 1986.

(5) A parent company shall not be treated as qualifying as a small company in relation to a financial year unless the group headed by it qualifies as a small group, and shall not be treated as qualifying as a medium-sized company in relation to a financial year unless that group qualifies as a medium-sized group (see section 249).

Qualification of company as small or medium-sized.

247.—(1) A company qualifies as small or medium-sized in relation to a financial year if the qualifying conditions are met—

(a) in the case of the company's first financial year, in that year, and

(b) in the case of any subsequent financial year, in that year and the preceding year.

(2) A company shall be treated as qualifying as small or medium-sized in relation to a financial year—

(a) if it so qualified in relation to the previous financial year under subsection (1); or

(b) if it was treated as so qualifying in relation to the previous year by virtue of paragraph (a) and the qualifying conditions are met in the year in question.

(3) The qualifying conditions are met by a company in a year in which it satisfies two or more of the following requirements—

Small company

1. Turnover	Not more than £2 million
2. Balance sheet total	Not more than £975,000
3. Number of employees	Not more than 50

Medium-sized company

1. Turnover	Not more than £8 million
2. Balance sheet total	Not more than £3.9 million
3. Number of employees	Not more than 250.

(4) For a period which is a company's financial year but not in fact a year the maximum figures for turnover shall be proportionately adjusted.

(5) The balance sheet total means—

> (a) where in the company's accounts Format 1 of the balance sheet formats set out in Part I of Schedule 4 is adopted, the aggregate of the amounts shown in the balance sheet under the headings corresponding to items A to D in that Format, and

> (b) where Format 2 is adopted, the aggregate of the amounts shown under the general heading "Assets".

(6) The number of employees means the average number of persons employed by the company in the year (determined on a weekly basis).

That number shall be determined by applying the method of calculation prescribed by paragraph 56(2) and (3) of Schedule 4 for determining the corresponding number required to be stated in a note to the company's accounts.

(2) Schedule 6 to this Act is substituted for Schedule 8 to the [1985 c. 6.] Companies Act 1985.

(3) The following sections are inserted in Part VII of the [1985 c. 6.] Companies Act 1985—

"Exemption for small and medium-sized groups.

248.—(1) A parent company need not prepare group accounts for a financial year in relation to which the group headed by that company qualifies as a small or medium-sized group and is not an ineligible group.

(2) A group is ineligible if any of its members is—

> (a) a public company or a body corporate which (not being a company) has power under its constitution to offer its shares or debentures to the public and may lawfully exercise that power,

> (b) an authorised institution under the Banking Act 1987,

> (c) an insurance company to which Part II of the Insurance Companies Act 1982 applies, or

(d) an authorised person under the Financial Services Act 1986.

(3) If the directors of a company propose to take advantage of the exemption conferred by this section, it is the auditors' duty to provide them with a report stating whether in their opinion the company is entitled to the exemption.

(4) The exemption does not apply unless—

(a) the auditors' report states that in their opinion the company is so entitled, and

(b) that report is attached to the individual accounts of the company.

Qualification of group as small or medium-sized.

249.—(1) A group qualifies as small or medium-sized in relation to a financial year if the qualifying conditions are met—

(a) in the case of the parent company's first financial year, in that year, and

(b) in the case of any subsequent financial year, in that year and the preceding year.

(2) A group shall be treated as qualifying as small or medium-sized in relation to a financial year—

(a) if it so qualified in relation to the previous financial year under subsection (1); or

(b) if it was treated as so qualifying in relation to the previous year by virtue of paragraph (a) and the qualifying conditions are met in the year in question.

(3) The qualifying conditions are met by a group in a year in which it satisfies two or more of the following requirements—
Small group

1. Aggregate turnover	Not more than £2 million net (or £2.4 million gross)
2. Aggregate balance sheet total	Not more than £1 million net (or £1.2 million gross)
3. Aggregate number of employees	Not more than 50

Medium-sized group

1. Aggregate turnover	Not more than £8 million net (or £9.6 million gross)
2. Aggregate balance sheet total	Not more than £3.9 million net (or £4.7 million gross)
3. Aggregate number of employees	Not more than 250.

(4) The aggregate figures shall be ascertained by aggregating the relevant figures determined in accordance with section 247 for each member of the group.

In relation to the aggregate figures for turnover and balance sheet total, "net" means with the set-offs and other adjustments required by Schedule 4A in the case of group accounts and "gross" means without those set-offs and other adjustments; and a company may satisfy the relevant requirement on the basis of either the net or the gross figure.

(5) The figures for each subsidiary undertaking shall be those included in its accounts for the relevant financial year, that is—

(a) if its financial year ends with that of the parent company, that financial year, and

(b) if not, its financial year ending last before the end of the financial year of the parent company.

(6) If those figures cannot be obtained without disproportionate expense or undue delay, the latest available figures shall be taken."

14. Dormant companies

The following section is inserted in Part VII of the [1985 c. 6.] Companies Act 1985—

"Dormant companies

Resolution not to appoint auditors.

250.—(1) A company may by special resolution make itself exempt from the provisions of this Part relating to the audit of accounts in the following cases—

(a) if the company has been dormant from the time of its formation, by a special resolution passed before the first general meeting of the company at which annual accounts are laid;

(b) if the company has been dormant since the end of the previous financial year and—

(i) is entitled in respect of its individual accounts for that year to the exemptions conferred by section 246 on a small company, or would be so entitled but for being a member of an ineligible group, and

(ii) is not required to prepare group accounts for that year,

by a special resolution passed at a general meeting of the company at which the annual accounts for that year are laid.

(2) A company may not pass such a resolution if it is—

(a) a public company,

(b) a banking or insurance company, or

(c) an authorised person under the Financial Services Act 1986.

(3) A company is "dormant" during a period in which no significant accounting transaction occurs, that is, no transaction which is required by section 221 to be entered in the company's accounting records; and a company ceases to be dormant on the occurrence of such a transaction.

For this purpose there shall be disregarded any transaction arising from the taking of shares in the company by a subscriber to the memorandum in pursuance of an undertaking of his in the memorandum.

(4) Where a company is, at the end of a financial year, exempt by virtue of this section from the provisions of this Part relating to the audit of accounts—

(a) sections 238 and 239 (right to receive or demand copies of accounts and reports) have effect with the omission of references to the auditors' report;

(b) no copies of an auditors' report need be laid before the company in general meeting;

(c) no copy of an auditors' report need be delivered to the registrar, and if none is delivered, the copy of the balance sheet so delivered shall contain a statement by the directors, in a position immediately above the signature required by section 233(4), that the company was dormant throughout the financial year; and

(d) the company shall be treated as entitled in respect of its individual accounts for that year to the exemptions conferred by section 246 on a small company notwithstanding that it is a member of an ineligible group.

(5) Where a company which is exempt by virtue of this section from the provisions of this Part relating to the audit of accounts—

(a) ceases to be dormant, or

(b) would no longer qualify (for any other reason) to make itself exempt by passing a resolution under this section,

it shall thereupon cease to be so exempt.

15. **Public listed companies: provision of summary financial statement**

The following section is inserted in Part VII of the [1985 c. 6.] Companies Act 1985—

Public listed companies

Provision of summary financial statement to shareholders.

251.—(1) A public company whose shares, or any class of whose shares, are listed need not, in such cases as may be specified by regulations made by the Secretary of State, and provided any conditions so specified are complied with, send copies of the documents referred to in section 238(1) to members of the company, but may instead send them a summary financial statement.

In this subsection "listed" means admitted to the Official List of The International Stock Exchange of the United Kingdom and the Republic of Ireland Limited.

(2) Copies of the documents referred to in section 238(1) shall, however, be sent to any member of the company who wishes to receive them; and the Secretary of State may by regulations make provision as to the manner in which it is to be ascertained whether a member of the company wishes to receive them.

(3) The summary financial statement shall be derived from the company's annual accounts and the directors' report and shall be in such form and contain such information as may be specified by regulations made by the Secretary of State.

(4) Every summary financial statement shall—

(a) state that it is only a summary of information in the company's annual accounts and the directors' report;

(b) contain a statement by the company's auditors of their opinion as to whether the summary financial statement is consistent with those accounts and that report and complies with the requirements of this section and regulations made under it;

(c) state whether the auditors' report on the annual accounts was unqualified or qualified, and if it was qualified set out the report in full together with any further material needed to understand the qualification;

(d) state whether the auditors' report on the annual accounts contained a statement under—

(i) section 237(2) (accounting records or returns inadequate or accounts not agreeing with records and returns), or

(ii) section 237(3) (failure to obtain necessary information and explanations),

and if so, set out the statement in full.

(5) Regulations under this section shall be made by statutory instrument which shall be subject to annulment in pursuance of a resolution of either House of Parliament.

(6) If default is made in complying with this section or regulations made under it, the company and every officer of it who is in default is guilty of an offence and liable to a fine.

(7) Section 240 (requirements in connection with publication of accounts) does not apply in relation to the provision to members of a company of a summary financial statement in accordance with this section."

16. **Private companies: election to dispense with laying of accounts and reports before general meeting**

The following sections are inserted in Part VII of the [1985 c. 6.] Companies Act 1985—

Private companies

Election to dispense with laying of accounts and reports before general meeting.	**252.**—(1) A private company may elect (by elective resolution in accordance with section 379A) to dispense with the laying of accounts and reports before the company in general meeting. (2) An election has effect in relation to the accounts and reports in respect of the financial year in which the election is made and subsequent financial years.

(3) Whilst an election is in force, the references in the following provisions of this Act to the laying of accounts before the company in general meeting shall be read as references to the sending of copies of the accounts to members and others under section 238(1)—

    (a) section 235(1) (accounts on which auditors are to report),

    (b) section 270(3) and (4) (accounts by reference to which distributions are justified), and

    (c) section 320(2) (accounts relevant for determining company's net assets for purposes of ascertaining whether approval required for certain transactions);

and the requirement in section 271(4) that the auditors' statement under that provision be laid before the company in general meeting shall be read as a requirement that it be sent to members and others along with the copies of the accounts sent to them under section 238(1).

(4) If an election under this section ceases to have effect, section 241 applies in relation to the accounts and reports in respect of the financial year in which the election ceases to have effect and subsequent financial years.

Right of shareholder to require laying of accounts.

253.—(1) Where an election under section 252 is in force, the copies of the accounts and reports sent out in accordance with section 238(1)—

    (a) shall be sent not less than 28 days before the end of the period allowed for laying and delivering accounts and reports, and

    (b) shall be accompanied, in the case of a member of the company, by a notice informing him of his right to require the laying of the accounts and reports before a general meeting;

and section 238(5) (penalty for default) applies in relation to the above requirements as to the requirements contained in that section.

(2) Before the end of the period of 28 days beginning with the day on which the accounts and reports are sent out in accordance with section 238(1), any member or auditor of the company may by notice in writing deposited at the registered office of the company require that a general meeting be held for the purpose of laying the accounts and reports before the company.

(3) If the directors do not within 21 days from the date of the deposit of such a notice proceed duly to convene a meeting, the person who deposited the notice may do so himself.

(4) A meeting so convened shall not be held more than three months from that date and shall be convened in the same manner, as nearly as possible, as that in which meetings are to be convened by directors.

(5) Where the directors do not duly convene a meeting, any reasonable expenses incurred by reason of that failure by the person who deposited the notice shall be made good to him by the company, and shall be recouped by the company out of any fees, or other remuneration in respect of their services, due or to become due to such of the directors as were in default.

(6) The directors shall be deemed not to have duly convened a meeting if they convene a meeting for a date more than 28 days after the date of the notice convening it."

17. Unlimited companies: exemption from requirement to deliver accounts and reports

The following section is inserted in Part VII of the [1985 c. 6.] Companies Act 1985—

Unlimited companies

Exemption from requirement to deliver accounts and reports.

254.—(1) The directors of an unlimited company are not required to deliver accounts and reports to the registrar in respect of a financial year if the following conditions are met.

(2) The conditions are that at no time during the relevant accounting reference period—

 (a) has the company been, to its knowledge, a subsidiary undertaking of an undertaking which was then limited, or

 (b) have there been, to its knowledge, exercisable by or on behalf of two or more undertakings which were then limited, rights which if exercisable by one of them would have made the company a subsidiary undertaking of it, or

 (c) has the company been a parent company of an undertaking which was then limited.

The references above to an undertaking being limited at a particular time are to an undertaking (under whatever law established) the liability of whose members is at that time limited.

(3) The exemption conferred by this section does not apply if at any time during the relevant accounting period the company carried on business as the promoter of a trading stamp scheme within the Trading Stamps Act 1964.

(4) Where a company is exempt by virtue of this section from the obligation to deliver accounts, section 240 (requirements in connection with publication of accounts) has effect with the following modifications—

 (a) in subsection (3)(b) for the words from "whether statutory accounts" to "have been delivered to the registrar" substitute "that the company is exempt from the requirement to deliver statutory accounts", and

(b) in subsection (5) for "as required to be delivered to the registrar under section 242" substitute "as prepared in accordance with this Part and approved by the board of directors"."

18. Banking and insurance companies and groups: special provisions

—(1) The following sections are inserted in Part VII of the [1985 c. 6.] Companies Act 1985—

Banking and insurance companies and groups

Special provisions for banking and insurance companies.

255.—(1) A banking or insurance company may prepare its individual accounts in accordance with Part I of Schedule 9 rather than Schedule 4.

(2) Accounts so prepared shall contain a statement that they are prepared in accordance with the special provisions of this Part relating to banking companies or insurance companies, as the case may be.

(3) In relation to the preparation of individual accounts in accordance with the special provisions of this Part relating to banking or insurance companies, the references to the provisions of Schedule 4 in section 226(4) and (5) (relationship between specific requirements and duty to give true and fair view) shall be read as references to the provisions of Part I of Schedule 9.

(4) The Secretary of State may, on the application or with the consent of the directors of a company which prepares individual accounts in accordance with the special provisions of this Part relating to banking or insurance companies, modify in relation to the company any of the requirements of this Part for the purpose of adapting them to the circumstances of the company.

This does not affect the duty to give a true and fair view.

Special provisions for banking and insurance groups.

255A.—(1) The parent company of a banking or insurance group may prepare group accounts in accordance with the provisions of this Part as modified by Part II of Schedule 9.

(2) Accounts so prepared shall contain a statement that they are prepared in accordance with the special provisions of this Part relating to banking groups or insurance groups, as the case may be.

(3) References in this Part to a banking group are to a group where—

(a) the parent company is a banking company, or

(b) at least one of the undertakings in the group is an authorised institution under the Banking Act 1987 and the predominant activities of the group are such as to make it inappropriate to prepare group accounts in accordance with the formats in Part I of Schedule 4.

(4) References in this Part to an insurance group are to a group where—

(a) the parent company is an insurance company, or

(b) the predominant activity of the group is insurance business and activities which are a direct extension of or ancillary to insurance business.

(5) In relation to the preparation of group accounts in accordance with the special provisions of this Part relating to banking or insurance groups, the references to the provisions of Schedule 4A in section 227(5) and (6) (relationship between specific requirements and duty to give true and fair view) shall be read as references to those provisions as modified by Part II of Schedule 9.

(6) The Secretary of State may, on the application or with the consent of the directors of a company which prepares group accounts in accordance with the special provisions of this Part relating to banking or insurance groups, modify in relation to the company any of the requirements of this Part for the purpose of adapting them to the circumstances of the company.

Modification of disclosure requirements in relation to banking company or group.

255B.—(1) In relation to a company which prepares accounts in accordance with the special provisions of this Part relating to banking companies or groups, the provisions of Schedule 5 (additional disclosure: related undertakings) have effect subject to Part III of Schedule 9.

(2) In relation to a banking company, or the parent company of a banking company, the provisions of Schedule 6 (disclosure: emoluments and other benefits of directors and others) have effect subject to Part IV of Schedule 9.

Directors' report where accounts prepared in accordance with special provisions.

255C.—(1) The following provisions apply in relation to the directors' report of a company for a financial year in respect of which it prepares accounts in accordance with the special provisions of this Part relating to banking or insurance companies or groups.

(2) The information required to be given by paragraph 6, 8 or 13 of Part I of Schedule 9 (which is allowed to be given in a statement or report annexed to the accounts), may be given in the directors' report instead.

Information so given shall be treated for the purposes of audit as forming part of the accounts.

(3) The reference in section 234(1)(b) to the amount proposed to be carried to reserves shall be construed as a reference to the amount proposed to be carried to reserves within the meaning of Part I of Schedule 9.

(4) If the company takes advantage, in relation to its individual or group

accounts, of the exemptions conferred by paragraph 27 or 28 of Part I of Schedule 9, paragraph 1 of Schedule 7 (disclosure of asset values) does not apply.

(5) The directors' report shall, in addition to complying with Schedule 7, also comply with Schedule 10 (which specifies additional matters to be disclosed)."

(2) The following section is inserted in Part VII of the [1985 c. 6.] Companies Act 1985—

"Power to apply provisions to banking partnerships.

255D.—(1) The Secretary of State may by regulations apply to banking partnerships, subject to such exceptions, adaptations and modifications as he considers appropriate, the provisions of this Part applying to banking companies.

(2) A "banking partnership" means a partnership which is an authorised institution under the Banking Act 1987.

(3) Regulations under this section shall be made by statutory instrument.

(4) No regulations under this section shall be made unless a draft of the instrument containing the regulations has been laid before Parliament and approved by a resolution of each House."

(3) Schedule 9 to the [1985 c. 6.] Companies Act 1985 (form and content of special category accounts) is amended in accordance with Schedule 7 to this Act.

(4) In that Schedule—

Part I contains amendments relating to the form and content of accounts of banking and insurance companies and groups,

Part II contains provisions with respect to the group accounts of banking and insurance groups,

Part III contains provisions adapting the requirements of Schedule 5 to the [1985 c. 6.] Companies Act 1985 (additional disclosure: related undertakings), and

Part IV contains provisions relating to the requirements of Schedule 6 to that Act (additional disclosure: emoluments and other benefits of directors and others).

(5) Schedule 8 to this Act (directors' report where accounts prepared in accordance with special provisions for banking and insurance companies and groups) is substituted for Schedule 10 to the [1985 c. 6.] Companies Act 1985.

Supplementary provisions

19. Accounting standards

The following section is inserted in Part VII of the [1985 c. 6.] Companies Act 1985, as the beginning of a Chapter III—

Accounting standards

Accounting standards.

256.—(1) In this Part "accounting standards" means statements of standard accounting practice issued by such body or bodies as may be prescribed by regulations.

(2) References in this Part to accounting standards applicable to a company's annual accounts are to such standards as are, in accordance with their terms, relevant to the company's circumstances and to the accounts.

(3) The Secretary of State may make grants to or for the purposes of bodies concerned with—

(a) issuing accounting standards,

(b) overseeing and directing the issuing of such standards, or

(c) investigating departures from such standards or from the accounting requirements of this Act and taking steps to secure compliance with them.

(4) Regulations under this section may contain such transitional and other supplementary and incidental provisions as appear to the Secretary of State to be appropriate.

20. Power to alter accounting requirements

The following section is inserted in Part VII of the [1985 c. 6.] Companies Act 1985—

"Power to alter accounting requirements

Power of Secretary of State to alter accounting requirements.

257.—(1) The Secretary of State may by regulations made by statutory instrument modify the provisions of this Part.

(2) Regulations which—

(a) add to the classes of documents required to be prepared, laid before the company in general meeting or delivered to the registrar,

(b) restrict the classes of company which have the benefit of any exemption, exception or special provision,

(c) require additional matter to be included in a document of any class, or

(d) otherwise render the requirements of this Part more onerous,

shall not be made unless a draft of the instrument containing the regulations has been laid before Parliament and approved by a resolution of each House.

(3) Otherwise, a statutory instrument containing regulations under this section shall be subject to annulment in pursuance of a resolution of either House of Parliament.

(4) Regulations under this section may—

(a) make different provision for different cases or classes of case,

(b) repeal and re-enact provisions with modifications of form or arrangement, whether or not they are modified in substance,

(c) make consequential amendments or repeals in other provisions of this Act, or in other enactments, and

(d) contain such transitional and other incidental and supplementary provisions as the Secretary of State thinks fit.

(5) Any modification by regulations under this section of section 258 or Schedule 10A (parent and subsidiary undertakings) does not apply for the purposes of enactments outside the Companies Acts unless the regulations so provide."

21. Parent and subsidiary undertakings

—(1) The following section is inserted in Part VII of the [1985 c. 6.] Companies Act 1985—

"Parent and subsidiary undertakings

Parent and subsidiary undertakings.

258.—(1) The expressions "parent undertaking" and "subsidiary undertaking" in this Part shall be construed as follows; and a "parent company" means a parent undertaking which is a company.

(2) An undertaking is a parent undertaking in relation to another undertak-

ing, a subsidiary undertaking, if—

    (a) it holds a majority of the voting rights in the undertaking, or

    (b) it is a member of the undertaking and has the right to appoint or remove a majority of its board of directors, or

    (c) it has the right to exercise a dominant influence over the undertaking—

        (i) by virtue of provisions contained in the undertaking's memorandum or articles, or

        (ii) by virtue of a control contract, or

    (d) it is a member of the undertaking and controls alone, pursuant to an agreement with other shareholders or members, a majority of the voting rights in the undertaking.

(3) For the purposes of subsection (2) an undertaking shall be treated as a member of another undertaking—

    (a) if any of its subsidiary undertakings is a member of that undertaking, or

    (b) if any shares in that other undertaking are held by a person acting on behalf of the undertaking or any of its subsidiary undertakings.

(4) An undertaking is also a parent undertaking in relation to another undertaking, a subsidiary undertaking, if it has a participating interest in the undertaking and—

    (a) it actually exercises a dominant influence over it, or

    (b) it and the subsidiary undertaking are managed on a unified basis.

(5) A parent undertaking shall be treated as the parent undertaking of undertakings in relation to which any of its subsidiary undertakings are, or are to be treated as, parent undertakings; and references to its subsidiary undertakings shall be construed accordingly.

(6) Schedule 10A contains provisions explaining expressions used in this section and otherwise supplementing this section."

(2) Schedule 9 to this Act (parent and subsidiary undertakings: supplementary provisions) is inserted after Schedule 10 to the [1985 c. 6.] Companies Act 1985, as Schedule 10A.

22. Other interpretation provisions

The following sections are inserted in Part VII of the [1985 c. 6.] Companies Act 1985—

Other interpretation provisions.

259.—(1) In this Part "undertaking" means—

(a) a body corporate or partnership, or

(b) an unincorporated association carrying on a trade or business, with or without a view to profit.

(2) In this Part references to shares—

(a) in relation to an undertaking with a share capital, are to allotted shares;

(b) in relation to an undertaking with capital but no share capital, are to rights to share in the capital of the undertaking; and

(c) in relation to an undertaking without capital, are to interests—

(i) conferring any right to share in the profits or liability to contribute to the losses of the undertaking, or

(ii) giving rise to an obligation to contribute to the debts or expenses of the undertaking in the event of a winding up.

(3) Other expressions appropriate to companies shall be construed, in relation to an undertaking which is not a company, as references to the corresponding persons, officers, documents or organs, as the case may be, appropriate to undertakings of that description.

This is subject to provision in any specific context providing for the translation of such expressions.

(4) References in this Part to "fellow subsidiary undertakings" are to undertakings which are subsidiary undertakings of the same parent undertaking but are not parent undertakings or subsidiary undertakings of each other.

(5) In this Part "group undertaking", in relation to an undertaking, means an undertaking which is—

(a) a parent undertaking or subsidiary undertaking of that undertaking, or

(b) a subsidiary undertaking of any parent undertaking of that undertaking.

260.—(1) In this Part a "participating interest" means an interest held by an undertaking in the shares of another undertaking which it holds on a long-term basis for the purpose of securing a contribution to its activities by the exercise of control or influence arising from or related to that interest.

(2) A holding of 20 per cent. or more of the shares of an undertaking shall be presumed to be a participating interest unless the contrary is shown.

(3) The reference in subsection (1) to an interest in shares includes—

    (a) an interest which is convertible into an interest in shares, and

    (b) an option to acquire shares or any such interest;

and an interest or option falls within paragraph (a) or (b) notwithstanding that the shares to which it relates are, until the conversion or the exercise of the option, unissued.

(4) For the purposes of this section an interest held on behalf of an undertaking shall be treated as held by it.

(5) For the purposes of this section as it applies in relation to the expression "participating interest" in section 258(4) (definition of "subsidiary undertaking")—

    (a) there shall be attributed to an undertaking any interests held by any of its subsidiary undertakings, and

    (b) the references in subsection (1) to the purpose and activities of an undertaking include the purposes and activities of any of its subsidiary undertakings and of the group as a whole.

(6) In the balance sheet and profit and loss formats set out in Part I of Schedule 4, "participating interest" does not include an interest in a group undertaking.

(7) For the purposes of this section as it applies in relation to the expression "participating interest"—

    (a) in those formats as they apply in relation to group accounts, and

    (b) in paragraph 20 of Schedule 4A (group accounts: undertakings to be accounted for as associated undertakings),

the references in subsections (1) to (4) to the interest held by, and the purposes and activities of, the undertaking concerned shall be construed as references to the interest held by, and the purposes and activities of, the group (within the meaning of paragraph 1 of that Schedule).

261.—(1) Information required by this Part to be given in notes to a company's annual accounts may be contained in the accounts or in a separate document annexed to the accounts. (2) References in this Part to a company's annual accounts, or to a balance sheet or profit and loss account, include notes to the accounts giving information which is required by any provision of this Act, and required or allowed by any such provision to be given in a note to company accounts.

262.—(1) In this Part—

"annual accounts" means—

(a) the individual accounts required by section 226, and

(b) any group accounts required by section 227,

(but see also section 230 (treatment of individual profit and loss account where group accounts prepared));

"annual report", in relation to a company, means the directors' report required by section 234;

"balance sheet date" means the date as at which the balance sheet was made up;

"capitalisation", in relation to work or costs, means treating that work or those costs as a fixed asset;

"credit institution" means an undertaking carrying on a deposit-taking business within the meaning of the Banking Act 1987;

"fixed assets" means assets of a company which are intended for use on a continuing basis in the company's activities, and "current assets" means assets not intended for such use;

"group" means a parent undertaking and its subsidiary undertakings;

"included in the consolidation", in relation to group accounts, or "included in consolidated group accounts", means that the undertaking is included in the accounts by the method of full (and not proportional) consolidation, and references to an undertaking excluded from consolidation shall be construed accordingly;

"purchase price", in relation to an asset of a company or any raw materials or consumables used in the production of such an asset, includes any consideration (whether in cash or otherwise) given by the company in respect of that asset or those materials or consumables, as the case may be;

"qualified", in relation to an auditors' report, means that the report does not state the auditors' unqualified opinion that the accounts have been properly prepared in accordance with this Act or, in the case of an undertaking not required to prepare accounts in accordance with this Act, under any corresponding legislation under which it is required to prepare accounts;

"true and fair view" refers—

(a) in the case of individual accounts, to the requirement of section 226(2), and

(b) in the case of group accounts, to the requirement of section 227(3);

"turnover", in relation to a company, means the amounts derived from the provision of goods and services falling within the company's ordinary activities, after deduction of—

(i) trade discounts,

(ii) value added tax, and

(iii) any other taxes based on the amounts so derived.

(2) In the case of an undertaking not trading for profit, any reference in this Part to a profit and loss account is to an income and expenditure account; and references to profit and loss and, in relation to group accounts, to a consolidated profit and loss account shall be construed accordingly.

(3) References in this Part to "realised profits" and "realised losses", in relation to a company's accounts, are to such profits or losses of the company as fall to be treated as realised in accordance with principles generally accepted, at the time when the accounts are prepared, with respect to the determination for accounting purposes of realised profits or losses.

This is without prejudice to—

(a) the construction of any other expression (where appropriate) by reference to accepted accounting principles or practice, or

(b) any specific provision for the treatment of profits or losses of any description as realised.

262A. The following Table shows the provisions of this Part defining or otherwise explaining expressions used in this Part (other than expressions used only in the same section or paragraph)—

accounting reference date and accounting reference period	section 224
accounting standards and applicable accounting standards	section 256
annual accounts	
(generally)	section 262(1)
(includes notes to the accounts)	section 261(2)
annual report	section 262(1)
associated undertaking (in Schedule 4A)	paragraph 20 of that Schedule
balance sheet (includes notes)	section 261(2)
balance sheet date	section 262(1)
banking group	section 255A(3)
capitalisation (in relation to work or costs)	section 262(1)

credit institution	section 262(1)
current assets	section 262(1)
fellow subsidiary undertaking	section 259(4)
financial year	section 223
fixed assets	section 262(1)
group	section 262(1)
group undertaking	section 259(5)
historical cost accounting rules (in Schedule 4)	paragraph 29 of that Schedule
included in the consolidation and related expressions	section 262(1)
individual accounts	section 262(1)
insurance group	section 255A(4)
land of freehold tenure and land of leasehold tenure (in relation to Scotland)	
—in Schedule 4	paragraph 93 of that Schedule
—in Schedule 9	paragraph 36 of that Schedule
lease, long lease and short lease	
—in Schedule 4	paragraph 83 of that Schedule
—in Schedule 9	paragraph 34 of that Schedule
listed investment	
—in Schedule 4	paragraph 84 of that Schedule
—in Schedule 9	paragraph 33 of that Schedule
notes to the accounts	section 261(1)
parent undertaking (and parent company)	section 258 and Schedule 10A
participating interest	section 260
pension costs (in Schedule 4)	paragraph 94(2) and (3) of that Schedule
period allowed for laying and delivering accounts and reports	section 244
profit and loss account	
(includes notes)	section 261(2)
(in relation to a company not trading for profit)	section 262(2)
provision	
—in Schedule 4	paragraphs 88 and 89 of that Schedule
—in Schedule 9	paragraph 32 of that Schedule
purchase price	section 262(1)

qualified	section 262(1)
realised losses and realised profits	section 262(3)
reserve (in Schedule 9)	paragraph 32 of that Schedule
shares	section 259(2)
social security costs (in Schedule 4)	paragraph 94(1) and (3) of that Schedule
special provisions for banking and insurance companies and groups	sections 255 and 255A
subsidiary undertaking	section 258 and Schedule 10A
true and fair view	section 262(1)
turnover	section 262(1)
undertaking and related expressions	section 259(1) to (3)

"

Consequential amendments

23. Consequential amendments

The enactments specified in Schedule 10 have effect with the amendments specified there, which are consequential on the amendments made by the preceding provisions of this Part.

Part II: Eligibility for Appointment as Company Auditor

24. Introduction

—(1) The main purposes of this Part are to secure that only persons who are properly supervised and appropriately qualified are appointed company auditors, and that audits by persons so appointed are carried out properly and with integrity and with a proper degree of independence.

(2) A "company auditor" means a person appointed as auditor under Chapter V of Part XI of the [1985 c. 6.] Companies Act 1985; and the expressions "company audit" and "company audit work" shall

be construed accordingly.

25. Eligibility for appointment

.—(1) A person is eligible for appointment as a company auditor only if he—

(a) is a member of a recognised supervisory body, and

(b) is eligible for the appointment under the rules of that body.

(2) An individual or a firm may be appointed a company auditor.

(3) In the cases to which section 34 applies (individuals retaining only 1967 Act authorisation) a person's eligibility for appointment as a company auditor is restricted as mentioned in that section.

26. Effect of appointment of partnership

.—(1) The following provisions apply to the appointment as company auditor of a partnership constituted under the law of England and Wales or Northern Ireland, or under the law of any other country or territory in which a partnership is not a legal person.

(2) The appointment is (unless a contrary intention appears) an appointment of the partnership as such and not of the partners.

(3) Where the partnership ceases, the appointment shall be treated as extending to—

(a) any partnership which succeeds to the practice of that partnership and is eligible for the appointment, and

(b) any person who succeeds to that practice having previously carried it on in partnership and is eligible for the appointment.

(4) For this purpose a partnership shall be regarded as succeeding to the practice of another partnership only if the members of the successor partnership are substantially the same as those of the former partnership; and a partnership or other person shall be regarded as succeeding to the practice of a partnership only if it or he succeeds to the whole or substantially the whole of the business of the former partnership.

(5) Where the partnership ceases and no person succeeds to the appointment under subsection (3), the appointment may with the consent of the company be treated as extending to a partnership or other person eligible for the appointment who succeeds to the business of the former partnership or to such part of it as is agreed by the company shall be treated as comprising the appointment.

27. Ineligibility on ground of lack of independence

—(1) A person is ineligible for appointment as company auditor of a company if he is—

(a) an officer or employee of the company, or

(b) a partner or employee of such a person, or a partnership of which such a person is a partner,

or if he is ineligible by virtue of paragraph (a) or (b) for appointment as company auditor of any associated undertaking of the company.

For this purpose an auditor of a company shall not be regarded as an officer or employee of the company.

(2) A person is also ineligible for appointment as company auditor of a company if there exists between him or any associate of his and the company or any associated undertaking a connection of any such description as may be specified by regulations made by the Secretary of State.

The regulations may make different provisions for different cases.

(3) In this section "associated undertaking", in relation to a company, means—

(a) a parent undertaking or subsidiary undertaking of the company, or

(b) a subsidiary undertaking of any parent undertaking of the company.

(4) Regulations under this section shall be made by statutory instrument which shall be subject to annulment in pursuance of a resolution of either House of Parliament.

28. Effect of ineligibility

—(1) No person shall act as a company auditor if he is ineligible for appointment to the office.

(2) If during his term of office a company auditor becomes ineligible for appointment to the office, he shall thereupon vacate office and shall forthwith give notice in writing to the company concerned that he has vacated it by reason of ineligibility.

(3) A person who acts as company auditor in contravention of subsection (1), or fails to give notice of vacating his office as required by subsection (2), is guilty of an offence and liable—

(a) on conviction on indictment, to a fine, and

(b) on summary conviction, to a fine not exceeding the statutory maximum.

(4) In the case of continued contravention he is liable on a second or subsequent summary conviction (instead of the fine mentioned in subsection (3)(b)) to a fine not exceeding one-tenth of the statutory maximum in respect of each day on which the contravention is continued.

(5) In proceedings against a person for an offence under this section it is a defence for him to show

that he did not know and had no reason to believe that he was, or had become, ineligible for appointment.

29. Power of Secretary of State to require second audit

—(1) Where a person appointed company auditor was, for any part of the period during which the audit was conducted, ineligible for appointment to that office, the Secretary of State may direct the company concerned to retain a person eligible for appointment as auditor of the company—

    (a) to audit the relevant accounts again, or

    (b) to review the first audit and to report (giving his reasons) whether a second audit is needed;

and the company shall comply with such a direction within 21 days of its being given.

(2) If a second audit is recommended the company shall forthwith take such steps as are necessary to comply with the recommendation.

(3) Where a direction is given under this section, the Secretary of State shall send a copy of the direction to the registrar of companies; and the company shall within 21 days of receiving any report under subsection (1)(b) send a copy of it to the registrar of companies.

The provisions of the [1985 c. 6.] Companies Act 1985 relating to the delivery of documents to the registrar apply for the purposes of this subsection.

(4) Any statutory or other provisions applying in relation to the first audit shall apply, so far as practicable, in relation to a second audit under this section.

(5) If a company fails to comply with the requirements of this section, it is guilty of an offence and liable on summary conviction to a fine not exceeding the statutory maximum; and in the case of continued contravention it is liable on a second or subsequent summary conviction (instead of the fine mentioned above) to a fine not exceeding one-tenth of the statutory maximum in respect of each day on which the contravention is continued.

(6) A direction under this section is, on the application of the Secretary of State, enforceable by injunction or, in Scotland, by an order under section 45 of the [1988 c. 36.] Court of Session Act 1988.

(7) If a person accepts an appointment, or continues to act, as company auditor at a time when he knows he is ineligible, the company concerned may recover from him any costs incurred by it in complying with the requirements of this section.

Recognition of supervisory bodies and professional qualifications

30. Supervisory bodies

—(1) In this Part a "supervisory body" means a body established in the United Kingdom (whether a body corporate or an unincorporated association) which maintains and enforces rules as to—

    (a) the eligibility of persons to seek appointment as company auditors, and

    (b) the conduct of company audit work,

which are binding on persons seeking appointment or acting as company auditors either because they are members of that body or because they are otherwise subject to its control.

(2) In this Part references to the members of a supervisory body are to the persons who, whether or not members of the body, are subject to its rules in seeking appointment or acting as company auditors.

(3) In this Part references to the rules of a supervisory body are to the rules (whether or not laid down by the body itself) which the body has power to enforce and which are relevant for the purposes of this Part.

This includes rules relating to the admission and expulsion of members of the body, so far as relevant for the purposes of this Part.

(4) In this Part references to guidance issued by a supervisory body are to guidance issued or any recommendation made by it to all or any class of its members or persons seeking to become members which would, if it were a rule, fall within subsection (3).

(5) The provisions of Parts I and II of Schedule 11 have effect with respect to the recognition of supervisory bodies for the purposes of this Part.

31. Meaning of "appropriate qualification"

(1) A person holds an appropriate qualification for the purposes of this Part if—

    (a) he was, by virtue of membership of a body recognised for the purposes of section 389(1)(a) of the [1985 c. 6.] Companies Act 1985, qualified for appointment as auditor of a company under that section immediately before 1st January 1990 and immediately before the commencement of section 25 above,

    (b) he holds a recognised professional qualification obtained in the United Kingdom, or

    (c) he holds an approved overseas qualification and satisfies any additional educational requirements applicable in accordance with section 33(4).

(2) A person who, immediately before 1st January 1990 and immediately before the commencement of section 25 above, was qualified for appointment as auditor of a company under section 389 of the [1985 c. 6.] Companies Act 1985 otherwise than by virtue of membership of a body recognised for the purposes of section 389(1)(a)—

    (a) shall be treated as holding an appropriate qualification for twelve months from the day on which section 25 comes into force, and

(b) shall continue to be so treated if within that period he notifies the Secretary of State that he wishes to retain the benefit of his qualification.

The notice shall be in writing and shall contain such information as the Secretary of State may require.

(3) If a person fails to give such notice within the time allowed he may apply to the Secretary of State, giving such information as would have been required in connection with a notice, and the Secretary of State may, if he is satisfied—

(a) that there was good reason why the applicant did not give notice in time, and

(b) that the applicant genuinely intends to practise as an auditor in Great Britain,

direct that he shall be treated as holding an appropriate qualification for the purposes of this Part.

(4) A person who—

(a) began before 1st January 1990 a course of study or practical training leading to a professional qualification in accountancy offered by a body established in the United Kingdom, and

(b) obtained that qualification on or after that date and before 1st January 1996,

shall be treated as holding an appropriate qualification if the qualification is approved by the Secretary of State for the purposes of this subsection.

(5) Approval shall not be given unless the Secretary of State is satisfied that the body concerned has or, as the case may be, had at the relevant time adequate arrangements to ensure that the qualification is, or was, awarded only to persons educated and trained to a standard equivalent to that required in the case of a recognised professional qualification.

(6) A person shall not be regarded as holding an appropriate qualification for the purposes of this Part except in the above cases.

32. Qualifying bodies and recognised professional qualifications

—(1) In this Part a "qualifying body" means a body established in the United Kingdom (whether a body corporate or an unincorporated association) which offers a professional qualification in accountancy.

(2) In this Part references to the rules of a qualifying body are to the rules (whether or not laid down by the body itself) which the body has power to enforce and which are relevant for the purposes of this Part.

This includes rules relating to—

(a) admission to or expulsion from a course of study leading to a qualification,

(b) the award or deprivation of a qualification, or

(c) the approval of a person for the purposes of giving practical training or the withdrawal of such approval,

so far as relevant for the purposes of this Part.

(3) In this Part references to guidance issued by any such body are to any guidance which the body issues, or any recommendation it makes to all or any class of persons holding or seeking to hold a qualification, or approved or seeking to be approved by the body for the purpose of giving practical training, which would, if it were a rule, fall within subsection (2).

(4) The provisions of Parts I and II of Schedule 12 have effect with respect to the recognition for the purposes of this Part of a professional qualification offered by a qualifying body.

33. Approval of overseas qualifications

—(1) The Secretary of State may declare that persons who—

(a) are qualified to audit accounts under the law of a specified country or territory outside the United Kingdom, or

(b) hold a specified professional qualification in accountancy recognised under the law of a country or territory outside the United Kingdom,

shall be regarded for the purposes of this Part as holding an approved overseas qualification.

(2) A qualification shall not be so approved by the Secretary of State unless he is satisfied that it affords an assurance of professional competence equivalent to that afforded by a recognised professional qualification.

(3) In exercising the power conferred by subsection (1) the Secretary of State may have regard to the extent to which persons—

(a) eligible under this Part for appointment as a company auditor, or

(b) holding a professional qualification recognised under this Part,

are recognised by the law of the country or territory in question as qualified to audit accounts there.

(4) The Secretary of State may direct that a person holding an approved overseas qualification shall not be treated as holding an appropriate qualification for the purposes of this Part unless he holds such additional educational qualifications as the Secretary of State may specify for the purpose of ensuring that such persons have an adequate knowledge of the law and practice in the United Kingdom relevant to the audit of accounts.

(5) Different directions may be given in relation to different qualifications.

(6) The Secretary of State may if he thinks fit, having regard to the considerations mentioned in subsections (2) and (3), withdraw his approval of an overseas qualification in relation to persons becom-

ing qualified as mentioned in subsection (1)(a), or obtaining such a qualification as is mentioned in subsection (1)(b), after such date as he may specify.

34. Eligibility of individuals retaining only 1967 Act authorisation

—(1) A person whose only appropriate qualification is that he retains an authorisation granted by the Board of Trade or the Secretary of State under section 13(1) of the Companies Act 1967 is eligible only for appointment as auditor of an unquoted company.

(2) A company is "unquoted" if, at the time of the person's appointment, no shares or debentures of the company, or of a parent undertaking of which it is a subsidiary undertaking, have been quoted on a stock exchange (in Great Britain or elsewhere) or offered (whether in Great Britain or elsewhere) to the public for subscription or purchase.

(3) This section does not authorise the appointment of such a person as auditor of a company that carries on business as the promoter of a trading stamp scheme within the meaning of the [1964 c. 71.] Trading Stamps Act 1964.

(4) References to a person eligible for appointment as company auditor under section 25 in enactments relating to eligibility for appointment as auditor of a body other than a company do not include a person to whom this section applies.

Duties of recognised bodies

35. The register of auditors

—(1) The Secretary of State shall make regulations requiring the keeping of a register of—

    (a) the individuals and firms eligible for appointment as company auditor, and

    (b) the individuals holding an appropriate qualification who are responsible for company audit work on behalf of such firms.

(2) The regulations shall provide that each person's entry in the register shall give—

    (a) his name and address, and

    (b) in the case of a person eligible as mentioned in subsection (1)(a), the name of the relevant supervisory body,

together with such other information as may be specified by the regulations.

(3) The regulations may impose such obligations as the Secretary of State thinks fit—

(a) on recognised supervisory bodies,

(b) on persons eligible for appointment as company auditor, and

(c) on any person with whom arrangements are made by one or more recognised supervisory bodies with respect to the keeping of the register.

(4) The regulations may include provision—

(a) requiring the register to be open to inspection at such times and places as may be specified in the regulations or determined in accordance with them,

(b) enabling a person to require a certified copy of an entry in the register, and

(c) authorising the charging of fees for inspection, or the provision of copies, of such reasonable amount as may be specified in the regulations or determined in accordance with them;

and may contain such other supplementary and incidental provisions as the Secretary of State thinks fit.

(5) Regulations under this section shall be made by statutory instrument which shall be subject to annulment in pursuance of a resolution of either House of Parliament.

(6) The obligations imposed by regulations under this section on such persons as are mentioned in subsection (3)(a) or (c) are enforceable on the application of the Secretary of State by injunction or, in Scotland, by an order under section 45 of the [1988 c. 36.] Court of Session Act 1988.

36. Information about firms to be available to public

—(1) The Secretary of State shall make regulations requiring recognised supervisory bodies to keep and make available to the public the following information with respect to the firms eligible under their rules for appointment as a company auditor—

(a) in relation to a body corporate, the name and address of each person who is a director of the body or holds any shares in it,

(b) in relation to a partnership, the name and address of each partner,

and such other information as may be specified in the regulations.

(2) The regulations may impose such obligations as the Secretary of State thinks fit—

(a) on recognised supervisory bodies,

(b) on persons eligible for appointment as company auditor, and

(c) on any person with whom arrangements are made by one or more recognised supervisory bodies with respect to the keeping of the information.

(3) The regulations may include provision—

(a) requiring that the information be open to inspection at such times and places as may be specified in the regulations or determined in accordance with them,

(b) enabling a person to require a certified copy of the information or any part of it, and

(c) authorising the charging of fees for inspection, or the provision of copies, of such reasonable amount as may be specified in the regulations or determined in accordance with them;

and may contain such other supplementary and incidental provisions as the Secretary of State thinks fit.

(4) The regulations may make different provision in relation to different descriptions of information and may contain such other supplementary and incidental provisions as the Secretary of State thinks fit.

(5) Regulations under this section shall be made by statutory instrument which shall be subject to annulment in pursuance of a resolution of either House of Parliament.

(6) The obligations imposed by regulations under this section on such persons as are mentioned in subsection (2)(a) or (c) are enforceable on the application of the Secretary of State by injunction or, in Scotland, by an order under section 45 of the [1988 c. 36.] Court of Session Act 1988.

37. Matters to be notified to the Secretary of State

—(1) The Secretary of State may require a recognised supervisory or qualifying body—

(a) to notify him forthwith of the occurrence of such events as he may specify in writing and to give him such information in respect of those events as is so specified;

(b) to give him, at such times or in respect of such periods as he may specify in writing, such information as is so specified.

(2) The notices and information required to be given shall be such as the Secretary of State may reasonably require for the exercise of his functions under this Part.

(3) The Secretary of State may require information given under this section to be given in a specified form or verified in a specified manner.

(4) Any notice or information required to be given under this section shall be given in writing unless the Secretary of State specifies or approves some other manner.

38. Power to call for information

—(1) The Secretary of State may by notice in writing require a recognised supervisory or qualifying body to give him such information as he may reasonably require for the exercise of his functions under this Part.

(2) The Secretary of State may require that any information which he requires under this section shall be given within such reasonable time and verified in such manner as he may specify.

39. Compliance orders

—(1) If at any time it appears to the Secretary of State—

> (a) in the case of a recognised supervisory body, that any requirement of Schedule 11 is not satisfied,
>
> (b) in the case of a recognised professional qualification, that any requirement of Schedule 12 is not satisfied, or
>
> (c) that a recognised supervisory or qualifying body has failed to comply with an obligation to which it is subject by virtue of this Part,

he may, instead of revoking the relevant recognition order, make an application to the court under this section.

(2) If on such application the court decides that the subsection or requirement in question is not satisfied or, as the case may be, that the body has failed to comply with the obligation in question it may order the supervisory or qualifying body in question to take such steps as the court directs for securing that the subsection or requirement is satisfied or that the obligation is complied with.

(3) The jurisdiction conferred by this section is exercisable by the High Court and the Court of Session.

40. Directions to comply with international obligations

—(1) If it appears to the Secretary of State—

> (a) that any action proposed to be taken by a recognised supervisory or qualifying body, or a body established by order under section 46, would be incompatible with Community obligations or any other international obligations of the United Kingdom, or
>
> (b) that any action which that body has power to take is required for the purpose of implementing any such obligations,

he may direct the body not to take or, as the case may be, to take the action in question.

(2) A direction may include such supplementary or incidental requirements as the Secretary of State thinks necessary or expedient.

(3) A direction under this section is enforceable on the application of the Secretary of State by injunction or, in Scotland, by an order under section 45 of the [1988 c. 36.] Court of Session Act 1988.

Offences

41. False and misleading statements

—(1) A person commits an offence if—

(a) for the purposes of or in connection with any application under this Part, or

(b) in purported compliance with any requirement imposed on him by or under this Part,

he furnishes information which he knows to be false or misleading in a material particular or recklessly furnishes information which is false or misleading in a material particular.

(2) It is an offence for a person whose name does not appear on the register of auditors kept under regulations under section 35 to describe himself as a registered auditor or so to hold himself out as to indicate, or be reasonably understood to indicate, that he is a registered auditor.

(3) It is an offence for a body which is not a recognised supervisory or qualifying body to describe itself as so recognised or so to describe itself or hold itself out as to indicate, or be reasonably understood to indicate, that it is so recognised.

(4) A person guilty of an offence under subsection (1) is liable—

(a) on conviction on indictment, to imprisonment for a term not exceeding two years or to a fine or both;

(b) on summary conviction, to imprisonment for a term not exceeding six months or to a fine not exceeding the statutory maximum or both.

(5) A person guilty of an offence under subsection (2) or (3) is liable on summary conviction to imprisonment for a term not exceeding six months or to a fine not exceeding level 5 on the standard scale or both.

Where a contravention of subsection (2) or (3) involves a public display of the offending description, the maximum fine that may be imposed is (in place of that mentioned above) an amount equal to level 5 on the standard scale multiplied by the number of days for which the display has continued.

(6) It is a defence for a person charged with an offence under subsection (2) or (3) to show that he took all reasonable precautions and exercised all due diligence to avoid the commission of the offence.

42. Offences by bodies corporate, partnerships and unincorporated associations

—(1) Where an offence under this Part committed by a body corporate is proved to have been committed with the consent or connivance of, or to be attributable to any neglect on the part of, a director, manager, secretary or other similar officer of the body, or a person purporting to act in any such capacity, he as well as the body corporate is guilty of the offence and liable to be proceeded against and punished accordingly.

(2) Where the affairs of a body corporate are managed by its members, subsection (1) applies in relation to the acts and defaults of a member in connection with his functions of management as to a director of a body corporate.

(3) Where an offence under this Part committed by a partnership is proved to have been committed with the consent or connivance of, or to be attributable to any neglect on the part of, a partner, he as well as the partnership is guilty of the offence and liable to be proceeded against and punished accordingly.

(4) Where an offence under this Part committed by an unincorporated association (other than a partnership) is proved to have been committed with the consent or connivance of, or to be attributable to any neglect on the part of, any officer of the association or any member of its governing body, he as well as the association is guilty of the offence and liable to be proceeded against and punished accordingly.

43. Time limits for prosecution of offences

—(1) An information relating to an offence under this Part which is triable by a magistrates' court in England and Wales may be so tried on an information laid at any time within twelve months after the date on which evidence sufficient in the opinion of the Director of Public Prosecutions or the Secretary of State to justify the proceedings comes to his knowledge.

(2) Proceedings in Scotland for an offence under this Part may be commenced at any time within twelve months after the date on which evidence sufficient in the Lord Advocate's opinion to justify the proceedings came to his knowledge or, where such evidence was reported to him by the Secretary of State, within twelve months after the date on which it came to the knowledge of the latter.

For the purposes of this subsection proceedings shall be deemed to be commenced on the date on which a warrant to apprehend or to cite the accused is granted, if the warrant is executed without undue delay.

(3) Subsection (1) does not authorise the trial of an information laid, and subsection (2) does not authorise the commencement of proceedings, more than three years after the commission of the offence.

(4) For the purposes of this section a certificate of the Director of Public Prosecutions, the Lord Advocate or the Secretary of State as to the date on which such evidence as is referred to above came to his knowledge is conclusive evidence.

(5) Nothing in this section affects proceedings within the time limits prescribed by section 127(1) of the [1980 c. 43.] Magistrates' Courts Act 1980 or section 331 of the [1975 c. 21.] Criminal Procedure (Scotland) Act 1975 (the usual time limits for criminal proceedings).

44. Jurisdiction and procedure in respect of offences

—(1) Summary proceedings for an offence under this Part may, without prejudice to any jurisdiction exercisable apart from this section, be taken against a body corporate or unincorporated association at any place at which it has a place of business and against an individual at any place where he is for the time being.

(2) Proceedings for an offence alleged to have been committed under this Part by an unincorporated association shall be brought in the name of the association (and not in that of any of its members), and for the purposes of any such proceedings any rules of court relating to the service of documents apply as in relation to a body corporate.

(3) Section 33 of the [1925 c. 86.] Criminal Justice Act 1925 and Schedule 3 to the Magistrates' Courts Act 1980 (procedure on charge of offence against a corporation) apply in a case in which an unincorporated association is charged in England and Wales with an offence under this Part as they apply in the case of a corporation.

(4) In relation to proceedings on indictment in Scotland for an offence alleged to have been committed under this Part by an unincorporated association, section 74 of the Criminal Procedure (Scotland) Act 1975 (proceedings on indictment against bodies corporate) applies as if the association were a body corporate.

(5) A fine imposed on an unincorporated association on its conviction of such an offence shall be paid out of the funds of the association.

Supplementary provisions

45. Fees

—(1) An applicant for a recognition order under this Part shall pay such fee in respect of his application as may be prescribed; and no application shall be regarded as duly made unless this subsection is complied with.

(2) Every recognised supervisory or qualifying body shall pay such periodical fees to the Secretary of State as may be prescribed.

(3) In this section "prescribed" means prescribed by regulations made by the Secretary of State, which may make different provision for different cases or classes of case.

(4) Regulations under this section shall be made by statutory instrument which shall be subject to annulment in pursuance of a resolution of either House of Parliament.

(5) Fees received by the Secretary of State by virtue of this Part shall be paid into the Consolidated Fund.

46. Delegation of functions of Secretary of State

—(1) The Secretary of State may by order (a "delegation order") establish a body corporate to exercise his functions under this Part.

(2) A delegation order has the effect of transferring to the body established by it, subject to such exceptions and reservations as may be specified in the order, all the functions of the Secretary of State under this Part except—

(a) such functions under Part I of Schedule 14 (prevention of restrictive practices) as are excepted by regulations under section 47, and

(b) his functions in relation to the body itself;

and the order may also confer on the body such other functions supplementary or incidental to those transferred as appear to the Secretary of State to be appropriate.

(3) Any transfer of the functions under the following provisions shall be subject to the reservation that they remain exercisable concurrently by the Secretary of State—

(a) section 38 (power to call for information), and

(b) section 40 (directions to comply with international obligations);

and any transfer of the function of refusing to approve an overseas qualification, or withdrawing such approval, on the grounds referred to in section 33(3) (lack of reciprocity) shall be subject to the reservation that the function is exercisable only with the consent of the Secretary of State.

(4) A delegation order may be amended or, if it appears to the Secretary of State that it is no longer in the public interest that the order should remain in force, revoked by a further order under this section.

(5) Where functions are transferred or resumed, the Secretary of State may by order confer or, as the case may be, take away such other functions supplementary or incidental to those transferred or resumed as appear to him to be appropriate.

(6) The provisions of Schedule 13 have effect with respect to the status, constitution and proceedings of a body established by a delegation order, the exercise by it of certain functions transferred to it and other supplementary matters.

(7) An order under this section shall be made by statutory instrument.

(8) An order which has the effect of transferring or resuming any functions shall not be made unless a draft of it has been laid before and approved by resolution of each House of Parliament; and any other description of order shall be subject to annulment in pursuance of a resolution of either House of Parliament.

47.   Restrictive practices

—(1) The provisions of Schedule 14 have effect with respect to certain matters relating to restrictive practices and competition law.

(2) The Secretary of State may make provision by regulations as to the discharge of the functions under paragraphs 1 to 7 of that Schedule when a delegation order is in force.

(3) The regulations may—

(a) except any function from the effect of the delegation order,

(b) modify any of the provisions mentioned in subsection (2), and

(c) impose such duties on the body established by the delegation order, the Secretary of State and Director General of Fair Trading as appear to the Secretary of State to be appropriate.

(4) The regulations shall contain such provision as appears to the Secretary of State to be necessary or expedient for reserving to him the decision—

(a) to refuse recognition on the ground mentioned in paragraph 1(3) of that Schedule, or

(b) to exercise the powers conferred by paragraph 6 of that Schedule.

(5) For that purpose the regulations may—

(a) prohibit the body from granting a recognition order without the leave of the Secretary of State, and

(b) empower the Secretary of State to direct the body to exercise its powers in such manner as may be specified in the direction.

(6) Regulations under this section shall be made by statutory instrument which shall be subject to annulment in pursuance of a resolution of either House of Parliament.

48.
Exemption from liability for damages

—(1) Neither a recognised supervisory body, nor any of its officers or employees or members of its governing body, shall be liable in damages for anything done or omitted in the discharge or purported discharge of functions to which this subsection applies, unless the act or omission is shown to have been in bad faith.

(2) Subsection (1) applies to the functions of the body so far as relating to, or to matters arising out of—

(a) such rules, practices, powers and arrangements of the body to which the requirements of Part II of Schedule 11 apply, or

(b) the obligations with which paragraph 16 of that Schedule requires the body to comply,

(c) any guidance issued by the body, or

(d) the obligations to which the body is subject by virtue of this Part.

(3) Neither a body established by a delegation order, nor any of its members, officers or employees, shall be liable in damages for anything done or omitted in the discharge or purported discharge of the functions exercisable by virtue of an order under section 46, unless the act or omission is shown to have been in bad faith.

49. Service of notices

—(1) This section has effect in relation to any notice, direction or other document required or authorised by or under this Part to be given to or served on any person other than the Secretary of State.

(2) Any such document may be given to or served on the person in question—

(a) by delivering it to him,

(b) by leaving it at his proper address, or

(c) by sending it by post to him at that address.

(3) Any such document may—

(a) in the case of a body corporate, be given to or served on the secretary or clerk of that body;

(b) in the case of a partnership, be given to or served on any partner;

(c) in the case of an unincorporated association other than a partnership, be given to or served on any member of the governing body of the association.

(4) For the purposes of this section and section 7 of the [1978 c. 30.] Interpretation Act 1978 (service of documents by post) in its application to this section, the proper address of any person is his last known address (whether of his residence or of a place where he carries on business or is employed) and also—

(a) in the case of a person who is eligible under the rules of a recognised supervisory body for appointment as company auditor and who does not have a place of business in the United Kingdom, the address of that body;

(b) in the case of a body corporate, its secretary or its clerk, the address of its registered or principal office in the United Kingdom;

(c) in the case of an unincorporated association (other than a partnership) or a member of its governing body, its principal office in the United Kingdom.

50. Power to make consequential amendments

—(1) The Secretary of State may by regulations make such amendments of enactments as appear to him to be necessary or expedient in consequence of the provisions of this Part having effect in place of section 389 of the [1985 c. 6.] Companies Act 1985.

(2) That power extends to making such amendments as appear to the Secretary of State necessary or expedient of—

    (a) enactments referring by name to the bodies of accountants recognised for the purposes of section 389(1)(a) of the [1985 c. 6.] Companies Act 1985, and

    (b) enactments making with respect to other statutory auditors provision as to the matters dealt with in relation to company auditors by section 389 of the [1985 c. 6.] Companies Act 1985.

(3) The provision which may be made with respect to other statutory auditors includes provision as to—

    (a) eligibility for the appointment,

    (b) the effect of appointing a partnership which is not a legal person and the manner of exercise of the auditor's rights in such a case, and

    (c) ineligibility on the ground of lack of independence or any other ground.

(4) The regulations may contain such supplementary, incidental and transitional provision as appears to the Secretary of State to be necessary or expedient.

(5) The Secretary of State shall not make regulations under this section with respect to any statutory auditors without the consent of—

    (a) the Minister responsible for their appointment or responsible for the body or person by, or in relation to whom, they are appointed, or

    (b) if there is no such Minister, the person by whom they are appointed.

(6) In this section a "statutory auditor" means a person appointed auditor in pursuance of any enactment authorising or requiring the appointment of an auditor or auditors.

(7) Regulations under this section shall be made by statutory instrument which shall be subject to annulment in pursuance of a resolution of either House of Parliament.

51.   **Power to make provisions in consequence of changes affecting accountancy bodies**

—(1) The Secretary of State may by regulations make such amendments of enactments as appear to him to be necessary or expedient in consequence of any change of name, merger or transfer of engagements affecting—

(a) a recognised supervisory or qualifying body under this Part, or

(b) a body of accountants referred to in, or approved, authorised or otherwise recognised for the purposes of, any other enactment.

(2) Regulations under this section shall be made by statutory instrument which shall be subject to annulment in pursuance of a resolution of either House of Parliament.

52. Meaning of "associate"

—(1) In this Part "associate", in relation to a person, shall be construed as follows.

(2) In relation to an individual "associate" means—

(a) that individual's spouse or minor child or step-child,

(b) any body corporate of which that individual is a director, and

(c) any employee or partner of that individual.

(3) In relation to a body corporate "associate" means—

(a) any body corporate of which that body is a director,

(b) any body corporate in the same group as that body, and

(c) any employee or partner of that body or of any body corporate in the same group.

(4) In relation to a Scottish firm, or a partnership constituted under the law of any other country or territory in which a partnership is a legal person, "associate" means—

(a) any body corporate of which the firm is a director,

(b) any employee of or partner in the firm, and

(c) any person who is an associate of a partner in the firm.

(5) In relation to a partnership constituted under the law of England and Wales or Northern Ireland, or the law of any other country or territory in which a partnership is not a legal person, "associate" means any person who is an associate of any of the partners.

53. Minor definitions

—(1) In this Part—

"address" means—

>(a) in relation to an individual, his usual residential or business address, and

>(b) in relation to a firm, its registered or principal office in Great Britain;

"company" means any company or other body to which section 384 of the [1985 c. 6.] Companies Act 1985 (duty to appoint auditors) applies;

"director", in relation to a body corporate, includes any person occupying in relation to it the position of a director (by whatever name called) and any person in accordance with whose directions or instructions (not being advice given in a professional capacity) the directors of the body are accustomed to act;

"enactment" includes an enactment contained in subordinate legislation within the meaning of the [1978 c. 30.] Interpretation Act 1978;

"firm" means a body corporate or a partnership;

"group", in relation to a body corporate, means the body corporate, any other body corporate which is its holding company or subsidiary and any other body corporate which is a subsidiary of that holding company; and

"holding company" and "subsidiary" have the meaning given by section 736 of the [1985 c. 6.] Companies Act 1985;

"parent undertaking" and "subsidiary undertaking" have the same meaning as in Part VII of the [1985 c. 6.] Companies Act 1985.

(2) For the purposes of this Part a body shall be regarded as ``established in the United Kingdom" if and only if—

>(a) it is incorporated or formed under the law of the United Kingdom or a part of the United Kingdom, or

>(b) its central management and control is exercised in the United Kingdom;

and any reference to a qualification ``obtained in the United Kingdom" is to a qualification obtained from such a body.

54. Index of defined expressions

The following Table shows provisions defining or otherwise explaining expressions used in this Part (other than provisions defining or explaining an expression used only in the same section)—

address	section 53(1)

appropriate qualification	section 31
associate	section 52
company	section 53(1)
company auditor, company audit and company audit work	section 24(2)
delegation order	section 46
director (of a body corporate)	section 53(1)
Director (in Schedule 14)	paragraph 1(1) of that Schedule
enactment	section 53(1)
established in the United Kingdom	section 53(2)
firm	section 53(1)
group (in relation to a body corporate)	section 53(1)
guidance	
–of a qualifying body	section 32(3)
-of a supervisory body	section 30(4)
holding company	section 53(1)
member (of a supervisory body)	section 30(2)
obtained in the United Kingdom	section 53(2)
parent undertaking	section 53(1)
purposes of this Part	section 24(1)
qualifying body	section 32(1)
recognised	
-in relation to a professional qualification	section 32(4) and Schedule 12
-in relation to a qualifying body	paragraph 2(1) of Schedule 12
-in relation to a supervisory body	section 30(5) and Schedule 11
rules	
-of a qualifying body	section 32(2)
-of a supervisory body	section 30(3)
subsidiary and subsidiary undertaking	section 53(1)
supervisory body	section 30(1)

Part III: Investigations and Powers to Obtain Information

55. Investigations by inspectors not leading to published report

In section 432 of the [1985 c. 6.] Companies Act 1985 (appointment of inspectors by Secretary of State), after subsection (2) (investigation of circumstances suggesting misconduct) insert—

> "(2A) Inspectors may be appointed under subsection (2) on terms that any report they may make is not for publication; and in such a case, the provisions of section 437(3) (availability and publication of inspectors' reports) do not apply." .

56. Production of documents and evidence to inspectors

—(1) Section 434 of the [1985 c. 66.] Companies Act 1985 (production of documents and evidence to inspectors) is amended as follows.

(2) In subsection (1) (duty of officers to assist inspectors), for "books and documents" substitute "documents".

(3) For subsection (2) (power to require production of documents, attendance or other assistance) substitute—

> "(2) If the inspectors consider that an officer or agent of the company or other body corporate, or any other person, is or may be in possession of information relating to a matter which they believe to be relevant to the investigation, they may require him—
>
>> (a) to produce to them any documents in his custody or power relating to that matter,
>>
>> (b) to attend before them, and
>>
>> (c) otherwise to give them all assistance in connection with the investigation which he is reasonably able to give;
>
> and it is that person's duty to comply with the requirement." .

(4) For subsection (3) (power to examine on oath) substitute—

> "(3) An inspector may for the purposes of the investigation examine any person on oath, and may administer an oath accordingly." .

(5) After subsection (5) insert—

> "(6) In this section "documents" includes information recorded in any form; and, in relation to information recorded otherwise than in legible form, the power to require its production includes power to require the production of a copy of the information in

legible form." .

(6) In section 436 of the [1985 c. 6.] Companies Act 1985 (obstruction of inspectors treated as contempt of court), for subsections (1) and (2) substitute—

"(1) If any person—

(a) fails to comply with section 434(1)(a) or (c),

(b) refuses to comply with a requirement under section 434(1)(b) or (2), or

(c) refuses to answer any question put to him by the inspectors for the purposes of the investigation,

the inspectors may certify that fact in writing to the court." .

57.   Duty of inspectors to report

In section 437 of the [1985 c. 6.] Companies Act 1985 (inspectors' reports), after subsection (1A) insert—

"(1B) If it appears to the Secretary of State that matters have come to light in the course of the inspectors' investigation which suggest that a criminal offence has been committed, and those matters have been referred to the appropriate prosecuting authority, he may direct the inspectors to take no further steps in the investigation or to take only such further steps as are specified in the direction.

(1C) Where an investigation is the subject of a direction under subsection (1B), the inspectors shall make a final report to the Secretary of State only where—

(a) they were appointed under section 432(1) (appointment in pursuance of an order of the court), or

(b) the Secretary of State directs them to do so."

58.   Power to bring civil proceedings on the company's behalf

In section 438 of the [1985 c. 6.] Companies Act 1985 (power to bring civil proceedings on the company's behalf), for the opening words of subsection (1) down to "it appears to the Secretary of State" substitute "If from any report made or information obtained under this Part it appears to the Secretary of State".

59.   Expenses of investigating a company's affairs

—(1) Section 439 of the [1985 c. 6.] Companies Act 1985 (expenses of investigating a company's affairs) is amended as follows.

(2) For subsection (1) substitute—

"(1) The expenses of an investigation under any of the powers conferred by this Part shall be defrayed in the first instance by the Secretary of State, but he may recover those expenses from the persons liable in accordance with this section.

There shall be treated as expenses of the investigation, in particular, such reasonable sums as the Secretary of State may determine in respect of general staff costs and overheads.

(3) In subsection (4) for "the inspectors' report" substitute "an inspectors' report".

(4) For subsection (5) substitute—

"(5) Where inspectors were appointed—

(a) under section 431, or

(b) on an application under section 442(3),

the applicant or applicants for the investigation is or are liable to such extent (if any) as the Secretary of State may direct." .

60. Power of Secretary of State to present winding-up petition

—(1) Section 440 of the [1985 c. 6.] Companies Act 1985 (power of Secretary of State to present winding-up petition) is repealed; but the following amendments have the effect of re-enacting that provision, with modifications.

(2) In section 124(4) of the [1986 c. 45.] Insolvency Act 1986 (application by Secretary of State for company to be wound up by the court), for paragraph (b) substitute—

"(b) in a case falling within section 124A below." .

(3) After that section insert—

"Petition for winding up on grounds of public interest.

124A.—(1) Where it appears to the Secretary of State from—

(a) any report made or information obtained under Part XIV of the [1985 c. 6.] Companies Act 1985 (company investigations, &c.),

(b) any report made under section 94 or 177 of the Financial Services Act 1986 or any information obtained under section 105 of that Act,

(c) any information obtained under section 2 of the Criminal Justice Act 1987 or section 52 of the Criminal Justice (Scotland) Act 1987 (fraud investigations), or

(d) any information obtained under section 83 of the Companies Act 1989 (powers exercisable for purpose of assisting overseas regulatory authorities),

that it is expedient in the public interest that a company should be wound up, he may present a petition for it to be wound up if the court thinks it just and equitable for it to be so.

(2) This section does not apply if the company is already being wound up by the court."

61. Inspectors' reports as evidence

In section 441 of the [1985 c. 6.] Companies Act 1985 (inspectors' reports to be evidence), in subsection (1) for "sections 431 or 432" substitute "this Part".

62. Investigation of company ownership

In section 442 of the [1985 c. 6.] Companies Act 1985 (power to investigate company ownership), for subsection (3) (investigation on application by members of company) substitute—

"(3) If an application for investigation under this section with respect to particular shares or debentures of a company is made to the Secretary of State by members of the company, and the number of applicants or the amount of shares held by them is not less than that required for an application for the appointment of inspectors under section 431(2)(a) or (b), then, subject to the following provisions, the Secretary of State shall appoint inspectors to conduct the investigation applied for.

(3A) The Secretary of State shall not appoint inspectors if he is satisfied that the application is vexatious; and where inspectors are appointed their terms of appointment shall exclude any matter in so far as the Secretary of State is satisfied that it is unreasonable for it to be investigated.

(3B) The Secretary of State may, before appointing inspectors, require the applicant or applicants to give security, to an amount not exceeding £5,000, or such other sum as he may by order specify, for payment of the costs of the investigation.

An order under this subsection shall be made by statutory instrument which shall be subject to annulment in pursuance of a resolution of either House of Parliament.

(3C) If on an application under subsection (3) it appears to the Secretary of State that the powers conferred by section 444 are sufficient for the purposes of investigating the matters which inspectors would be appointed to investigate, he may instead conduct the investigation under that section.".

63. Secretary of State's power to require production of documents

—(1) Section 447 of the [1985 c. 6.] Companies Act 1985 (power of Secretary of State to require production of documents) is amended as follows.

(2) Omit subsection (1) (bodies in relation to which powers exercisable), and—

(a) in subsections (2) and (3) for "any such body" substitute "a company",

(b) in subsections (4) and (5) for "any body" and "a body" substitute "a company", and

(c) in subsections (5) and (6) for "the body" substitute "the company".

(3) For "books or papers", wherever occurring, substitute "documents".

(4) In subsection (3) (power to authorise officer to require production of documents) after "an officer of his" insert "or any other competent person", after "the officer" in the first place where it occurs insert "or other person" and for "the officer" in the second place where it occurs substitute "he (the officer or other person)".

(5) In subsection (4) (power to require production of documents in possession of third party) after "an officer of his" and after "the officer" (twice) insert "or other person".

(6) In subsection (6), for the second sentence substitute—

"Sections 732 (restriction on prosecutions), 733 (liability of individuals for corporate default) and 734 (criminal proceedings against unincorporated bodies) apply to this offence."

(7) After subsection (8) insert—

"(9) In this section "documents" includes information recorded in any form; and, in relation to information recorded otherwise than in legible form, the power to require its production includes power to require the production of a copy of it in legible form.".

(8) In Schedule 24 to the [1985 c. 6.] Companies Act 1985 (punishment of offences), in the entry relating to section 447(6), for "books and papers" substitute "documents".

64. Entry and search of premises

—(1) For section 448 of the [1985 c. 6.] Companies Act 1985 (entry and search of premises) substitute—

"Entry and search of premises.

448.—(1) A justice of the peace may issue a warrant under this section if satisfied on information on oath given by or on behalf of the Secretary of State, or by a person appointed or authorised to exercise powers under this Part, that there are reasonable grounds for believing that there are on any premises documents whose production has been required under this Part and which have not been produced in compliance with the requirement.

(2) A justice of the peace may also issue a warrant under this section if satisfied on information on oath given by or on behalf of the Secretary of State, or by a person appointed or authorised to exercise powers under this Part—

(a) that there are reasonable grounds for believing that an offence has been committed for which the penalty on conviction on indictment is imprisonment for a term of not less than two years and that there are on any premises documents relating to whether the offence has been committed,

(b) that the Secretary of State, or the person so appointed or authorised, has power to require the production of the documents under this Part, and

(c) that there are reasonable grounds for believing that if production was so required the documents would not be produced but would be removed from the premises, hidden, tampered with or destroyed.

(3) A warrant under this section shall authorise a constable, together with any other person named in it and any other constables—

(a) to enter the premises specified in the information, using such force as is reasonably necessary for the purpose;

(b) to search the premises and take possession of any documents appearing to be such documents as are mentioned in subsection (1) or (2), as the case may be, or to take, in relation to any such documents, any other steps which may appear to be necessary for preserving them or preventing interference with them;

(c) to take copies of any such documents; and

(d) to require any person named in the warrant to provide an explanation of them or to state where they may be found.

(4) If in the case of a warrant under subsection (2) the justice of the peace is satisfied on information on oath that there are reasonable grounds for believing that there are also on the premises other documents relevant to the investigation, the warrant shall also authorise the actions mentioned in subsection (3) to be taken in relation to such documents.

(5) A warrant under this section shall continue in force until the end of the period of one month beginning with the day on which it is issued.

(6) Any documents of which possession is taken under this section may be retained—

    (a) for a period of three months; or

    (b) if within that period proceedings to which the documents are relevant are commenced against any person for any criminal offence, until the conclusion of those proceedings.

(7) Any person who intentionally obstructs the exercise of any rights conferred by a warrant issued under this section or fails without reasonable excuse to comply with any requirement imposed in accordance with subsection (3)(d) is guilty of an offence and liable to a fine.

Sections 732 (restriction on prosecutions), 733 (liability of individuals for corporate default) and 734 (criminal proceedings against unincorporated bodies) apply to this offence.

(8) For the purposes of sections 449 and 451A (provision for security of information) documents obtained under this section shall be treated as if they had been obtained under the provision of this Part under which their production was or, as the case may be, could have been required.

(9) In the application of this section to Scotland for the references to a justice of the peace substitute references to a justice of the peace or a sheriff, and for the references to information on oath substitute references to evidence on oath.

(10) In this section "document" includes information recorded in any form."

(2) In Schedule 24 to the [1985 c. 6.] Companies Act 1985 (punishment of offences), in the entry relating to section 448(5)—

    (a) in the first column for "448(5)" substitute "448(7)", and

    (b) for the entry in the second column substitute—

"

> Obstructing the exercise of any rights conferred by a warrant or failing to comply with a requirement imposed under subsection (3)(d).

"

65. Provision for security of information obtained

—(1) Section 449 of the [1985 c. 6.] Companies Act 1985 (provision for security of information obtained) is amended as follows.

(2) In subsection (1) (purposes for which disclosure permitted)—

(a) in the opening words for "body" (twice) substitute "company";

(b) for paragraph (c) substitute—

"(c) for the purposes of enabling or assisting any inspector appointed under this Part, or under section 94 or 177 of the Financial Services Act 1986, to discharge his functions;" ;

(c) after that paragraph insert —

"(cc) for the purpose of enabling or assisting any person authorised to exercise powers under section 44 of the Insurance Companies Act 1982, section 447 of this Act, section 106 of the Financial Services Act 1986 or section 84 of the Companies Act 1989 to discharge his functions;" ;

(d) in paragraph (d) for "or the Financial Services Act 1986" substitute ", the Financial Services Act 1986 or Part II, III or VII of the Companies Act 1989,";

(e) omit paragraph (e);

(f) in paragraph (h) for "(n) or (p)" substitute "or (n)";

(g) after that paragraph insert—

"(hh) for the purpose of enabling or assisting a body established by order under section 46 of the Companies Act 1989 to discharge its functions under Part II of that Act, or of enabling or assisting a recognised supervisory or qualifying body within the meaning of that Part to discharge its functions as such;" ;

(h) after paragraph (l) insert—

"(ll) with a view to the institution of, or otherwise for the purposes of, any disciplinary proceedings relating to the discharge by a public servant of his duties;";

(i) for paragraph (m) substitute—

"(m) for the purpose of enabling or assisting an overseas regulatory authority to exercise its regulatory functions." .

(3) For subsection (1A) substitute—

"(1A) In subsection (1)—

(a) in paragraph (ll) "public servant" means an officer or servant of the Crown or of any public or other authority for the time being designated for the purposes of that paragraph by the Secretary of State by order made by statutory instrument; and

(b) in paragraph (m) "overseas regulatory authority" and "regulatory functions" have the same meaning as in section 82 of the Companies Act 1989."

(4) In subsection (1B) (disclosure to designated public authorities) for "designated for the purposes of this section" substitute "designated for the purposes of this subsection".

(5) In subsection (2), for the second sentence substitute—

"Sections 732 (restriction on prosecutions), 733 (liability of individuals for corporate default) and 734 (criminal proceedings against unincorporated bodies) apply to this offence."

(6) For subsection (3) substitute—

"(3) For the purposes of this section each of the following is a competent authority—

(a) the Secretary of State,

(b) an inspector appointed under this Part or under section 94 or 177 of the Financial Services Act 1986,

(c) any person authorised to exercise powers under section 44 of the Insurance Companies Act 1982, section 447 of this Act, section 106 of the Financial Services Act 1986 or section 84 of the Companies Act 1989,

(d) the Department of Economic Development in Northern Ireland,

(e) the Treasury,

(f) the Bank of England,

(g) the Lord Advocate,

(h) the Director of Public Prosecutions, and the Director of Public Prosecutions for Northern Ireland,

(i) any designated agency or transferee body within the meaning of the Financial Services Act 1986, and any body administering a scheme under section 54 of or paragraph 18 of Schedule 11 to that Act (schemes for compensation of investors),

(j) the Chief Registrar of friendly societies and the Registrar of Friendly Societies for Northern Ireland,

(k) the Industrial Assurance Commissioner and the Industrial Assurance Commissioner for Northern Ireland,

(l) any constable,

(m) any procurator fiscal.

(3A) Any information which may by virtue of this section be disclosed to a competent authority may be disclosed to any officer or servant of the authority." .

(7) In subsection (4) (orders) for "subsection (1B)" substitute "subsection (1A)(a) or (1B)".

66. Punishment for destroying, mutilating, &c. company documents

—(1) Section 450 of the [1985 c. 6.] Companies Act 1985 (punishment for destroying, mutilating, &c. company documents) is amended as follows.

(2) In subsection (1) for the opening words down to "insurance company" substitute "An officer of a company, or of an insurance company", for "body's" substitute "company's" and for "the body" substitute "the company".

(3) For subsection (4) substitute—

"(4) Sections 732 (restriction on prosecutions), 733 (liability of individuals for corporate default) and 734 (criminal proceedings against unincorporated bodies) apply to an offence under this section." .

(4) After that subsection insert—

"(5) In this section "document" includes information recorded in any form." .

67. Punishment for furnishing false information

In section 451 of the [1985 c. 6.] Companies Act 1985 (punishment for furnishing false information), for the second sentence substitute—

"Sections 732 (restriction on prosecutions), 733 (liability of individuals for corporate default) and 734 (criminal proceedings against unincorporated bodies) apply to this offence."

68. Disclosure of information by Secretary of State or inspector

For section 451A of the [1985 c. 6.] Companies Act 1985 (disclosure of information by the Secretary of State) substitute—

"Disclosure of information by Secretary of State or inspector.

451A.—(1) This section applies to information obtained under sections 434 to 446.

(2) The Secretary of State may, if he thinks fit—

(a) disclose any information to which this section applies to any person to whom, or for any purpose for which, disclosure is permitted under section 449, or

(b) authorise or require an inspector appointed under this Part to disclose such information to any such person or for any such purpose.

(3) Information to which this section applies may also be disclosed by an inspector appointed under this Part to—

(a) another inspector appointed under this Part or an inspector appointed under section 94 or 177 of the Financial Services Act 1986, or

(b) a person authorised to exercise powers under section 44 of the Insurance Companies Act 1982, section 447 of this Act, section 106 of the Financial Services Act 1986 or section 84 of the Companies Act 1989.

(4) Any information which may by virtue of subsection (3) be disclosed to any person may be disclosed to any officer or servant of that person.

(5) The Secretary of State may, if he thinks fit, disclose any information obtained under section 444 to—

(a) the company whose ownership was the subject of the investigation,

(b) any member of the company,

(c) any person whose conduct was investigated in the course of the investigation,

(d) the auditors of the company, or

(e) any person whose financial interests appear to the Secretary of State to be affected by matters covered by the investigation."

69.   Protection of banking information

—(1) Section 452 of the [1985 c. 6.] Companies Act 1985 (privileged information) is amended as follows.

(2) In subsection (1), omit paragraph (b) (disclosure by bankers of information relating to their customers).

(3) After that subsection insert—

"(1A) Nothing in section 434, 443 or 446 requires a person (except as mentioned in subsection (1B) below) to disclose information or produce documents in respect of which he owes an obligation of confidence by virtue of carrying on the business of banking unless—

(a) the person to whom the obligation of confidence is owed is the company or other body corporate under investigation,

(b) the person to whom the obligation of confidence is owed consents to the disclosure or production, or

(c) the making of the requirement is authorised by the Secretary of State.

(1B) Subsection (1A) does not apply where the person owing the obligation of confidence is the company or other body corporate under investigation under section 431, 432 or 433.".

(4) In subsection (3) after "officer of his" insert "or other person".

70. Investigation of oversea companies

In section 453 of the [1985 c. 6.] Companies Act 1985 (investigation of oversea companies), for subsection (1) substitute—

"(1) The provisions of this Part apply to bodies corporate incorporated outside Great Britain which are carrying on business in Great Britain, or have at any time carried on business there, as they apply to companies under this Act; but subject to the following exceptions, adaptations and modifications.

(1A) The following provisions do not apply to such bodies—

(a) section 431 (investigation on application of company or its members),

(b) section 438 (power to bring civil proceedings on the company's behalf),

(c) sections 442 to 445 (investigation of company ownership and power to obtain information as to those interested in shares, &c.), and

(d) section 446 (investigation of share dealings).

(1B) The other provisions of this Part apply to such bodies subject to such adaptations and modifications as may be specified by regulations made by the Secretary of State." .

71. Investigation of unregistered companies

In Schedule 22 to the [1985 c. 6.] Companies Act 1985 (provisions applying to unregistered companies), for the entry relating to Part XIV substitute—

"

Part XIV (except section 446)	Investigation of companies and their affairs; requisition of documents.

"

Amendments of the Financial Services Act 1986

72. Investigations into collective investment schemes

—(1) Section 94 of the [1986 c. 60.] Financial Services Act 1986 (investigations into collective investment schemes) is amended as follows.

(2) For subsection (7) (privilege on grounds of banker's duty of confidentiality) substitute—

"(7) Nothing in this section requires a person (except as mentioned in subsection (7A) below) to disclose any information or produce any document in respect of which he owes an obligation of confidence by virtue of carrying on the business of banking unless—

(a) the person to whom the obligation of confidence is owed consents to the disclosure or production, or

(b) the making of the requirement was authorised by the Secretary of State.

(7A) Subsection (7) does not apply where the person owing the obligation of confidence or the person to whom it is owed is—

(a) the manager, operator or trustee of the scheme under investigation, or

(b) a manager, operator or trustee whose own affairs are under investigation."

(3) After subsection (8) (duty of inspectors to report) insert—

"(8A) If it appears to the Secretary of State that matters have come to light in the course of the inspectors' investigation which suggest that a criminal offence has been committed, and those matters have been referred to the appropriate prosecuting authority, he may direct the inspectors to take no further steps in the investigation or to take only such further steps as are specified in the direction.

(8B) Where an investigation is the subject of a direction under subsection (8A), the inspectors shall make a final report to the Secretary of State only where the Secretary of State directs them to do so." .

(4) After subsection (9) add—

"(10) A person who is convicted on a prosecution instituted as a result of an investigation under this section may in the same proceedings be ordered to pay the expenses of the investigation to such extent as may be specified in the order.

There shall be treated as expenses of the investigation, in particular, such reasonable sums as the Secretary of State may determine in respect of general staff costs and overheads.

" .

73. Investigations into affairs of persons carrying on investment business

—(1) Section 105 of the Financial Services Act 1986 (investigation into affairs of person carrying on investment business) is amended as follows.

(2) Omit subsection (7) (privilege on grounds of banker's duty of confidentiality).

(3) In subsection (9) (interpretation), in the definition of "documents", for "references to its production include references to producing" substitute "the power to require its production includes power to require the production of".

(4) After subsection (10) add—

"(11) A person who is convicted on a prosecution instituted as a result of an investigation under this section may in the same proceedings be ordered to pay the expenses of the investigation to such extent as may be specified in the order.

There shall be treated as expenses of the investigation, in particular, such reasonable sums as the Secretary of State may determine in respect of general staff costs and overheads.

".

(5) In section 106 of the [1986 c. 60.] Financial Services Act 1986 (exercise of investigation powers by officer, &c.), after subsection (2) insert—

"(2A) A person shall not by virtue of an authority under this section be required to disclose any information or produce any documents in respect of which he owes an obligation of confidence by virtue of carrying on the business of banking unless—

(a) he is the person under investigation or a related company,

(b) the person to whom the obligation of confidence is owed is the person under investigation or a related company,

(c) the person to whom the obligation of confidence is owed consents to the disclosure or production, or

(d) the imposing on him of a requirement with respect to such information or documents has been specifically authorised by the Secretary of State.

In this subsection "documents", "person under investigation" and "related company" have the same meaning as in section 105.

"

74. Investigations into insider dealing

—(1) Section 177 of the Financial Services Act 1986 (investigations into insider dealing) is amended as follows.

(2) After subsection (2) (power to limit period or scope of investigation) insert—

"(2A) At any time during the investigation the Secretary of State may vary the appointment by limiting or extending the period during which the inspector is to continue his investigation or by confining the investigation to particular matters." .

(3) After subsection (5) (duty of inspectors to report) insert—

"(5A) If the Secretary of State thinks fit, he may direct the inspector to take no further steps in the investigation or to take only such further steps as are specified in the direction; and where an investigation is the subject of such a direction, the inspectors shall make a final report to the Secretary of State only where the Secretary of State directs them to do so." .

(4) For subsection (8) (privilege on grounds of banker's duty of confidentiality) substitute—

"(8) A person shall not under this section be required to disclose any information or produce any document in respect of which he owes an obligation of confidence by virtue of carrying on the business of banking unless—

(a) the person to whom the obligation of confidence is owed consents to the disclosure or production, or

(b) the making of the requirement was authorised by the Secretary of State."

(5) In subsection (10) (definition of "documents") for "references to its production include references to producing" substitute "the power to require its production includes power to require the production of".

(6) After subsection (10) add—

"(11) A person who is convicted on a prosecution instituted as a result of an investigation under this section may in the same proceedings be ordered to pay the expenses of the investigation to such extent as may be specified in the order.

There shall be treated as expenses of the investigation, in particular, such reasonable sums as the Secretary of State may determine in respect of general staff costs and overheads.

".

75. Restrictions on disclosure of information

—(1) In section 179(3) of the [1986 c. 60.] Financial Services Act 1986 (persons who are "primary recipients" for purposes of provisions restricting disclosure of information)—

(a) omit the word "and" preceding paragraph (i);

(b) in that paragraph, after "any such person" insert "as is mentioned in paragraphs (a) to (h) above";

(c) after that paragraph insert—

"(j) any constable or other person named in a warrant issued under this Act." .

(2) Section 180 of the Financial Services Act 1986 (exceptions from restrictions on disclosure) is amended as follows.

(3) In subsection (1) (purposes for which disclosure permitted)—

(a) in paragraph (c), after "insolvency" insert "or by Part II, III or VII of the Companies Act 1989";

(b) for paragraph (e) substitute—

"(e) for the purpose—

(i) of enabling or assisting a designated agency to discharge its functions under this Act or Part VII of the Companies Act 1989,

(ii) of enabling or assisting a transferee body or the competent authority to discharge its functions under this Act, or

(iii) of enabling or assisting the body administering a scheme under section 54 above to discharge its functions under the scheme;"

(c) after paragraph (h) insert—

"(hh) for the purpose of enabling or assisting a body established by order under section 46 of the Companies Act 1989 to discharge its functions under Part II of that Act, or of enabling or assisting a recognised supervisory or qualifying body within the meaning of that Part to discharge its functions as such;" ;

(d) after paragraph (o) insert—

"(oo) with a view to the institution of, or otherwise for the purposes of, any disciplinary proceedings relating to the discharge by a public servant of his duties;" ;

(e) in paragraph (p), after "under" insert "section 44 of the Insurance Companies Act 1982, section 447 of the [1985 c. 6.] Companies Act 1985," and after "above" insert "or section 84 of the Companies Act 1989";

(f) after paragraph (q) insert—

"(qq) for the purpose of enabling or assisting an overseas regulatory authority to exercise its regulatory functions;" .

(4) After that subsection insert—

"(1A) In subsection (1)—

(a) in paragraph (oo) "public servant" means an officer or servant of the Crown or of any public or other authority for the time being designated for the purposes of that paragraph by order of the Secretary of State; and

(b) in paragraph (qq) "overseas regulatory authority" and "regulatory functions" have the same meaning as in section 82 of the Companies Act 1989."

(5) In subsection (3) (disclosure to designated public authorities) for "designated for the purposes of this section" substitute "designated for the purposes of this subsection".

(6) Omit subsection (6) (disclosure to certain overseas authorities).

(7) In subsection (9) (orders) for "subsection (3) or (8)" substitute "subsection (1A)(a), (3) or (8)."

76.   Entry and search of premises

—(1) Section 199 of the [1986 c. 60.] Financial Services Act 1986 (powers of entry) is amended as follows.

(2) For subsections (1) and (2) substitute—

"(1) A justice of the peace may issue a warrant under this section if satisfied on information on oath given by or on behalf of the Secretary of State that there are reasonable grounds for believing that an offence has been committed—

(a) under section 4, 47, 57, 130, 133 or 171(2) or (3) above, or

(b) section 1, 2, 4 or 5 of the Company Securities (Insider Dealing) Act 1985,

and that there are on any premises documents relevant to the question whether that offence has been committed.

(2) A justice of the peace may also issue a warrant under this section if satisfied on information on oath given by or on behalf of the Secretary of State, or by a person appointed or authorised to exercise powers under section 94, 106 or 177 above, that there are reasonable grounds for believing that there are on any premises documents whose production has been required under section 94, 105 or 177 above and which have not been produced in compliance with the requirement." .

(3) In subsection (3)(b) for "subsection (1)(a) or (b)" substitute "subsection (1)".

(4) In subsection (5) (period for which documents may be retained), for paragraph (b) substitute—

"(b) if within that period proceedings to which the documents are relevant are commenced against any person for any criminal offence, until the conclusion of those proceedings." .

(5) In subsection (6) (offences) after "Any person who" insert "intentionally".

(6) In subsection (7) for "subsection (1)(a) above" substitute "subsection (1) above".

(7) For subsection (8) substitute—

"(8) In the application of this section to Scotland for the references to a justice of the peace substitute references to a justice of the peace or a sheriff, and for the references to information on oath substitute references to evidence on oath." .

(8) In subsection (9) (definition of "documents"), omit the words from "and, in relation" to the end.

Amendments of other enactments

77. Amendments of the Insurance Companies Act 1982

—(1) Part II of the [1982 c. 50.] Insurance Companies Act 1982 is amended as follows.

(2) In section 44 (power to obtain information and require production of documents), for "books or papers" (wherever occurring) substitute "documents", and for subsection (6) substitute—

"(6) In this section "document" includes information recorded in any form; and, in relation to information recorded otherwise than in legible form, the power to require its production includes power to require the production of a copy of the information in legible form." .

(3) After that section insert—

"Entry and search of premises.   **44A.**—(1) A justice of the peace may issue a warrant under this section if satisfied on information on oath given by or on behalf of the Secretary of State, or by a person authorised to exercise powers under section 44 above, that there are reasonable grounds for believing that there are on any premises documents whose production has been required under section 44(2) to (4) above and which have not been produced in compliance with the requirement.

(2) A justice of the peace may also issue a warrant under this section if satisfied on information on oath given by or on behalf of the Secretary of State, or by a person authorised to exercise powers under section 44 above—

(a) that there are reasonable grounds for believing that an offence has been committed for which the penalty on conviction on indictment is imprisonment for a term of not less than two years and that there are on any premises documents relating to whether the offence has been committed,

(b) that the Secretary of State or, as the case may be, the authorised person has power to require the production of the documents under section 44(2) to (4) above, and

(c) that there are reasonable grounds for believing that if production was so required the documents would not be produced but would be removed from the premises, hidden, tampered with or destroyed.

(3) A warrant under this section shall authorise a constable, together with any other person named in it and any other constables—

(a) to enter the premises specified in the information, using such force as is reasonably necessary for the purpose;

(b) to search the premises and take possession of any documents appearing to be such documents as are mentioned in subsection (1) or (2), as the case may be, or to take, in relation to any such documents, any other steps which may appear to be necessary for preserving them or preventing interference with them;

(c) to take copies of any such documents; and

(d) to require any person named in the warrant to provide an explanation of them or to state where they may be found.

(4) If in the case of a warrant under subsection (2) the justice of the peace is satisfied on information on oath that there are reasonable grounds for believing that there are also on the premises other documents relevant to the investigation, the warrant shall also authorise the actions mentioned in subsection (3) to be taken in relation to such documents.

(5) A warrant under this section shall continue in force until the end of the period of one month beginning with the day on which it is issued.

(6) Any documents of which possession is taken under this section may be retained—

(a) for a period of three months; or

(b) if within that period proceedings to which the documents are relevant are commenced against any person for any criminal offence, until the conclusion of those proceedings.

(7) In the application of this section to Scotland for the references to a justice of the peace substitute references to a justice of the peace or a sheriff, and for the references to information on oath substitute references to evidence on oath.

(8) In this section "document" includes information recorded in any form."

(4) In section 47A(1) (restriction on disclosure of information), after "section 44(2) to (4)" insert "or 44A".

(5) In section 71 (offences and penalties), after subsection (2) insert—

"(2A) A person who intentionally obstructs the exercise of any rights conferred by a warrant issued under section 44A above or fails without reasonable excuse to comply with any requirement imposed in accordance with subsection (3)(d) of that section is guilty of an offence and liable—

(a) on conviction on indictment, to a fine, and

(b) on summary conviction, to a fine not exceeding the statutory maximum."

(6) In section 71(6) (defence to failure to comply with requirement to produce books or papers) for "books or papers" substitute "documents".

78. Amendment of the Insolvency Act 1986

In section 218(5) of the [1986 c. 45.] Insolvency Act 1986 (investigation by Secretary of State on report by liquidator), for paragraph (a) substitute—

"(a) shall thereupon investigate the matter reported to him and such other matters relating to the affairs of the company as appear to him to require investigation, and".

79. Amendment of the Company Directors Disqualification Act 1986

In section 8 of the [1996 c. 46.] Company Directors Disqualification Act 1986 (disqualification after investigation of company), after "section 52 of the Criminal Justice (Scotland) Act 1987" insert "or section 83 of the Companies Act 1989".

80. Amendment of the Building Societies Act 1986

In section 53 of the [1986 c. 53.] Building Societies Act 1986 (confidentiality of information obtained by the Building Societies Commission), in subsection (7)(b) (functions of Secretary of State for purposes of which disclosure may be made) after sub-paragraph (ii) insert—

", or

(iii) Part II, III or VII of the Companies Act 1989;".

81. Amendments of the Banking Act 1987

—(1) In section 84(1) of the [1987 c. 22.] Banking Act 1987 (disclosure of information obtained under that Act), the Table showing the authorities to which, and functions for the purposes of which, disclosure may be made is amended as follows.

(2) In the entry relating to the Secretary of State, in column 2, for "or the Financial Services Act 1986" substitute ", the Financial Services Act 1986 or Part II, III or VII of the Companies Act 1989".

(3) For the entry relating to inspectors appointed by the Secretary of State substitute—

"

| An inspector appointed under Part XIV of the [1985 c. 6.] | Functions under that |

Companies Act 1985 or section 94 or 177 of the Financial Services Act 1986.	Part or that section.

"

(4) For the entry beginning "A person authorised by the Secretary of State" substitute—

"

A person authorised to exercise powers under section 44 of the Insurance Companies Act 1982, section 447 of the [1985 c. 6.] Companies Act 1985, section 106 of the Financial Services Act 1986 or section 84 of the Companies Act 1989.	Functions under that section.

"

(5) For the entry relating to a designated agency or transferee body or the competent authority (within the meaning of the [1986 c. 60.] Financial Services Act 1986) substitute—

A designated agency (within the meaning of the Financial Services Act 1986).	Functions under the Financial Services Act 1986 or Part VII of the Companies Act 1989.
A transferee body or the competent authority (within the meaning of the Financial Services Act 1986).	Functions under the Financial Services Act 1986.

Powers exercisable to assist overseas regulatory authorities

82. Request for assistance by overseas regulatory authorities

—(1) The powers conferred by section 83 are exercisable by the Secretary of State for the purpose of assisting an overseas regulatory authority which has requested his assistance in connection with inquiries being carried out by it or on its behalf.

(2) An "overseas regulatory authority" means an authority which in a country or territory outside the United Kingdom exercises—

    (a) any function corresponding to—

(i) a function under the Financial Services Act 1986 of a designated agency, transferee body or competent authority (within the meaning of that Act),

(ii) a function of the Secretary of State under the [1982 c. 50.] Insurance Companies Act 1982, the [1985 c. 6.] Companies Act 1985 or the Financial Services Act 1986, or

(iii) a function of the Bank of England under the [1987 c. 22.] Banking Act 1987, or

(b) any function in connection with the investigation of, or the enforcement of rules (whether or not having the force of law) relating to, conduct of the kind prohibited by the [1985 c. 9.] Company Securities (Insider Dealing) Act 1985, or

(c) any function prescribed for the purposes of this subsection by order of the Secretary of State, being a function which in the opinion of the Secretary of State relates to companies or financial services.

An order under paragraph (c) shall be made by statutory instrument which shall be subject to annulment in pursuance of a resolution of either House of Parliament.

(3) The Secretary of State shall not exercise the powers conferred by section 83 unless he is satisfied that the assistance requested by the overseas regulatory authority is for the purposes of its regulatory functions.

An authority's "regulatory functions" means any functions falling within subsection (2) and any other functions relating to companies or financial services.

(4) In deciding whether to exercise those powers the Secretary of State may take into account, in particular—

(a) whether corresponding assistance would be given in that country or territory to an authority exercising regulatory functions in the United Kingdom;

(b) whether the inquiries relate to the possible breach of a law, or other requirement, which has no close parallel in the United Kingdom or involves the assertion of a jurisdiction not recognised by the United Kingdom;

(c) the seriousness of the matter to which the inquiries relate, the importance to the inquiries of the information sought in the United Kingdom and whether the assistance could be obtained by other means;

(d) whether it is otherwise appropriate in the public interest to give the assistance sought.

(5) Before deciding whether to exercise those powers in a case where the overseas regulatory authority is a banking supervisor, the Secretary of State shall consult the Bank of England.

A "banking supervisor" means an overseas regulatory authority with respect to which the Bank of England has notified the Secretary of State, for the purposes of this subsection, that it exercises functions corresponding to those of the Bank under the [1987 c. 22.] Banking Act 1987.

(6) The Secretary of State may decline to exercise those powers unless the overseas regulatory authority undertakes to make such contribution towards the costs of their exercise as the Secretary of State considers appropriate.

(7) References in this section to financial services include, in particular, investment business, insurance and banking.

83. Power to require information, documents or other assistance

—(1) The following powers may be exercised in accordance with section 82, if the Secretary of State considers there is good reason for their exercise.

(2) The Secretary of State may require any person—

(a) to attend before him at a specified time and place and answer questions or otherwise furnish information with respect to any matter relevant to the inquiries,

(b) to produce at a specified time and place any specified documents which appear to the Secretary of State to relate to any matter relevant to the inquiries, and

(c) otherwise to give him such assistance in connection with the inquiries as he is reasonably able to give.

(3) The Secretary of State may examine a person on oath and may administer an oath accordingly.

(4) Where documents are produced the Secretary of State may take copies or extracts from them.

(5) A person shall not under this section be required to disclose information or produce a document which he would be entitled to refuse to disclose or produce on grounds of legal professional privilege in proceedings in the High Court or on grounds of confidentiality as between client and professional legal adviser in proceedings in the Court of Session, except that a lawyer may be required to furnish the name and address of his client.

(6) A statement by a person in compliance with a requirement imposed under this section may be used in evidence against him.

(7) Where a person claims a lien on a document, its production under this section is without prejudice to his lien.

(8) In this section "documents" includes information recorded in any form; and, in relation to information recorded otherwise than in legible form, the power to require its production includes power to require the production of a copy of it in legible form.

84. Exercise of powers by officer, &c

—(1) The Secretary of State may authorise an officer of his or any other competent person to exercise on his behalf all or any of the powers conferred by section 83.

(2) No such authority shall be granted except for the purpose of investigating—

    (a) the affairs, or any aspects of the affairs, of a person specified in the authority, or

    (b) a subject-matter so specified,

being a person who, or subject-matter which, is the subject of the inquiries being carried out by or on behalf of the overseas regulatory authority.

(3) No person shall be bound to comply with a requirement imposed by a person exercising powers by virtue of an authority granted under this section unless he has, if required, produced evidence of his authority.

(4) A person shall not by virtue of an authority under this section be required to disclose any information or produce any documents in respect of which he owes an obligation of confidence by virtue of carrying on the business of banking unless—

    (a) the imposing on him of a requirement with respect to such information or documents has been specifically authorised by the Secretary of State, or

    (b) the person to whom the obligation of confidence is owed consents to the disclosure or production.

In this subsection "documents" has the same meaning as in section 83.

(5) Where the Secretary of State authorises a person other than one of his officers to exercise any powers by virtue of this section, that person shall make a report to the Secretary of State in such manner as he may require on the exercise of those powers and the results of exercising them.

85. Penalty for failure to comply with requirement, &c

—(1) A person who without reasonable excuse fails to comply with a requirement imposed on him under section 83 commits an offence and is liable on summary conviction to imprisonment for a term not exceeding six months or to a fine not exceeding level 5 on the standard scale, or both.

(2) A person who in purported compliance with any such requirement furnishes information which he knows to be false or misleading in a material particular, or recklessly furnishes information which is false or misleading in a material particular, commits an offence and is liable—

    (a) on conviction on indictment, to imprisonment for a term not exceeding two years or to a fine, or both;

    (b) on summary conviction, to imprisonment for a term not exceeding six months or to a fine not exceeding the statutory maximum, or both.

86.   Restrictions on disclosure of information

—(1) This section applies to information relating to the business or other affairs of a person which—

    (a) is supplied by an overseas regulatory authority in connection with a request for assistance, or

    (b) is obtained by virtue of the powers conferred by section 83, whether or not any requirement to supply it is made under that section.

(2) Except as permitted by section 87 below, such information shall not be disclosed for any purpose—

    (a) by the primary recipient, or

    (b) by any person obtaining the information directly or indirectly from him,

without the consent of the person from whom the primary recipient obtained the information and, if different, the person to whom it relates.

(3) The "primary recipient" means, as the case may be—

    (a) the Secretary of State,

    (b) any person authorised under section 84 to exercise powers on his behalf, and

    (c) any officer or servant of any such person.

(4) Information shall not be treated as information to which this section applies if it has been made available to the public by virtue of being disclosed in any circumstances in which, or for any purpose for which, disclosure is not precluded by this section.

(5) A person who contravenes this section commits an offence and is liable—

    (a) on conviction on indictment, to imprisonment for a term not exceeding two years or to a fine, or both;

    (b) on summary conviction, to imprisonment for a term not exceeding three months or to a fine not exceeding the statutory maximum, or both.

87.   Exceptions from restrictions on disclosure

—(1) Information to which section 86 applies may be disclosed—

    (a) to any person with a view to the institution of, or otherwise for the purposes of, relevant proceedings,

(b) for the purpose of enabling or assisting a relevant authority to discharge any relevant function (including functions in relation to proceedings),

(c) to the Treasury, if the disclosure is made in the interests of investors or in the public interest,

(d) if the information is or has been available to the public from other sources,

(e) in a summary or collection of information framed in such a way as not to enable the identity of any person to whom the information relates to be ascertained, or

(f) in pursuance of any Community obligation.

(2) The relevant proceedings referred to in subsection (1)(a) are—

(a) any criminal proceedings,

(b) civil proceedings arising under or by virtue of the [1986 c. 60.] Financial Services Act 1986 and proceedings before the Financial Services Tribunal, and

(c) disciplinary proceedings relating to—

(i) the exercise by a solicitor, auditor, accountant, valuer or actuary of his professional duties, or

(ii) the discharge by a public servant of his duties.

(3) In subsection (2)(c)(ii) "public servant" means an officer or servant of the Crown or of any public or other authority for the time being designated for the purposes of that provision by order of the Secretary of State.

(4) The relevant authorities referred to in subsection (1)(b), and the relevant functions in relation to each such authority, are as follows—

Authority	Functions
The Secretary of State.	Functions under the enactments relating to companies, insurance companies or insolvency, or under the Financial Services Act 1986 or Part II, this Part or Part VII of this Act.
An inspector appointed under Part XIV of the [1985 c. 6.] Companies Act 1985 or section 94 or 177 of the Financial Services Act 1986.	Functions under [1985 c. 6.] that Part or that section.
A person authorised to exercise powers under section 44 of the Insurance [1982 c. 50.] Companies Act 1982, section 447 of the [1985 c. 6.] Companies Act 1985, section 106 of the Financial Services Act 1986 or section	Functions under that section.

84 of this Act.	
An overseas regulatory authority.	Its regulatory functions (within the meaning of section 82 of this Act).
The Department of Economic Development in Northern Ireland or a person appointed or authorised by that Department.	Functions conferred on it or him by the enactments relating to companies or insolvency.
A designated agency within the meaning of the [1986 c. 60.] Financial Services Act 1986.	Functions under that Act or Part VII of this Act.
A transferee body or the competent authority within the meaning of the Financial Services Act 1986.	Functions under that Act.
The body administering a scheme under section 54 of the Financial Services Act 1986.	Functions under the scheme.
A recognised self-regulating organisation, recognised professional body, recognised investment exchange, recognised clearing house or recognised self-regulating organisation for friendly societies (within the meaning of the Financial Services Act 1986).	Functions in its capacity as an organisation, body, exchange or clearing house recognised under that Act.
The Chief Registrar of friendly societies, the Registrar of Friendly Societies for Northern Ireland and the Assistant Registrar of Friendly Societies for Scotland.	Functions under the Financial Services Act 1986 or the enactments relating to friendly societies or building societies.
The Bank of England.	Functions under the Banking [1987 c. 22.] Act 1987 and any other functions.
The Deposit Protection Board.	Functions under the Banking Act 1987.
A body established by order under section 46 of this Act.	Functions under Part II of this Act.
A recognised supervisory or qualifying body within the meaning of Part II of this Act.	Functions as such a body.
The Industrial Assurance Commissioner and the Industrial Assurance Commissioner for Northern Ireland.	Functions under the enactments relating to industrial assurance.
The Insurance Brokers Registration Council.	Functions under the Insurance [1977 c. 46.] Brokers (Registration) Act 1977.
The Official Receiver or, in Northern Ireland, the Official Assignee for company liquidations or for bankruptcy.	Functions under the enactments relating to insolvency.
A recognised professional body (within the meaning of section 391 of the [1986 c. 53.] Insolvency Act 1986).	Functions in its capacity as such a body under the [1986 c. 45.] Insolvency Act 1986.
The Building Societies Commission.	Functions under the Building [1986 c. 53.] Societies Act 1986.
The Director General of Fair Trading.	Functions under the [1986 c. 53.] Financial Services Act 1986.

(5) The Secretary of State may by order amend the Table in subsection (4) so as to—

    (a) add any public or other authority to the Table and specify the relevant functions of that authority,

(b) remove any authority from the Table, or

(c) add functions to, or remove functions from, those which are relevant functions in relation to an authority specified in the Table;

and the order may impose conditions subject to which, or otherwise restrict the circumstances in which, disclosure is permitted.

(6) An order under this section shall be made by statutory instrument which shall be subject to annulment in pursuance of a resolution of either House of Parliament.

88. Exercise of powers in relation to Northern Ireland

—(1) The following provisions apply where it appears to the Secretary of State that a request for assistance by an overseas regulatory authority may involve the powers conferred by section 83 being exercised in Northern Ireland in relation to matters which are transferred matters within the meaning of the [1973 c. 36.] Northern Ireland Constitution Act 1973.

(2) The Secretary of State shall before deciding whether to accede to the request consult the Department of Economic Development in Northern Ireland, and if he decides to accede to the request and it appears to him—

(a) that the powers should be exercised in Northern Ireland, and

(b) that the purposes for which they should be so exercised relate wholly or primarily to transferred matters,

he shall by instrument in writing authorise the Department to exercise in Northern Ireland his powers under section 83.

(3) The following provisions have effect in relation to the exercise of powers by virtue of such an authority with the substitution for references to the Secretary of State of references to the Department of Economic Development in Northern Ireland—

(a) section 84 (exercise of powers by officer, &c.),

(b) section 449 of the [1985 c. 6.] Companies Act 1985, section 53 or 54 of the [1985 c. 6.] Building [1986 c. 53.] Societies Act 1986, sections 179 and 180 of the [1986 c. 60.] Financial Services Act 1986, section 84 of the [1987 c. 22.] Banking Act 1987 and sections 86 and 87 above (restrictions on disclosure of information), and

(c) section 89 (authority for institution of criminal proceedings);

and references to the Secretary of State in other enactments which proceed by reference to those provisions shall be construed accordingly as being or including references to the Department.

(4) The Secretary of State may after consultation with the Department of Economic Development in Northern Ireland revoke an authority given to the Department under this section.

(5) In that case nothing in the provisions referred to in subsection (3)(b) shall apply so as to prevent

the Department from giving the Secretary of State any information obtained by virtue of the authority; and (without prejudice to their application in relation to disclosure by the Department) those provisions shall apply to the disclosure of such information by the Secretary of State as if it had been obtained by him in the first place.

(6) Nothing in this section affects the exercise by the Secretary of State of any powers in Northern Ireland—

> (a) in a case where at the time of acceding to the request it did not appear to him that the circumstances were such as to require him to authorise the Department of Economic Development in Northern Ireland to exercise those powers, or

> (b) after the revocation by him of any such authority;

and no objection shall be taken to anything done by or in relation to the Secretary of State or the Department on the ground that it should have been done by or in relation to the other.

89. Prosecutions

Proceedings for an offence under section 85 or 86 shall not be instituted—

> (a) in England and Wales, except by or with the consent of the Secretary of State or the Director of Public Prosecutions;

> (b) in Northern Ireland, except by or with the consent of the Secretary of State or the Director of Public Prosecutions for Northern Ireland.

90. Offences by bodies corporate, partnerships and unincorporated associations

—(1) Where an offence under section 85 or 86 committed by a body corporate is proved to have been committed with the consent or connivance of, or to be attributable to any neglect on the part of, a director, manager, secretary or other similar officer of the body, or a person purporting to act in any such capacity, he as well as the body corporate is guilty of the offence and liable to be proceeded against and punished accordingly.

(2) Where the affairs of a body corporate are managed by its members, subsection (1) applies in relation to the acts and defaults of a member in connection with his functions of management as to a director of a body corporate.

(3) Where an offence under section 85 or 86 committed by a partnership is proved to have been committed with the consent or connivance of, or to be attributable to any neglect on the part of, a partner, he as well as the partnership is guilty of the offence and liable to be proceeded against and punished accordingly.

(4) Where an offence under section 85 or 86 committed by an unincorporated association (other than a partnership) is proved to have been committed with the consent or connivance of, or to be attributable to any neglect on the part of, any officer of the association or any member of its governing body, he as well as the association is guilty of the offence and liable to be proceeded against and punished accordingly.

91. Jurisdiction and procedure in respect of offences

—(1) Summary proceedings for an offence under section 85 may, without prejudice to any jurisdiction exercisable apart from this section, be taken against a body corporate or unincorporated association at any place at which it has a place of business and against an individual at any place where he is for the time being.

(2) Proceedings for an offence alleged to have been committed under section 85 or 86 by an unincorporated association shall be brought in the name of the association (and not in that of any of its members), and for the purposes of any such proceedings any rules of court relating to the service of documents apply as in relation to a body corporate.

(3) Section 33 of the [1925 c. 86.] Criminal Justice Act 1925 and Schedule 3 to the [1980 c. 43.] Magistrates' Courts Act 1980 (procedure on charge of offence against a corporation) apply in a case in which an unincorporated association is charged in England and Wales with an offence under section 85 or 86 as they apply in the case of a corporation.

(4) In relation to proceedings on indictment in Scotland for an offence alleged to have been committed under section 85 or 86 by an unincorporated association, section 74 of the [1975 c. 21.] Criminal Procedure (Scotland) Act 1975 (proceedings on indictment against bodies corporate) applies as if the association were a body corporate.

(5) Section 18 of the [1945 c. 15. (N.I.)] Criminal Justice Act (Northern Ireland) 1945 and Schedule 4 to the [S.I. 1981/1675 (N.I. 26.)] Magistrates' Courts (Northern Ireland) Order 1981 (procedure on charge of offence against a corporation) apply in a case in which an unincorporated association is charged in Northern Ireland with an offence under section 85 or 86 as they apply in the case of a corporation.

(6) A fine imposed on an unincorporated association on its conviction of such an offence shall be paid out of the funds of the association.

Part IV: Registration of Company Charges

92. Introduction

The provisions of this Part amend the provisions of the [1985 c. 6.] Companies Act 1985 relating to the registration of company charges—

    (a) by inserting in Part XII of that Act (in place of sections 395 to 408 and 410 to 423) new provisions with respect to <u>companies registered in Great Britain</u>, and

    (b) by inserting as Chapter III of Part XXIII of that Act (in place of sections 409 and 424) new provisions with respect to oversea companies.

Registration in the companies charges register

93. Charges requiring registration

The following sections are inserted in Part XII of the [1985 c. 6.] Companies Act 1985—

"Registration in the company charges register

Introductory provisions.	**395.**—(1) The purpose of this Part is to secure the registration of charges on a company's property.

(2) In this Part—

"charge" means any form of security interest (fixed or floating) over property, other than an interest arising by operation of law; and

"property", in the context of what is the subject of a charge, includes future property.

(3) It is immaterial for the purposes of this Part where the property subject to a charge is situated.

(4) References in this Part to "the registrar" are—

(a) in relation to a company registered in England and Wales, to the <u>registrar of companies for England and Wales</u>, and

(b) in relation to a company registered in Scotland, to the registrar of companies for Scotland;

and references to registration, in relation to a charge, are to registration in the register kept by him under this Part.

Charges requiring registration.	**396.**—(1) The charges requiring registration under this Part are—

(a) a charge on land or any interest in land, other than—

(i) in England and Wales, a charge for rent or any other periodical sum issuing out of the land,

(ii) in Scotland, a charge for any rent, ground annual or other periodical sum payable in respect of the land;

(b) a charge on goods or any interest in goods, other than a charge under which the chargee is entitled to possession either of the goods or of a document of title to them;

(c) a charge on intangible movable property (in Scotland, incorporeal moveable property) of any of the following descriptions—

    (i) goodwill,

    (ii) intellectual property,

    (iii) book debts (whether book debts of the company or assigned to the company),

    (iv) uncalled share capital of the company or calls made but not paid;

(d) a charge for securing an issue of debentures; or

(e) a floating charge on the whole or part of the company's property.

(2) The descriptions of charge mentioned in subsection (1) shall be construed as follows—

(a) a charge on a debenture forming part of an issue or series shall not be treated as falling within paragraph (a) or (b) by reason of the fact that the debenture is secured by a charge on land or goods (or on an interest in land or goods);

(b) in paragraph (b) "goods" means any tangible movable property (in Scotland, corporeal moveable property) other than money;

(c) a charge is not excluded from paragraph (b) because the chargee is entitled to take possession in case of default or on the occurrence of some other event;

(d) in paragraph (c)(ii) "intellectual property" means—

    (i) any patent, trade mark, service mark, registered design, copyright or design right, or

    (ii) any licence under or in respect of any such right;

(e) a debenture which is part of an issue or series shall not be treated as a book debt for the purposes of paragraph (c)(iii);

(f) the deposit by way of security of a negotiable instrument given to secure the payment of book debts shall not be treated for the purposes of paragraph (c)(iii) as a charge on book debts;

(g) a shipowner's lien on subfreights shall not be treated as a charge on book debts for the purposes of paragraph (c)(iii) or as a floating charge for the purposes of paragraph (e).

(3) Whether a charge is one requiring registration under this Part shall be determined—

(a) in the case of a charge created by a company, as at the date the charge is created, and

(b) in the case of a charge over property acquired by a company, as at the date of the acquisition.

(4) The Secretary of State may by regulations amend subsections (1) and (2) so as to add any description of charge to, or remove any description of charge from, the charges requiring registration under this Part.

(5) Regulations under this section shall be made by statutory instrument which shall be subject to annulment in pursuance of a resolution of either House of Parliament.

(6) In the following provisions of this Part references to a charge are, unless the context otherwise requires, to a charge requiring registration under this Part.

Where a charge not otherwise requiring registration relates to property by virtue of which it requires to be registered and to other property, the references are to the charge so far as it relates to property of the former description.

"

94. The companies charges register

The following section is inserted in Part XII of the [1985 c. 6.] Companies Act 1985—

"The companies charges register.

397.—(1) The registrar shall keep for each company a register, in such form as he thinks fit, of charges on property of the company.

(2) The register shall consist of a file containing with respect to each charge the particulars and other information delivered to the registrar under the provisions of this Part.

(3) Any person may require the registrar to provide a certificate stating the date on which any specified particulars of, or other information relating to, a charge were delivered to him.

(4) The certificate shall be signed by the registrar or authenticated by his official seal.

(5) The certificate shall be conclusive evidence that the specified particulars or other information were delivered to the registrar no later than the date stated in the certificate; and it shall be presumed unless the contrary is proved that they were not delivered earlier than that date."

95. Delivery of particulars for registration

The following sections are inserted in Part XII of the [1985 c. 6.] Companies Act 1985—

"Company's duty to deliver particulars of charge for registration.

398.—(1) It is the duty of a company which creates a charge, or acquires property subject to a charge—

(a) to deliver the prescribed particulars of the charge, in the prescribed form, to the registrar for registration, and

(b) to do so within 21 days after the date of the charge's creation or, as the case may be, the date of the acquisition;

but particulars of a charge may be delivered for registration by any person interested in the charge.

(2) Where the particulars are delivered for registration by a person other than the company concerned, that person is entitled to recover from the company the amount of any fees paid by him to the registrar in connection with the registration.

(3) If a company fails to comply with subsection (1), then, unless particulars of the charge have been delivered for registration by another person, the company and every officer of it who is in default is liable to a fine.

(4) Where prescribed particulars in the prescribed form are delivered to the registrar for registration, he shall file the particulars in the register and shall note, in such form as he thinks fit, the date on which they were delivered to him.

(5) The registrar shall send to the company and any person appearing from the particulars to be the chargee, and if the particulars were delivered by another person interested in the charge to that person, a copy of the particulars filed by him and of the note made by him as to the date on which they were delivered.

Effect of failure to deliver particulars

399.—(1) Where a charge is created by a company and no prescribed particulars in the prescribed form are delivered for registration within the period of 21 days after the date of the charge's creation, the charge is void against—

for registration.

        (a) an administrator or liquidator of the company, and

        (b) any person who for value acquires an interest in or right over property subject to the charge,

where the relevant event occurs after the creation of the charge, whether before or after the end of the 21 day period.

This is subject to section 400 (late delivery of particulars).

(2) In this Part "the relevant event" means—

        (a) in relation to the voidness of a charge as against an administrator or liquidator, the beginning of the insolvency proceedings, and

        (b) in relation to the voidness of a charge as against a person acquiring an interest in or right over property subject to a charge, the acquisition of that interest or right;

and references to "a relevant event" shall be construed accordingly.

(3) Where a relevant event occurs on the same day as the charge is created, it shall be presumed to have occurred after the charge is created unless the contrary is proved.

Late delivery of particulars.

400.—(1) Where prescribed particulars of a charge created by a company, in the prescribed form, are delivered for registration more than 21 days after the date of the charge's creation, section 399(1) does not apply in relation to relevant events occurring after the particulars are delivered.

(2) However, where in such a case—

        (a) the company is at the date of delivery of the particulars unable to pay its debts, or subsequently becomes unable to pay its debts in consequence of the transaction under which the charge is created, and

        (b) insolvency proceedings begin before the end of the relevant period beginning with the date of delivery of the particulars,

the charge is void as against the administrator or liquidator.

(3) For this purpose—

        (a) the company is "unable to pay its debts" in the circumstances specified in section 123 of the Insolvency Act 1986; and

(b) the "relevant period" is—

(i) two years in the case of a floating charge created in favour of a person connected with the company (within the meaning of section 249 of that Act),

(ii) one year in the case of a floating charge created in favour of a person not so connected, and

(iii) six months in any other case.

(4) Where a relevant event occurs on the same day as the particulars are delivered, it shall be presumed to have occurred before the particulars are delivered unless the contrary is proved."

96. Delivery of further particulars

The following section is inserted in Part XII of the [1985 c. 6.] Companies Act 1985—

"Delivery of further particulars.

401.—(1) Further particulars of a charge, supplementing or varying the registered particulars, may be delivered to the registrar for registration at any time.

(2) Further particulars must be in the prescribed form signed by or on behalf of both the company and the chargee.

(3) Where further particulars are delivered to the registrar for registration and appear to him to be duly signed, he shall file the particulars in the register and shall note, in such form as he thinks fit, the date on which they were delivered to him.

(4) The registrar shall send to the company and any person appearing from the particulars to be the chargee, and if the particulars were delivered by another person interested in the charge to that other person, a copy of the further particulars filed by him and of the note made by him as to the date on which they were delivered."

97. Effect of omissions and errors in registered particulars

The following section is inserted in Part XII of the [1985 c. 6.] Companies Act 1985—

"Effect of omissions and errors in registered particulars.

402.—(1) Where the registered particulars of a charge created by a company are not complete and accurate, the charge is void, as mentioned below, to the extent that rights are not disclosed by the registered particulars which would be disclosed if they were complete and accurate.

(2) The charge is void to that extent, unless the court on the application of the chargee orders otherwise, as against—

(a) an administrator or liquidator of the company, and

(b) any person who for value acquires an interest in or right over property subject to the charge,

where the relevant event occurs at a time when the particulars are incomplete or inaccurate in a relevant respect.

(3) Where a relevant event occurs on the same day as particulars or further particulars are delivered, it shall be presumed to have occurred before those particulars are delivered unless the contrary is proved.

(4) The court may order that the charge is effective as against an administrator or liquidator of the company if it is satisfied—

(a) that the omission or error is not likely to have misled materially to his prejudice any unsecured creditor of the company, or

(b) that no person became an unsecured creditor of the company at a time when the registered particulars of the charge were incomplete or inaccurate in a relevant respect.

(5) The court may order that the charge is effective as against a person acquiring an interest in or right over property subject to the charge if it is satisfied that he did not rely, in connection with the acquisition, on registered particulars which were incomplete or inaccurate in a relevant respect.

(6) For the purposes of this section an omission or inaccuracy with respect to the name of the chargee shall not be regarded as a failure to disclose the rights of the chargee."

98. Memorandum of charge ceasing to affect company's property

The following section is inserted in Part XII of the [1985 c. 6.] Companies Act 1985—

"Memorandum of charge ceasing to affect company's property.

403.—(1) Where a charge of which particulars have been delivered ceases to affect the company's property, a memorandum to that effect may be delivered to the registrar for registration.

(2) The memorandum must be in the prescribed form signed by or on behalf of both the company and the chargee.

(3) Where a memorandum is delivered to the registrar for registration and appears to him to be duly signed, he shall file it in the register, and shall note, in such form as he thinks fit, the date on which it was delivered to him.

(4) The registrar shall send to the company and any person appearing from the memorandum to be the chargee, and if the memorandum was delivered by

another person interested in the charge to that person, a copy of the memorandum filed by him and of the note made by him as to the date on which it was delivered.

(5) If a duly signed memorandum is delivered in a case where the charge in fact continues to affect the company's property, the charge is void as against—

    (a) an administrator or liquidator of the company, and

    (b) any person who for value acquires an interest in or right over property subject to the charge,

where the relevant event occurs after the delivery of the memorandum.

(6) Where a relevant event occurs on the same day as the memorandum is delivered, it shall be presumed to have occurred before the memorandum is delivered unless the contrary is proved."

The following sections are inserted in Part XII of the [1985 c. 6.] Companies Act 1985—

99.   'Further provisions with respect to voidness of charges

Exclusion of voidness as against unregistered charges.

404.—(1) A charge is not void by virtue of this Part as against a subsequent charge unless some or all of the relevant particulars of that charge are duly delivered for registration—

    (a) within 21 days after the date of its creation, or

    (b) before complete and accurate relevant particulars of the earlier charge are duly delivered for registration.

(2) Where relevant particulars of the subsequent charge so delivered are incomplete or inaccurate, the earlier charge is void as against that charge only to the extent that rights are disclosed by registered particulars of the subsequent charge duly delivered for registration before the corresponding relevant particulars of the earlier charge.

(3) The relevant particulars of a charge for the purposes of this section are those prescribed particulars relating to rights inconsistent with those conferred by or in relation to the other charge.

Restrictions on voidness by virtue of this Part.

405.—(1) A charge is not void by virtue of this Part as against a person acquiring an interest in or right over property where the acquisition is expressly subject to the charge.

(2) Nor is a charge void by virtue of this Part in relation to any property by reason of a relevant event occurring after the company which created the

charge has disposed of the whole of its interest in that property.

Effect of exercise of power of sale.

406.–(1) A chargee exercising a power of sale may dispose of property to a purchaser freed from any interest or right arising from the charge having become void to any extent by virtue of this Part—

    (a) against an administrator or liquidator of the company, or

    (b) against a person acquiring a security interest over property subject to the charge;

and a purchaser is not concerned to see or inquire whether the charge has become so void.

(2) The proceeds of the sale shall be held by the chargee in trust to be applied—

    First, in discharge of any sum effectively secured by prior incumbrances to which the sale is not made subject;

    Second, in payment of all costs, charges and expenses properly incurred by him in connection with the sale, or any previous attempted sale, of the property;

    Third, in discharge of any sum effectively secured by the charge and incumbrances ranking *pari passu* with the charge;

    Fourth, in discharge of any sum effectively secured by incumbrances ranking after the charge;

and any residue is payable to the company or to a person authorised to give a receipt for the proceeds of the sale of the property.

(3) For the purposes of subsection (2)—

    (a) prior incumbrances include any incumbrance to the extent that the charge is void as against it by virtue of this Part; and

    (b) no sum is effectively secured by a charge to the extent that it is void as against an administrator or liquidator of the company.

(4) In this section—

    (a) references to things done by a chargee include things done by a receiver appointed by him, whether or not the receiver acts as his agent;

    (b) "power of sale" includes any power to dispose of, or grant an interest out of, property for the purpose of enforcing a charge (but in relation to Scotland does not include the power to grant a lease), and references to "sale" shall be construed accordingly; and

(c) "purchaser" means a person who in good faith and for valuable consideration acquires an interest in property.

(5) The provisions of this section as to the order of application of the proceeds of sale have effect subject to any other statutory provision (in Scotland, any other statutory provision or rule of law) applicable in any case.

(6) Where a chargee exercising a power of sale purports to dispose of property freed from any such interest or right as is mentioned in subsection (1) to a person other than a purchaser, the above provisions apply, with any necessary modifications, in relation to a disposition to a purchaser by that person or any successor in title of his.

(7) In Scotland, subsections (2) and (7) of section 27 of the Conveyancing and Feudal Reform (Scotland) Act 1970 apply to a chargee unable to obtain a discharge for any payment which he is required to make under subsection (2) above as they apply to a creditor in the circumstances mentioned in those subsections.

Effect of voidness on obligation secured.

407.—(1) Where a charge becomes void to any extent by virtue of this Part, the whole of the sum secured by the charge is payable forthwith on demand; and this applies notwithstanding that the sum secured by the charge is also the subject of other security.

(2) Where the charge is to secure the repayment of money, the references in subsection (1) to the sum secured include any interest payable."

. **100.** The following sections are inserted in Part XII of the [1985 c. 6.] Companies Act 1985—

100. "**Additional information to be registered**

Particulars of taking up of issue of debentures.

408.—(1) Where particulars of a charge for securing an issue of debentures have been delivered for registration, it is the duty of the company—

(a) to deliver to the registrar for registration particulars in the prescribed form of the date on which any debentures of the issue are taken up, and of the amount taken up, and

(b) to do so before the end of the period of 21 days after the date on which they are taken up.

(2) Where particulars in the prescribed form are delivered to the registrar for registration under this section, he shall file them in the register.

(3) If a company fails to comply with subsection (1), the company and every officer of it who is in default is liable to a fine.

Notice of appointment of receiver or manager, &c.

409.—(1) If a person obtains an order for the appointment of a receiver or manager of a company's property, or appoints such a receiver or manager under powers contained in an instrument, he shall within seven days of the order or of the appointment under those powers, give notice of that fact in the prescribed form to the registrar for registration.

(2) Where a person appointed receiver or manager of a company's property under powers contained in an instrument ceases to act as such receiver or manager, he shall, on so ceasing, give notice of that fact in the prescribed form to the registrar for registration.

(3) Where a notice under this section in the prescribed form is delivered to the registrar for registration, he shall file it in the register.

(4) If a person makes default in complying with the requirements of subsection (1) or (2), he is liable to a fine.

(5) This section does not apply in relation to companies registered in Scotland (for which corresponding provision is made by sections 53, 54 and 62 of the Insolvency Act 1986).

Notice of crystallisation of floating charge, &c.

410.—(1) The Secretary of State may by regulations require notice in the prescribed form to be given to the registrar of—

 (a) the occurrence of such events as may be prescribed affecting the nature of the security under a floating charge of which particulars have been delivered for registration, and

 (b) the taking of such action in exercise of powers conferred by a fixed or floating charge of which particulars have been delivered for registration, or conferred in relation to such a charge by an order of the court, as may be prescribed.

(2) The regulations may make provision as to—

 (a) the persons by whom notice is required to be, or may be, given, and the period within which notice is required to be given;

 (b) the filing in the register of the particulars contained in the notice and the noting of the date on which the notice was given; and

 (c) the consequences of failure to give notice.

(3) As regards the consequences of failure to give notice of an event causing a floating charge to crystallise, the regulations may include provision to the

effect that the crystallisation—

(a) shall be treated as ineffective until the prescribed particulars are delivered, and

(b) if the prescribed particulars are delivered after the expiry of the prescribed period, shall continue to be ineffective against such persons as may be prescribed,

subject to the exercise of such powers as may be conferred by the regulations on the court.

(4) The regulations may provide that if there is a failure to comply with such of the requirements of the regulations as may be prescribed, such persons as may be prescribed are liable to a fine.

(5) Regulations under this section shall be made by statutory instrument which shall be subject to annulment in pursuance of a resolution of either House of Parliament.

(6) Regulations under this section shall not apply in relation to a floating charge created under the law of Scotland by a company registered in Scotland."

Copies of instruments and register to be kept by company

101. Copies of instruments and register to be kept by company

The following sections are inserted in Part XII of the [1985 c. 6.] Companies Act 1985—

"*Copies of instruments and register to be kept by company*

Duty to keep copies of instruments and register.

411.—(1) Every company shall keep at its registered office a copy of every instrument creating or evidencing a charge over the company's property.

In the case of a series of uniform debentures, a copy of one debenture of the series is sufficient.

(2) Every company shall also keep at its registered office a register of all such charges, containing entries for each charge giving a short description of the property charged, the amount of the charge and (except in the case of securities to bearer) the names of the persons entitled to it.

(3) This section applies to any charge, whether or not particulars are required to be delivered to the registrar for registration.

(4) If a company fails to comply with any requirement of this section, the company and every officer of it who is in default is liable to a fine.

Inspection of copies and register.

412.—(1) The copies and the register referred to in section 411 shall be open to the inspection of any creditor or member of the company without fee; and to the inspection of any other person on payment of such fee as may be prescribed.

(2) Any person may request the company to provide him with a copy of—

(a) any instrument creating or evidencing a charge over the company's property, or

(b) any entry in the register of charges kept by the company, on payment of such fee as may be prescribed.

This subsection applies to any charge, whether or not particulars are required to be delivered to the registrar for registration.

(3) The company shall send the copy to him not later than ten days after the day on which the request is received or, if later, on which payment is received.

(4) If inspection of the copies or register is refused, or a copy requested is not sent within the time specified above—

(a) the company and every officer of it who is in default is liable to a fine, and

(b) the court may by order compel an immediate inspection of the copies or register or, as the case may be, direct that the copy be sent immediately."

Supplementary provisions

102. Power to make further provision by regulations

The following section is inserted in Part XII of the [1985 c. 6.] Companies Act 1985—

"Supplementary provisions

Power to make further provi-

413.—(1) The Secretary of State may by regulations make further provision as to the application of the provisions of this Part in relation to charges of any

sion by regula-   description specified in the regulations.
tions.

Nothing in the following provisions shall be construed as restricting the generality of that power.

(2) The regulations may require that where the charge is contained in or evidenced or varied by a written instrument there shall be delivered to the registrar for registration, instead of particulars or further particulars of the charge, the instrument itself or a certified copy of it together with such particulars as may be prescribed.

(3) The regulations may provide that a memorandum of a charge ceasing to affect property of the company shall not be accepted by the registrar unless supported by such evidence as may be prescribed, and that a memorandum not so supported shall be treated as not having been delivered.

(4) The regulations may also provide that where the instrument creating the charge is delivered to the registrar in support of such a memorandum, the registrar may mark the instrument as cancelled before returning it and shall send copies of the instrument cancelled to such persons as may be prescribed.

(5) The regulations may exclude or modify, in such circumstances and to such extent as may be prescribed, the operation of the provisions of this Part relating to the voidness of a charge.

(6) The regulations may require, in connection with the delivery of particulars, further particulars or a memorandum of the charge's ceasing to affect property of the company, the delivery of such supplementary information as may be prescribed, and may—

(a) apply in relation to such supplementary information any provisions of this Part relating to particulars, further particulars or such a memorandum, and

(b) provide that the particulars, further particulars or memorandum shall be treated as not having been delivered until the required supplementary information is delivered.

(7) Regulations under this section shall be made by statutory instrument which shall be subject to annulment in pursuance of a resolution of either House of Parliament."

103. Other supplementary provisions

The following sections are inserted in Part XII of the [1985 c. 6.] Companies Act 1985—

"Date of   **414.**—(1) References in this Part to the date of creation of a charge by a company shall be construed as follows.
creation of
charge.

(2) A charge created under the law of England and Wales shall be taken to be

created—

(a) in the case of a charge created by an instrument in writing, when the instrument is executed by the company or, if its execution by the company is conditional, upon the conditions being fulfilled, and

(b) in any other case, when an enforceable agreement is entered into by the company conferring a security interest intended to take effect forthwith or upon the company acquiring an interest in property subject to the charge.

(3) A charge created under the law of Scotland shall be taken to be created—

(a) in the case of a floating charge, when the instrument creating the floating charge is executed by the company, and

(b) in any other case, when the right of the person entitled to the benefit of the charge is constituted as a real right.

(4) Where a charge is created in the United Kingdom but comprises property outside the United Kingdom, any further proceedings necessary to make the charge valid or effectual under the law of the country where the property is situated shall be disregarded in ascertaining the date on which the charge is to be taken to be created.

Prescribed particulars and related expressions.

415.—(1) References in this Part to the prescribed particulars of a charge are to such particulars of, or relating to, the charge as may be prescribed.

(2) The prescribed particulars may, without prejudice to the generality of subsection (1), include—

(a) whether the company has undertaken not to create other charges ranking in priority to or *pari passu* with the charge, and

(b) whether the charge is a market charge within the meaning of Part VII of the Companies Act 1989 or a charge to which the provisions of that Part apply as they apply to a market charge.

(3) References in this Part to the registered particulars of a charge at any time are to such particulars and further particulars of the charge as have at that time been duly delivered for registration.

(4) References in this Part to the registered particulars of a charge being complete and accurate at any time are to their including all the prescribed particulars which would be required to be delivered if the charge were then newly created.

Notice of matters

416.—(1) A person taking a charge over a company's property shall be taken to have notice of any matter requiring registration and disclosed on the register at the disclosed on register. time the charge is created.

(2) Otherwise, a person shall not be taken to have notice of any matter by reason of its being disclosed on the register or by reason of his having failed to search the register in the course of making such inquiries as ought reasonably to be made.

(3) The above provisions have effect subject to any other statutory provision as to whether a person is to be taken to have notice of any matter disclosed on the register.

Power of court to dispense with signature.

417.—(1) Where it is proposed to deliver further particulars of a charge, or to deliver a memorandum of a charge ceasing to affect the company's property, and—

    (a) the chargee refuses to sign or authorise a person to sign on his behalf, or cannot be found, or

    (b) the company refuses to authorise a person to sign on its behalf,

the court may on the application of the company or the chargee, or of any other person having a sufficient interest in the matter, authorise the delivery of the particulars or memorandum without that signature.

(2) The order may be made on such terms as appear to the court to be appropriate.

(3) Where particulars or a memorandum are delivered to the registrar for registration in reliance on an order under this section, they must be accompanied by an office copy of the order.

In such a case the references in sections 401 and 403 to the particulars or memorandum being duly signed are to their being otherwise duly signed.

(4) The registrar shall file the office copy of the court order along with the particulars or memorandum."

104.   **Interpretation, &c**

The following sections are inserted in Part XII of the [1985 c. 6.] Companies Act 1985—

"Regulations.   **418.** Regulations under any provision of this Part, or prescribing anything for the purposes of any such provision—

    (a) may make different provision for different cases, and

    (b) may contain such supplementary, incidental and transitional provisions as appear to the Secretary of State to be appropriate.

Minor definitions.   **419.**—(1) In this Part—

"chargee" means the person for the time being entitled to exercise the security rights conferred by the charge;

"issue of debentures" means a group of debentures, or an amount of debenture stock, secured by the same charge; and

"series of debentures" means a group of debentures each containing or giving by reference to another instrument a charge to the benefit of which the holders of debentures of the series are entitled *pari passu*.

(2) References in this Part to the creation of a charge include the variation of a charge which is not registrable so as to include property by virtue of which it becomes registrable.

The provisions of section 414 (construction of references to date of creation of charge) apply in such a case with any necessary modifications.

(3) References in this Part to the date of acquisition of property by a company are—

(a) in England and Wales, to the date on which the acquisition is completed, and

(b) in Scotland, to the date on which the transaction is settled.

(4) In the application of this Part to a floating charge created under the law of Scotland, references to crystallisation shall be construed as references to the attachment of the charge.

(5) References in this Part to the beginning of insolvency proceedings are to—

(a) the presentation of a petition on which an administration order or winding-up order is made, or

(b) the passing of a resolution for voluntary winding up.

Index of defined expressions.   **420.** The following Table shows the provisions of this Part defining or otherwise explaining expressions used in this Part (other than expressions used only in the same section)—

| charge | sections 395(2) |

	and 396(6)
	section 396
charge requiring registration	
chargee	section 419(1)
complete and accurate (in relation to registered particulars)	section 415(4)
creation of charge	section 419(2)
crystallisation (in relation to Scottish floating charge)	section 419(4)
date of acquisition (of property by a company)	section 419(3)
date of creation of charge	section 414
further particulars	section 401
insolvency proceedings, beginning of	section 419(5)
issue of debentures	section 419(1)
memorandum of charge ceasing to affect company's property	section 403
prescribed particulars	section 415(1) and (2)
property	section 395(2)
registered particulars	section 415(3)
registrar and registration in relation to a charge	section 395(4)
relevant event	section 399(2)
series of debentures	section 419(1).

"

105. Charges on property of oversea company

The provisions set out in Schedule 15 are inserted in Part XXIII of the [1985 c. 6.] Companies Act 1985 (oversea companies), as a Chapter III (registration of charges).

106. Application of provisions to unregistered companies

In Schedule 22 to the [1985 c. 6.] Companies Act 1985 (provisions applying to unregistered companies), at the appropriate place insert—

| Part XII | Registration of company charges; copies of instruments and register to be kept by company. | Subject to section 718(3). |

107. Consequential amendments

The enactments specified in Schedule 16 have effect with the amendments specified there, which are consequential on the amendments made by the preceding provisions of this Part.

Part V: Other amendments of Company Law

108. A company's capacity and the power of the directors to bind it

—(1) In Chapter III of Part I of the [1985 c. 6.] Companies Act 1985 (a company's capacity; formalities of carrying on business), for section 35 substitute—

"A company's capacity not limited by its memorandum.

35.—(1) The validity of an act done by a company shall not be called into question on the ground of lack of capacity by reason of anything in the company's memorandum.

(2) A member of a company may bring proceedings to restrain the doing of an act which but for subsection (1) would be beyond the company's capacity; but no such proceedings shall lie in respect of an act to be done in fulfilment of a legal obligation arising from a previous act of the company.

(3) It remains the duty of the directors to observe any limitations on their powers flowing

from the company's memorandum; and action by the directors which but for subsection (1) would be beyond the company's capacity may only be ratified by the company by special resolution.

A resolution ratifying such action shall not affect any liability incurred by the directors or any other person; relief from any such liability must be agreed to separately by special resolution.

(4) The operation of this section is restricted by section 30B(1) of the [1960 c. 58.] Charities Act 1960 and section 112(3) of the Companies Act 1989 in relation to companies which are charities; and section 322A below (invalidity of certain transactions to which directors or their associates are parties) has effect notwithstanding this section.

Power of directors to bind the company.

35A.—(1) In favour of a person dealing with a company in good faith, the power of the board of directors to bind the company, or authorise others to do so, shall be deemed to be free of any limitation under the company's constitution.

(2) For this purpose—

(a) a person "deals with" a company if he is a party to any transaction or other act to which the company is a party;

(b) a person shall not be regarded as acting in bad faith by reason only of his knowing that an act is beyond the powers of the directors under the company's constitution; and

(c) a person shall be presumed to have acted in good faith unless the contrary is proved.

(3) The references above to limitations on the directors' powers under the company's constitution include limitations deriving—

(a) from a resolution of the company in general meeting or a meeting of any class of shareholders, or

(b) from any agreement between the members of the company or of any class of shareholders.

(4) Subsection (1) does not affect any right of a member of the company to bring proceedings to restrain the doing of an act which is beyond the powers of the directors; but no such proceedings shall lie in respect of an act to be done in fulfilment of a legal obligation arising from a previous act of the company.

(5) Nor does that subsection affect any liability incurred by the directors, or any other person, by reason of the directors' exceeding their powers.

(6) The operation of this section is restricted by section 30B(1) of the [1960 c. 58.] Charities Act 1960 and section 112(3) of the Companies Act 1989 in relation to companies which are charities; and section 322A below (invalidity of certain transactions to which directors or their associates are parties) has effect notwithstanding this section.

No duty to enquire as to capacity of company or authority of directors.	**35B.** A party to a transaction with a company is not bound to enquire as to whether it is permitted by the company's memorandum or as to any limitation on the powers of the board of directors to bind the company or authorise others to do so.".

(2) In Schedule 21 to the [1985 c. 6.] Companies Act 1985 (effect of registration of companies not formed under that Act), in paragraph 6 (general application of provisions of Act), after sub-paragraph (5) insert—

"(6) Where by virtue of sub-paragraph (4) or (5) a company does not have power to alter a provision, it does not have power to ratify acts of the directors in contravention of the provision.".

(3) In Schedule 22 to the [1985 c. 6.] Companies Act 1985 (provisions applying to unregistered companies), in the entries relating to Part I, in the first column for "section 35" substitute "sections 35 to 35B".

109. Invalidity of certain transactions involving directors

.—(1) In Part X of the [1985 c. 6.] Companies Act 1985 (enforcement of fair dealing by directors), after section 322 insert—

"Invalidity of certain transactions involving directors, etc.

322A.—(1) This section applies where a company enters into a transaction to which the parties include—

(a) a director of the company or of its holding company, or

(b) a person connected with such a director or a company with whom such a director is associated,

and the board of directors, in connection with the transaction, exceed any limitation on their powers under the company's constitution.

(2) The transaction is voidable at the instance of the company.

(3) Whether or not it is avoided, any such party to the transaction as is mentioned in subsection (1)(a) or (b), and any director of the company who authorised the transaction, is liable—

(a) to account to the company for any gain which he has made directly or indirectly by the transaction, and

(b) to indemnify the company for any loss or damage resulting from the transaction.

(4) Nothing in the above provisions shall be construed as excluding the operation of any other enactment or rule of law by virtue of which the transaction may be called in question or any liability to the company may arise.

(5) The transaction ceases to be voidable if—

(a) restitution of any money or other asset which was the subject-matter of the transaction is no longer possible, or

(b) the company is indemnified for any loss or damage resulting from the transaction, or

(c) rights acquired bona fide for value and without actual notice of the directors' exceeding their powers by a person who is not party to the transaction would be affected by the avoidance, or

(d) the transaction is ratified by the company in general meeting, by ordinary or special resolution or otherwise as the case may require.

(6) A person other than a director of the company is not liable under subsection (3) if he shows that at the time the transaction was entered into he did not know that the directors were exceeding their powers.

(7) This section does not affect the operation of section 35A in relation to any party to the transaction not within subsection (1)(a) or (b).

But where a transaction is voidable by virtue of this section and valid by virtue of that section in favour of such a person, the court may, on the application of that person or of the company, make such order affirming, severing or setting aside the transaction, on such terms, as appear to the court to be just.

(8) In this section "transaction" includes any act; and the reference in subsection (1) to limitations under the company's constitution includes limitations deriving—

(a) from a resolution of the company in general meeting or a meeting of any class of shareholders, or

(b) from any agreement between the members of the company or of any class of shareholders."

(2) In Schedule 22 to the [1985 c. 6.] Companies Act 1985 (provisions applying to unregistered companies), in the entries relating to Part X, insert—

"

| section 322A | Invalidity of certain transactions involving directors, etc. | Subject to section 718(3). |

"

110. Statement of company's objects

In Chapter I of Part I of the [1985 c. 6.] Companies Act 1985 (company formation), after section 3 (forms of memorandum) insert—

"Statement of company's objects: general commercial company.

    3A. Where the company's memorandum states that the object of the company is to carry on business as a general commercial company—

    (a) the object of the company is to carry on any trade or business whatsoever, and

    (b) the company has power to do all such things as are incidental or conducive to the carrying on of any trade or business by it."

(2) In the same Chapter, for section 4 (resolution to alter objects) substitute—

"Resolution to alter objects.

    4.— (1) A company may by special resolution alter its memorandum with respect to the statement of the company's objects.

    (2) If an application is made under the following section, an alteration does not have effect except in so far as it is confirmed by the court."

111. Charitable companies

—(1) In the [1960 c. 58.] Charities Act 1960, for section 30 (charitable companies) substitute—

"Charitable companies: winding

    30. Where a charity may be wound up by the High Court under the Insolvency Act 1986, a petition for it to be wound up under that Act by any court in up. England or Wales having jurisdiction may be presented by the Attorney General, as well as by any person authorised by that Act.

Charitable companies: alteration of objects clause.

30A.—(1) Where a charity is a company or other body corporate having power to alter the instruments establishing or regulating it as a body corporate, no exercise of that power which has the effect of the body ceasing to be a charity shall be valid so as to affect the application of—

(a) any property acquired under any disposition or agreement previously made otherwise than for full consideration in money or money's worth, or any property representing property so acquired,

(b) any property representing income which has accrued before the alteration is made, or

(c) the income from any such property as aforesaid.

(2) Where a charity is a company, any alteration by it of the objects clause in its memorandum of association is ineffective without the prior written consent of the Commissioners; and it shall deliver a copy of that consent to the registrar of companies under section 6(1)(a) or (b) of the [1985 c. 6.] Companies Act 1985 along with the printed copy of the memorandum as altered.

(3) Section 6(3) of that Act (offences) applies in relation to a default in complying with subsection (2) as regards the delivery of a copy of the Commissioners' consent."

30B.—(1) Sections 35 and 35A of the [1985 c. 6.] Companies Act 1985 (capacity of company not limited by its memorandum; power of directors to bind company) do not apply to the acts of a company which is a charity except in favour of a person who—

(a) gives full consideration in money or money's worth in relation to the act in question, and

(b) does not know that the act is not permitted by the company's memorandum or, as the case may be, is beyond the powers of the directors,

or who does not know at the time the act is done that the company is a charity.

(2) However, where such a company purports to transfer or grant an interest in property, the fact that the act was not permitted by the company's memorandum or, as the case may be, that the directors in connection with the act exceeded any limitation on their powers under the company's constitution, does not affect the title of a person who subsequently acquires the property or any interest in it for full consideration without actual notice of any such circumstances affecting the validity of the company's act.

(3) In any proceedings arising out of subsection (1) the burden of proving—

>   (a) that a person knew that an act was not permitted by the company's memorandum or was beyond the powers of the directors, or

>   (b) that a person knew that the company was a charity,

lies on the person making that allegation.

(4) Where a company is a charity, the ratification of an act under section 35(3) of the [1985 c. 6.] Companies Act 1985, or the ratification of a transaction to which section 322A of that Act applies (invalidity of certain transactions to which directors or their associates are parties), is ineffective without the prior written consent of the Commissioners.

30C.—(1) Where a company is a charity and its name does not include the word "charity" or the word "charitable", the fact that the company is a charity shall be stated in English in legible characters—

>   (a) in all business letters of the company,

>   (b) in all its notices and other official publications,

>   (c) in all bills of exchange, promissory notes, endorsements, cheques and orders for money or goods purporting to be signed by or on behalf of the company,

>   (d) in all conveyances purporting to be executed by the company, and

>   (e) in all its bills of parcels, invoices, receipts and letters of

credit.

(2) In subsection (1)(d) "conveyance" means any instrument creating, transferring, varying or extinguishing an interest in land.

(3) Section 349(2) to (4) of the [1985 c. 6.] Companies Act 1985 (offences in connection with failure to include required particulars in business letters, &c.) apply in relation to a contravention of subsection (1) above.

(2) In section 46 of the [1960 c. 58.] Charities Act 1960 (definitions), at the appropriate place insert—

""company" means a company formed and registered under the [1985 c. 6.] Companies Act 1985, or to which the provisions of that Act apply as they apply to such a company;."

112. Charitable companies (Scotland)

—(1) In the following provisions (which extend to Scotland only)—

(a) "company" means a company formed and registered under the [1985 c. 6.] Companies Act 1985, or to which the provisions of that Act apply as they apply to such a company; and

(b) "charity" means a body established for charitable purposes only (that expression having the same meaning as in the Income Tax Acts).

(2) Where a charity is a company or other body corporate having power to alter the instruments establishing or regulating it as a body corporate, no exercise of that power which has the effect of the body ceasing to be a charity shall be valid so as to affect the application of—

(a) any property acquired by virtue of any transfer, contract or obligation previously effected otherwise than for full consideration in money or money's worth, or any property representing property so acquired,

(b) any property representing income which has accrued before the alteration is made, or

(c) the income from any such property as aforesaid.

(3) Sections 35 and 35A of the [1985 c. 6.] Companies Act 1985 (capacity of company not limited by its memorandum; power of directors to bind company) do not apply to the acts of a company which is a charity except in favour of a person who—

(a) gives full consideration in money or money's worth in relation to the act in question, and

(b) does not know that the act is not permitted by the company's memorandum or, as the case may be, is beyond the powers of the directors,

or who does not know at the time the act is done that the company is a charity.

(4) However, where such a company purports to transfer or grant an interest in property, the fact that the act was not permitted by the company's memorandum or, as the case may be, that the directors in connection with the act exceeded any limitation on their powers under the company's constitution, does not affect the title of a person who subsequently acquires the property or any interest in it for full consideration without actual notice of any such circumstances affecting the validity of the company's act.

(5) In any proceedings arising out of subsection (3) the burden of proving—

(a) that a person knew that an act was not permitted by the company's memorandum or was beyond the powers of the directors, or

(b) that a person knew that the company was a charity,

lies on the person making that allegation.

(6) Where a company is a charity and its name does not include the word "charity" or the word "charitable", the fact that the company is a charity shall be stated in English in legible characters—

(a) in all business letters of the company,

(b) in all its notices and other official publications,

(c) in all bills of exchange, promissory notes, endorsements, cheques and orders for money or goods purporting to be signed by or on behalf of the company,

(d) in all conveyances purporting to be executed by the company, and

(e) in all its bills of parcels, invoices, receipts and letters of credit.

(7) In subsection (6)(d) "conveyance" means any document for the creation, transfer, variation or extinction of an interest in land.

(8) Section 349(2) to (4) of the [1985 c. 6.] Companies Act 1985 (offences in connection with failure to include required particulars in business letters, &c.) apply in relation to a contravention of subsection (6) above.

De-regulation of private companies

113. Written resolutions of private companies

—(1) Chapter IV of Part XI of the [1985 c. 6.] Companies Act 1985 (meetings and resolutions) is amended as follows.

(2) After section 381 insert—

Written resolutions of private companies

Written resolutions of private companies.

381A.—(1) Anything which in the case of a private company may be done—

(a) by resolution of the company in general meeting, or

(b) by resolution of a meeting of any class of members of the company,

may be done, without a meeting and without any previous notice being required, by resolution in writing signed by or on behalf of all the members of the company who at the date of the resolution would be entitled to attend and vote at such meeting.

(2) The signatures need not be on a single document provided each is on a document which accurately states the terms of the resolution.

(3) The date of the resolution means when the resolution is signed by or on behalf of the last member to sign.

(4) A resolution agreed to in accordance with this section has effect as if passed—

(a) by the company in general meeting, or

(b) by a meeting of the relevant class of members of the company,

as the case may be; and any reference in any enactment to a meeting at which a resolution is passed or to members voting in favour of a resolution shall be construed accordingly.

(5) Any reference in any enactment to the date of passing of a resolution is, in relation to a resolution agreed to in accordance with this section, a reference to the date of the resolution, unless section 381B(4) applies in which case it shall be construed as a reference to the date from which the resolution has effect.

(6) A resolution may be agreed to in accordance with this section which would otherwise be required to be passed as a special, extraordinary or elective resolution; and any reference in any enactment to a special, extraordinary or elective resolution includes such a resolution.

(7) This section has effect subject to the exceptions specified in Part I of Schedule 15A; and in relation to certain descriptions of resolution under this section the procedural requirements of this Act have effect with the adaptations specified in Part II of that Schedule.

Rights of auditors in relation to written resolution.	**381B.**—(1) A copy of any written resolution proposed to be agreed to in accordance with section 381A shall be sent to the company's auditors.

(2) If the resolution concerns the auditors as auditors, they may within seven days from the day on which they receive the copy give notice to the company stating their opinion that the resolution should be considered by the company in general meeting or, as the case may be, by a meeting of the relevant class of members of the company.

(3) A written resolution shall not have effect unless—

    (a) the auditors notify the company that in their opinion the resolution—

        (i) does not concern them as auditors, or

        (ii) does so concern them but need not be considered by the company in general meeting or, as the case may be, by a meeting of the relevant class of members of the company, or

    (b) the period for giving a notice under subsection (2) expires without any notice having been given in accordance with that subsection.

(4) A written resolution previously agreed to in accordance with section 381A shall not have effect until that notification is given or, as the case may be, that period expires. |
| Written resolutions: supplementary provisions. | **381C.**—(1) Sections 381A and 381B have effect notwithstanding any provision of the company's memorandum or articles.

(2) Nothing in those sections affects any enactment or rule of law as to—

    (a) things done otherwise than by passing a resolution, or

    (b) cases in which a resolution is treated as having been passed, or a person is precluded from alleging that a resolution has not been duly passed." |

(3) After section 382 insert—

"Recording of written resolutions.	**382A.**—(1) Where a written resolution is agreed to in accordance with section 381A which has effect as if agreed by the company in general meeting, the company shall cause a record of the resolution (and of the signatures) to be entered in a book in the same way as minutes of proceedings of a general meeting of the company.

(2) Any such record, if purporting to be signed by a director of the company or by the company secretary, is evidence of the proceedings in agreeing to the resolution; and where a record is made in accordance with this section, then, until the contrary is proved, the requirements of this Act with respect to those proceedings shall be deemed to be complied with.

(3) Section 382(5) (penalties) applies in relation to a failure to comply with subsection (1) above as it applies in relation to a failure to comply with subsection (1) of that section; and section 383 (inspection of minute books) applies in relation to a record made in accordance with this section as it applies in relation to the minutes of a general meeting."

114.   Written resolutions: supplementary provisions

—(1) In the [1985 c. 6.] Companies Act 1985 the following Schedule is inserted after Schedule 15—

Written Resolutions of Private Companies

Part I

Exceptions

"**1.**   Section 381A does not apply to—

(a) a resolution under section 303 removing a director before the expiration of his period of office, or

(b) a resolution under section 391 removing an auditor before the expiration of his term of office.

Part II

Adaptation of Procedural Requirements

Introductory

2.—(1) In this Part of this Schedule (which adapts certain requirements of this Act in relation to proceedings under section 381A)—

(a) a "written resolution" means a resolution agreed to, or proposed to be agreed to, in accordance with that section, and

(b) a "relevant member" means a member by whom, or on whose

behalf, the resolution is required to be signed in accordance with that section.

(2) A written resolution is not effective if any of the requirements of this Part of this Schedule is not complied with.

Section 95 (disapplication of pre-emption rights)

3.—(1) The following adaptations have effect in relation to a written resolution under section 95(2) (disapplication of pre-emption rights), or renewing a resolution under that provision.

(2) So much of section 95(5) as requires the circulation of a written statement by the directors with a notice of meeting does not apply, but such a statement must be supplied to each relevant member at or before the time at which the resolution is supplied to him for signature.

(3) Section 95(6) (offences) applies in relation to the inclusion in any such statement of matter which is misleading, false or deceptive in a material particular.

Section 155 (financial assistance for purchase of company's own shares or those of holding company)

4. In relation to a written resolution giving approval under section 155(4) or (5) (financial assistance for purchase of company's own shares or those of holding company), section 157(4)(a) (documents to be available at meeting) does not apply, but the documents referred to in that provision must be supplied to each relevant member at or before the time at which the resolution is supplied to him for signature.

Sections 164, 165 and 167 (authority for off-market purchase or contingent purchase contract of company's own shares)

5.—(1) The following adaptations have effect in relation to a written resolution—

(a) conferring authority to make an off-market purchase of the company's own shares under section 164(2),

(b) conferring authority to vary a contract for an off-market purchase of the company's own shares under section 164(7), or

(c) varying, revoking or renewing any such authority under section 164(3).

(2) Section 164(5) (resolution ineffective if passed by exercise of voting rights by member holding shares to which the resolution relates) does not apply; but for the purposes of section 381A(1) a member holding shares to

which the resolution relates shall not be regarded as a member who would be entitled to attend and vote.

(3) Section 164(6) (documents to be available at company's registered office and at meeting) does not apply, but the documents referred to in that provision and, where that provision applies by virtue of section 164(7), the further documents referred to in that provision must be supplied to each relevant member at or before the time at which the resolution is supplied to him for signature.

(4) The above adaptations also have effect in relation to a written resolution in relation to which the provisions of section 164(3) to (7) apply by virtue of—

(a) section 165(2) (authority for contingent purchase contract), or

(b) section 167(2) (approval of release of rights under contract approved under section 164 or 165).

Section 173 (approval for payment out of capital)

6.—(1) The following adaptations have effect in relation to a written resolution giving approval under section 173(2) (redemption or purchase of company's own shares out of capital).

(2) Section 174(2) (resolution ineffective if passed by exercise of voting rights by member holding shares to which the resolution relates) does not apply; but for the purposes of section 381A(1) a member holding shares to which the resolution relates shall not be regarded as a member who would be entitled to attend and vote.

(3) Section 174(4) (documents to be available at meeting) does not apply, but the documents referred to in that provision must be supplied to each relevant member at or before the time at which the resolution is supplied to him for signature.

Section 319 (approval of director's service contract)

7. In relation to a written resolution approving any such term as is mentioned in section 319(1) (director's contract of employment for more than five years), section 319(5) (documents to be available at company's registered office and at meeting) does not apply, but the documents referred to in that provision must be supplied to each relevant member at or before the time at which the resolution is supplied to him for signature.

Section 337 (funding of director's expenditure in performing his duties)

8. In relation to a written resolution giving approval under section 337(3)(a) (funding a director's expenditure in performing his duties), the requirement of that provision that certain matters be disclosed at the meeting at which the resolution is passed does not apply, but those matters must be disclosed to each relevant member at or before the time at which the resolution is supplied to him for signature.

(2) The Schedule inserted after Schedule 15 to the [1985 c. 6.] Companies Act 1985 by the [S.I. 1987/1991] Companies (Mergers and Divisions) Regulations 1987 is renumbered "15B"; and accordingly, in section 427A of that Act (also inserted by those regulations), in subsections (1) and (8) for "15A" substitute "15B".

115. Election by private company to dispense with certain requirements

—(1) In Part IV of the [1985 c. 6.] Companies Act 1985 (allotment of shares and debentures), in section 80(1) (authority of company required for certain allotments) after "this section" insert "or section 80A"; and after that section insert—

"Election by private company as to duration of authority.

80A.—(1) A private company may elect (by elective resolution in accordance with section 379A) that the provisions of this section shall apply, instead of the provisions of section 80(4) and (5), in relation to the giving or renewal, after the election, of an authority under that section.

(2) The authority must state the maximum amount of relevant securities that may be allotted under it and may be given—

(a) for an indefinite period, or

(b) for a fixed period, in which case it must state the date on which it will expire.

(3) In either case an authority (including an authority contained in the articles) may be revoked or varied by the company in general meeting.

(4) An authority given for a fixed period may be renewed or further renewed by the company in general meeting.

(5) A resolution renewing an authority—

(a) must state, or re-state, the amount of relevant securities which may be allotted under the authority or, as the case may be, the amount remaining to be allotted under it, and

(b) must state whether the authority is renewed for an indefinite period or for a fixed period, in which case it must state the date on which the renewed authority will expire.

(6) The references in this section to the maximum amount of relevant securities that may be allotted shall be construed in accordance with section 80(6).

(7) If an election under this section ceases to have effect, an authority then in force which was given for an indefinite period or for a fixed period of more than

five years—

      (a) if given five years or more before the election ceases to have effect, shall expire forthwith, and

      (b) otherwise, shall have effect as if it had been given for a fixed period of five years."

(2) In Chapter IV of Part XI of the [1985 c. 6.] Companies Act 1985 (meetings and resolutions), after section 366 (annual general meeting) insert—

"Election by private company to dispense with annual general meetings.

366A.—(1) A private company may elect (by elective resolution in accordance with section 379A) to dispense with the holding of annual general meetings.

(2) An election has effect for the year in which it is made and subsequent years, but does not affect any liability already incurred by reason of default in holding an annual general meeting.(3) In any year in which an annual general meeting would be required to be held but for the election, and in which no such meeting has been held, any member of the company may, by notice to the company not later than three months before the end of the year, require the holding of an annual general meeting in that year.

(4) If such a notice is given, the provisions of section 366(1) and (4) apply with respect to the calling of the meeting and the consequences of default.

(5) If the election ceases to have effect, the company is not obliged under section 366 to hold an annual general meeting in that year if, when the election ceases to have effect, less than three months of the year remains.

This does not affect any obligation of the company to hold an annual general meeting in that year in pursuance of a notice given under subsection (3).

"

(3) In the same Chapter, in sections 369(4) and 378(3) (majority required to sanction short notice of meeting) insert—

"A private company may elect (by elective resolution in accordance with section 379A) that the above provisions shall have effect in relation to the company as if for the references to 95 per cent. there were substituted references to such lesser percentage, but not less than 90 per cent., as may be specified in the resolution or subsequently determined by the company in general meeting."

116.   **Elective Resolution of private company**

—(1) Chapter IV of Part XI of the [1985 c. 6.] Companies Act 1985 (meetings and resolutions) is amended as follows.

(2) After section 379 insert—

"Elective resolution of private company.

379A.—(1) An election by a private company for the purposes of—

(a) section 80A (election as to duration of authority to allot shares),

(b) section 252 (election to dispense with laying of accounts and reports before general meeting),

(c) section 366A (election to dispense with holding of annual general meeting),

(d) section 369(4) or 378(3) (election as to majority required to authorise short notice of meeting), or

(e) section 386 (election to dispense with appointment of auditors annually),

shall be made by resolution of the company in general meeting in accordance with this section.

Such a resolution is referred to in this Act as an "elective resolution".

(2) An elective resolution is not effective unless—

(a) at least 21 days' notice in writing is given of the meeting, stating that an elective resolution is to be proposed and stating the terms of the resolution, and

(b) the resolution is agreed to at the meeting, in person or by proxy, by all the members entitled to attend and vote at the meeting.

(3) The company may revoke an elective resolution by passing an ordinary resolution to that effect.

(4) An elective resolution shall cease to have effect if the company is re-registered as a public company.

(5) An elective resolution may be passed or revoked in accordance with this section, and the provisions referred to in subsection (1) have effect, notwithstanding any contrary provision in the company's articles of association."

(3) In section 380 (registration of resolutions), in subsection (4) (resolutions to which the section applies), after paragraph (b) insert—

"(bb) an elective resolution or a resolution revoking such a resolution;".

117. Power to make further provision by regulations

—(1) The Secretary of State may by regulations make provision enabling private companies to elect, by elective resolution in accordance with section 379A of the [1985 c. 6.] Companies Act 1985, to dispense with compliance with such requirements of that Act as may be specified in the regulations, being requirements which appear to the Secretary of State to relate primarily to the internal administration and procedure of companies.

(2) The regulations may add to, amend or repeal provisions of that Act; and may provide for any such provision to have effect, where an election is made, subject to such adaptations and modifications as appear to the Secretary of State to be appropriate.

(3) The regulations may make different provision for different cases and may contain such supplementary, incidental and transitional provisions as appear to the Secretary of State to be appropriate.

(4) Regulations under this section shall be made by statutory instrument.

(5) No regulations under this section shall be made unless a draft of the instrument containing the regulations has been laid before Parliament and approved by a resolution of each House.

Appointment and removal of auditors and related matters

118. Introduction

—(1) The following sections amend the provisions of the [1985 c. 6.] Companies Act 1985 relating to auditors by inserting new provisions in Chapter V of Part XI of that Act.

(2) The new provisions, together with the amendment made by section 124, replace the present provisions of that Chapter except section 389 (qualification for appointment as auditor) which is replaced by provisions in Part II of this Act.

119. Appointment of auditors

—(1) The following sections are inserted in Chapter V of Part XI of the [1985 c. 6.] Companies Act 1985 (auditors)—

"Appointment of auditors

Duty to appoint auditors.	**384.**—(1) Every company shall appoint an auditor or auditors in accordance with this Chapter.

This is subject to section 388A (dormant company exempt from obligation to appoint auditors).

(2) Auditors shall be appointed in accordance with section 385 (appointment at general meeting at which accounts are laid), except in the case of a private company which has elected to dispense with the laying of accounts in which case the appointment shall be made in accordance with section 385A.

(3) References in this Chapter to the end of the time for appointing auditors are to the end of the time within which an appointment must be made under section 385(2) or 385A(2), according to whichever of those sections applies.

(4) Sections 385 and 385A have effect subject to section 386 under which a private company may elect to dispense with the obligation to appoint auditors annually.

Appointment at general meeting at which accounts laid.	**385.**—(1) This section applies to every public company and to a private company which has not elected to dispense with the laying of accounts.

(2) The company shall, at each general meeting at which accounts are laid, appoint an auditor or auditors to hold office from the conclusion of that meeting until the conclusion of the next general meeting at which accounts are laid.

(3) The first auditors of the company may be appointed by the directors at any time before the first general meeting of the company at which accounts are laid; and auditors so appointed shall hold office until the conclusion of that meeting.

(4) If the directors fail to exercise their powers under subsection (3), the powers may be exercised by the company in general meeting.

Appointment by private company which is not obliged to lay accounts.	**385A.**—(1) This section applies to a private company which has elected in accordance with section 252 to dispense with the laying of accounts before the company in general meeting.

(2) Auditors shall be appointed by the company in general meeting before the end of the period of 28 days beginning with the day on which copies of the company's annual accounts for the previous financial year are sent to members under section 238 or, if notice is given under section 253(2) requiring the laying of the accounts before the company in general meeting, the conclusion of that meeting.

Auditors so appointed shall hold office from the end of that period or, as the case may be, the conclusion of that meeting until the end of the time for appointing auditors for the next financial year.

(3) The first auditors of the company may be appointed by the directors at any time before—

> (a) the end of the period of 28 days beginning with the day on which copies of the company's first annual accounts are sent to members under section 238, or

> (b) if notice is given under section 253(2) requiring the laying of the accounts before the company in general meeting, the beginning of that meeting;

and auditors so appointed shall hold office until the end of that period or, as the case may be, the conclusion of that meeting.

(4) If the directors fail to exercise their powers under subsection (3), the powers may be exercised by the company in general meeting.

(5) Auditors holding office when the election is made shall, unless the company in general meeting determines otherwise, continue to hold office until the end of the time for appointing auditors for the next financial year; and auditors holding office when an election ceases to have effect shall continue to hold office until the conclusion of the next general meeting of the company at which accounts are laid.

Election by private company to dispense with annual appointment.

386.—(1) A private company may elect (by elective resolution in accordance with section 379A) to dispense with the obligation to appoint auditors annually.

(2) When such an election is in force the company's auditors shall be deemed to be re-appointed for each succeeding financial year on the expiry of the time for appointing auditors for that year, unless—

> (a) a resolution has been passed under section 250 by virtue of which the company is exempt from the obligation to appoint auditors, or

> (b) a resolution has been passed under section 393 to the effect that their appointment should be brought to an end.

(3) If the election ceases to be in force, the auditors then holding office shall continue to hold office—

> (a) where section 385 then applies, until the conclusion of the next general meeting of the company at which accounts are laid;

> (b) where section 385A then applies, until the end of the time for appointing auditors for the next financial year under that section.

(4) No account shall be taken of any loss of the opportunity of further

deemed re-appointment under this section in ascertaining the amount of any compensation or damages payable to an auditor on his ceasing to hold office for any reason.

Appointment by Secretary of State in default of appointment by company.

387.—(1) If in any case no auditors are appointed, re-appointed or deemed to be re-appointed before the end of the time for appointing auditors, the Secretary of State may appoint a person to fill the vacancy.

(2) In such a case the company shall within one week of the end of the time for appointing auditors give notice to the Secretary of State of his power having become exercisable.

If a company fails to give the notice required by this subsection, the company and every officer of it who is in default is guilty of an offence and liable to a fine and, for continued contravention, to a daily default fine.

Filling of casual vacancies.

388.—(1) The directors, or the company in general meeting, may fill a casual vacancy in the office of auditor.

(2) While such a vacancy continues, any surviving or continuing auditor or auditors may continue to act.

(3) Special notice is required for a resolution at a general meeting of a company—

(a) filling a casual vacancy in the office of auditor, or

(b) re-appointing as auditor a retiring auditor who was appointed by the directors to fill a casual vacancy.

(4) On receipt of notice of such an intended resolution the company shall forthwith send a copy of it—

(a) to the person proposed to be appointed, and

(b) if the casual vacancy was caused by the resignation of an auditor, to the auditor who resigned.

Dormant company exempt from obligation to appoint auditors.

388A.—(1) A company which by virtue of section 250 (dormant companies: exemption from provisions as to audit of accounts) is exempt from the provisions of Part VII relating to the audit of accounts is also exempt from the obligation to appoint auditors.

(2) The following provisions apply if the exemption ceases.

(3) Where section 385 applies (appointment at general meeting at which accounts are laid), the directors may appoint auditors at any time before the next meeting of the company at which accounts are to be laid; and auditors so appointed shall hold office until the conclusion of that meeting.

(4) Where section 385A applies (appointment by private company not obliged to lay accounts), the directors may appoint auditors at any time before—

(a) the end of the period of 28 days beginning with the day on which copies of the company's annual accounts are next sent to members under section 238, or

(b) if notice is given under section 253(2) requiring the laying of the accounts before the company in general meeting, the beginning of that meeting;

and auditors so appointed shall hold office until the end of that period or, as the case may be, the conclusion of that meeting.

(5) If the directors fail to exercise their powers under subsection (3) or (4), the powers may be exercised by the company in general meeting."

(2) In Schedule 24 to the [1985 c. 6.] Companies Act 1985 (punishment of offences), at the appropriate place insert—

387(2)	Company failing to give Secretary of State notice of non-appointment of auditors.	Summary.	One-fifth of the statutory maximum.	One-fiftieth of the statutory maximum.

(3) In section 46(2) of the [1987 c. 22.] Banking Act 1987 (duty of auditor of authorised institution to give notice to Bank of England of certain matters) for "appointed under section 384" substitute "appointed under Chapter V of Part XI"; and in section 46(4) (adaptation of references in relation to Northern Ireland) for "sections 384," substitute "Chapter V of Part XI and sections".

120. Rights of auditors

—(1) The following sections are inserted in Chapter V of Part XI of the [1985 c. 6.] Companies Act 1985 (auditors)—

"Rights of auditors

Rights to information.

389A.—(1) The auditors of a company have a right of access at all times to the company's books, accounts and vouchers, and are entitled to require from the company's officers such information and explanations as they think necessary for the performance of their duties as auditors.

(2) An officer of a company commits an offence if he knowingly or recklessly makes to the company's auditors a statement (whether written or oral) which—

(a) conveys or purports to convey any information or explanations which the auditors require, or are entitled to require, as auditors of the company, and

(b) is misleading, false or deceptive in a material particular.

A person guilty of an offence under this subsection is liable to imprisonment or a fine, or both.

(3) A subsidiary undertaking which is a body corporate incorporated in Great Britain, and the auditors of such an undertaking, shall give to the auditors of any parent company of the undertaking such information and explanations as they may reasonably require for the purposes of their duties as auditors of that company.

If a subsidiary undertaking fails to comply with this subsection, the undertaking and every officer of it who is in default is guilty of an offence and liable to a fine; and if an auditor fails without reasonable excuse to comply with this subsection he is guilty of an offence and liable to a fine.

(4) A parent company having a subsidiary undertaking which is not a body corporate incorporated in Great Britain shall, if required by its auditors to do so, take all such steps as are reasonably open to it to obtain from the subsidiary undertaking such information and explanations as they may reasonably require for the purposes of their duties as auditors of that company.

If a parent company fails to comply with this subsection, the company and every officer of it who is in default is guilty of an offence and liable to a fine.

(5) Section 734 (criminal proceedings against unincorporated bodies) applies to an offence under subsection (3).

Right to attend company meetings, &c.

390.—(1) A company's auditors are entitled—

(a) to receive all notices of, and other communications relating to, any general meeting which a member of the company is entitled to receive;

(b) to attend any general meeting of the company; and

(c) to be heard at any general meeting which they attend on any part of the business of the meeting which concerns them as auditors.

(2) In relation to a written resolution proposed to be agreed to by a private company in accordance with section 381A, the company's auditors are enti-

tled—

    (a) to receive all such communications relating to the resolution as, by virtue of any provision of Schedule 15A, are required to be supplied to a member of the company,

    (b) to give notice in accordance with section 381B of their opinion that the resolution concerns them as auditors and should be considered by the company in general meeting or, as the case may be, by a meeting of the relevant class of members of the company,

    (c) to attend any such meeting, and

    (d) to be heard at any such meeting which they attend on any part of the business of the meeting which concerns them as auditors.

    (3) The right to attend or be heard at a meeting is exercisable in the case of a body corporate or partnership by an individual authorised by it in writing to act as its representative at the meeting."

(2) In section 734 of the [1985 c. 6.] Companies Act 1985 (criminal proceedings against unincorporated bodies), in subsection (1) (offences in relation to which the provisions apply), after "under" insert "section 389A(3) or".

(3) In Schedule 24 to the [1985 c. 6.] Companies Act 1985 (punishment of offences) at the appropriate place insert—

"

389A(2)	Officer of company making false, misleading or deceptive statement to auditors.	1. On indictment. 2. Summary.	2 years or a fine; or both. 6 months or the statutory maximum; or both.
389A(3)	Subsidiary undertaking or its auditor failing to give information to auditors of parent company.	Summary.	One-fifth of the statutory maximum.
389A(4)	Parent company failing to obtain from subsidiary undertaking information for purposes of audit.	Summary.	One-fifth of the statutory maximum.

"

attend and be heard at general meetings, &c.) for "387(1)" substitute "390(1)".

121. Remuneration of auditors

The following sections are inserted in Chapter V of Part XI of the [1985 c. 6.] Companies Act 1985 (auditors)—

'Remuneration of auditors

Remuneration of auditors.

390A.—(1) The remuneration of auditors appointed by the company in general meeting shall be fixed by the company in general meeting or in such manner as the company in general meeting may determine.

(2) The remuneration of auditors appointed by the directors or the Secretary of State shall be fixed by the directors or the Secretary of State, as the case may be.

(3) There shall be stated in a note to the company's annual accounts the amount of the remuneration of the company's auditors in their capacity as such.

(4) For the purposes of this section "remuneration" includes sums paid in respect of expenses.

(5) This section applies in relation to benefits in kind as to payments in cash, and in relation to any such benefit references to its amount are to its estimated money value.

The nature of any such benefit shall also be disclosed.

Remuneration of auditors or their associates for non-audit work.

390B.—(1) The Secretary of State may make provision by regulations for securing the disclosure of the amount of any remuneration received or receivable by a company's auditors or their associates in respect of services other than those of auditors in their capacity as such.

(2) The regulations may—

(a) provide that "remuneration" includes sums paid in respect of expenses,

(b) apply in relation to benefits in kind as to payments in cash, and in relation to any such benefit require disclosure of its nature and its estimated money value,

(c) define "associate" in relation to an auditor,

(d) require the disclosure of remuneration in respect of services rendered to associated undertakings of the company, and

(e) define "associated undertaking" for that purpose.

(3) The regulations may require the auditors to disclose the relevant information in their report or require the relevant information to be disclosed in a note to the company's accounts and require the auditors to supply the directors of the company with such information as is necessary to enable that disclosure to be made.

(4) The regulations may make different provision for different cases.

(5) Regulations under this section shall be made by statutory instrument which shall be subject to annulment in pursuance of a resolution of either House of Parliament."

122.   Removal, resignation, &c. of auditors

—(1) The following sections are inserted in Chapter V of Part XI of the [1985 c. 6.] Companies Act 1985 (auditors)—

"Removal, resignation, &c. of auditors

Removal of auditors.

391.—(1) A company may by ordinary resolution at any time remove an auditor from office, notwithstanding anything in any agreement between it and him.

(2) Where a resolution removing an auditor is passed at a general meeting of a company, the company shall within 14 days give notice of that fact in the prescribed form to the registrar.

If a company fails to give the notice required by this subsection, the company and every officer of it who is in default is guilty of an offence and liable to a fine and, for continued contravention, to a daily default fine.

(3) Nothing in this section shall be taken as depriving a person removed under it of compensation or damages payable to him in respect of the termination of his appointment as auditor or of any appointment terminating with that as auditor.

(4) An auditor of a company who has been removed has, notwithstanding his removal, the rights conferred by section 390 in relation to any general meeting of the company—

(a) at which his term of office would otherwise have expired, or

(b) at which it is proposed to fill the vacancy caused by his removal.

In such a case the references in that section to matters concerning the auditors as auditors shall be construed as references to matters concerning him as a former auditor.

Rights of auditors who are removed or not re-appointed.

391A.—(1) Special notice is required for a resolution at a general meeting of a company—

 (a) removing an auditor before the expiration of his term of office, or

 (b) appointing as auditor a person other than a retiring auditor.

(2) On receipt of notice of such an intended resolution the company shall forthwith send a copy of it to the person proposed to be removed or, as the case may be, to the person proposed to be appointed and to the retiring auditor.

(3) The auditor proposed to be removed or (as the case may be) the retiring auditor may make with respect to the intended resolution representations in writing to the company (not exceeding a reasonable length) and request their notification to members of the company.

(4) The company shall (unless the representations are received by it too late for it to do so)—

 (a) in any notice of the resolution given to members of the company, state the fact of the representations having been made, and

 (b) send a copy of the representations to every member of the company to whom notice of the meeting is or has been sent.

(5) If a copy of any such representations is not sent out as required because received too late or because of the company's default, the auditor may (without prejudice to his right to be heard orally) require that the representations be read out at the meeting.

(6) Copies of the representations need not be sent out and the representations need not be read at the meeting if, on the application either of the company or of any other person claiming to be aggrieved, the court is satisfied that the rights conferred by this section are being abused to secure needless publicity for defamatory matter; and the court may order the company's costs on the application to be paid in whole or in part by the auditor, notwithstanding that he is not a party to the application.

Resignation of auditors.

392.—(1) An auditor of a company may resign his office by depositing a notice in writing to that effect at the company's registered office.

The notice is not effective unless it is accompanied by the statement required by section 394.

(2) An effective notice of resignation operates to bring the auditor's term of

office to an end as of the date on which the notice is deposited or on such later date as may be specified in it.

(3) The company shall within 14 days of the deposit of a notice of resignation send a copy of the notice to the registrar of companies.

If default is made in complying with this subsection, the company and every officer of it who is in default is guilty of an offence and liable to a fine and, for continued contravention, a daily default fine.

Rights of resigning auditors.	**392A.**—(1) This section applies where an auditor's notice of resignation is accompanied by a statement of circumstances which he considers should be brought to the attention of members or creditors of the company.

(2) He may deposit with the notice a signed requisition calling on the directors of the company forthwith duly to convene an extraordinary general meeting of the company for the purpose of receiving and considering such explanation of the circumstances connected with his resignation as he may wish to place before the meeting.

(3) He may request the company to circulate to its members—

(a) before the meeting convened on his requisition, or

(b) before any general meeting at which his term of office would otherwise have expired or at which it is proposed to fill the vacancy caused by his resignation,

a statement in writing (not exceeding a reasonable length) of the circumstances connected with his resignation.

(4) The company shall (unless the statement is received too late for it to comply)—

(a) in any notice of the meeting given to members of the company, state the fact of the statement having been made, and

(b) send a copy of the statement to every member of the company to whom notice of the meeting is or has been sent.

(5) If the directors do not within 21 days from the date of the deposit of a requisition under this section proceed duly to convene a meeting for a day not more than 28 days after the date on which the notice convening the meeting is given, every director who failed to take all reasonable steps to secure that a meeting was convened as mentioned above is guilty of an offence and liable to a fine.

(6) If a copy of the statement mentioned above is not sent out as required because received too late or because of the company's default, the auditor may (without prejudice to his right to be heard orally) require that the statement be

read out at the meeting.

(7) Copies of a statement need not be sent out and the statement need not be read out at the meeting if, on the application either of the company or of any other person who claims to be aggrieved, the court is satisfied that the rights conferred by this section are being abused to secure needless publicity for defamatory matter; and the court may order the company's costs on such an application to be paid in whole or in part by the auditor, notwithstanding that he is not a party to the application.

(8) An auditor who has resigned has, notwithstanding his resignation, the rights conferred by section 390 in relation to any such general meeting of the company as is mentioned in subsection (3)(a) or (b).

In such a case the references in that section to matters concerning the auditors as auditors shall be construed as references to matters concerning him as a former auditor.

Termination of appointment of auditors not appointed annually.

393.—(1) When an election is in force under section 386 (election by private company to dispense with annual appointment), any member of the company may deposit notice in writing at the company's registered office proposing that the appointment of the company's auditors be brought to an end.

No member may deposit more than one such notice in any financial year of the company.

(2) If such a notice is deposited it is the duty of the directors—

(a) to convene a general meeting of the company for a date not more than 28 days after the date on which the notice was given, and

(b) to propose at the meeting a resolution in a form enabling the company to decide whether the appointment of the company's auditors should be brought to an end.

(3) If the decision of the company at the meeting is that the appointment of the auditors should be brought to an end, the auditors shall not be deemed to be re-appointed when next they would be and, if the notice was deposited within the period immediately following the distribution of accounts, any deemed re-appointment for the financial year following that to which those accounts relate which has already occurred shall cease to have effect.

The period immediately following the distribution of accounts means the period beginning with the day on which copies of the company's annual accounts are sent to members of the company under section 238 and ending 14 days after that day.

(4) If the directors do not within 14 days from the date of the deposit of the notice proceed duly to convene a meeting, the member who deposited the notice (or, if there was more than one, any of them) may himself convene the meeting; but any meeting so convened shall not be held after the expiration of three months from that date.

(5) A meeting convened under this section by a member shall be convened in the same manner, as nearly as possible, as that in which meetings are to be convened by directors.

(6) Any reasonable expenses incurred by a member by reason of the failure of the directors duly to convene a meeting shall be made good to him by the company; and any such sums shall be recouped by the company from such of the directors as were in default out of any sums payable, or to become payable, by the company by way of fees or other remuneration in respect of their services.

(7) This section has effect notwithstanding anything in any agreement between the company and its auditors; and no compensation or damages shall be payable by reason of the auditors' appointment being terminated under this section."

(2) In Schedule 24 to the [1985 c. 6.] Companies Act 1985 (punishment of offences), at the appropriate place insert—

"

391(2)	Failing to give notice to registrar of removal of auditor.	Summary.	One-fifth of the statutory maximum.	One-fiftieth of the statutory maximum.
392(3)	Company failing to forward notice of auditor's resignation to registrar.	1. On indictment. 2. Summary.	A fine. The statutory maximum.	One-tenth of the statutory maximum.
392A(5)	Directors failing to convene meeting requisitioned by resigning auditor.	1. On indictment. 2. Summary.	A fine. The statutory maximum.	

"

123. Statement by person ceasing to hold office as auditor

—(1) The following section is inserted in Chapter V of Part XI of the [1985 c. 6.] Companies Act 1985 (auditors)—

"Statement   **394.**—(1) Where an auditor ceases for any reason to hold office, he shall deposit by person ceasing to hold office as auditor. at the company's registered office a statement of any circumstances connected with his ceasing to hold office which he considers should be brought to the attention of the members or creditors of the company or, if he considers that there are no such circumstances, a statement that there are none.

(2) In the case of resignation, the statement shall be deposited along with the notice of resignation; in the case of failure to seek re-appointment, the statement shall be deposited not less than 14 days before the end of the time allowed for next appointing auditors; in any other case, the statement shall be deposited not later than the end of the period of 14 days beginning with the date on which he ceases to hold office.

(3) If the statement is of circumstances which the auditor considers should be brought to the attention of the members or creditors of the company, the company shall within 14 days of the deposit of the statement either—

(a) send a copy of it to every person who under section 238 is entitled to be sent copies of the accounts, or

(b) apply to the court.

(4) The company shall if it applies to the court notify the auditor of the application.

(5) Unless the auditor receives notice of such an application before the end of the period of 21 days beginning with the day on which he deposited the statement, he shall within a further seven days send a copy of the statement to the registrar.

(6) If the court is satisfied that the auditor is using the statement to secure needless publicity for defamatory matter—

(a) it shall direct that copies of the statement need not be sent out, and

(b) it may further order the company's costs on the application to be paid in whole or in part by the auditor, notwithstanding that he is not a party to the application;

and the company shall within 14 days of the court's decision send to the persons mentioned in subsection (3)(a) a statement setting out the effect of the order.

(7) If the court is not so satisfied, the company shall within 14 days of the court's decision—

(a) send copies of the statement to the persons mentioned in subsection (3)(a), and

(b) notify the auditor of the court's decision;

and the auditor shall within seven days of receiving such notice send a copy of the statement to the registrar.

Offences of failing to comply with s.394.

394A.—(1) If a person ceasing to hold office as auditor fails to comply with section 394 he is guilty of an offence and liable to a fine.

(2) In proceedings for an offence under subsection (1) it is a defence for the person charged to show that he took all reasonable steps and exercised all due diligence to avoid the commission of the offence.

(3) Sections 733 (liability of individuals for corporate default) and 734 (criminal proceedings against unincorporated bodies) apply to an offence under subsection (1).

(4) If a company makes default in complying with section 394, the company and every officer of it who is in default is guilty of an offence and liable to a fine and, for continued contravention, to a daily default fine."

(2) In Schedule 24 to the [1985 c. 65.] Companies Act 1985 (punishment of offences), at the appropriate place insert—

"

394A(1)	Person ceasing to hold office as auditor failing to deposit statement as to circumstances.	1. On indictment. 2. Summary.	A fine. The statutory maximum.	
394A(4)	Company failing to comply with requirements as to statement of person ceasing to hold office as auditor.	1. On indictment. 2. Summary.	A fine. The statutory maximum.	One-tenth of the statutory maximum.

"

(3) In section 733 of the [1985 c. 6.] Companies Act 1985 (liability of individuals for corporate default), in subsection (1) (offences in relation to which provisions apply) after "216(3)" insert ", 394A(1)".

(4) In section 734 of the [1985 c. 6.] Companies Act 1985 (criminal proceedings against unincorporated bodies), in subsection (1) (offences in relation to which the provisions apply), after "under" insert "section 394A(1) or".

(5) In Schedule 22 to the [1985 c. 6.] Companies Act 1985 (unregistered companies), in the entry for sections 384 to 393, for "393" substitute "394A".

124. Auditors of trade unions and employers' associations

In section 11 of the [1974 c. 52.] Trade Union and Labour Relations Act 1974 (duties of trade unions and employers' associations as to auditors, &c.), after subsection (8) insert—

"(9) Where a trade union or employers' association to which this section applies is a company within the meaning of the [1985 c. 6.] Companies Act 1985—

(a) subsection (3) above, and the provisions of paragraphs 6 to 15 of Schedule 2 to this Act, do not apply, and

(b) the rights and powers conferred, and duties imposed, by paragraphs 16 to 21 of that Schedule belong to the auditors of the company appointed under Chapter V of Part XI of that Act."

Company records and related matters

125. Delivery of documents to the registrar

—(1) For section 706 of the [1985 c. 6.] Companies Act 1985 (size, durability, &c. of documents delivered to the registrar) substitute—

"Delivery to the registrar of documents in legible form.

706.—(1) This section applies to the delivery to the registrar under any provision of the Companies Acts of documents in legible form.

(2) The document must—

(a) state in a prominent position the registered number of the company to which it relates,

(b) satisfy any requirements prescribed by regulations for the purposes of this section, and

(c) conform to such requirements as the registrar may specify for the purpose of enabling him to copy the document.

(3) If a document is delivered to the registrar which does not comply with the requirements of this section, he may serve on the person by whom the document was delivered (or, if there are two or more such persons, on any of them) a notice indicating the respect in which the document does not comply.

(4) Where the registrar serves such a notice, then, unless a replacement document—

(a) is delivered to him within 14 days after the service of the notice, and

(b) complies with the requirements of this section (or section 707) or is not rejected by him for failure to comply with those requirements,

the original document shall be deemed not to have been delivered to him.

But for the purposes of any enactment imposing a penalty for failure to deliver, so far as it imposes a penalty for continued contravention, no account shall be taken of the period between the delivery of the original document and the end of the period of 14 days after service of the registrar's notice.

(5) Regulations made for the purposes of this section may make different provision with respect to different descriptions of document."

(2) For section 707 of the [1985 c. 6.] Companies Act 1985 (power of registrar to accept information on microfilm, &c.) substitute—

"Delivery to the registrar of documents otherwise than in legible form.

707.—(1) This section applies to the delivery to the registrar under any provision of the Companies Acts of documents otherwise than in legible form.

(2) Any requirement to deliver a document to the registrar, or to deliver a document in the prescribed form, is satisfied by the communication to the registrar of the requisite information in any non-legible form prescribed for the purposes of this section by regulations or approved by the registrar.

(3) Where the document is required to be signed or sealed, it shall instead be authenticated in such manner as may be prescribed by regulations or approved by the registrar.

(4) The document must—

(a) contain in a prominent position the registered number of the company to which it relates,

(b) satisfy any requirements prescribed by regulations for the purposes of this section, and

(c) be furnished in such manner, and conform to such requirements, as the registrar may specify for the purpose of enabling him to read and copy the document.

(5) If a document is delivered to the registrar which does not comply with the requirements of this section, he may serve on the person by whom the document was delivered (or, if there are two or more such persons, on any of them) a notice indicating the respect in which the document does not comply.

(6) Where the registrar serves such a notice, then, unless a replacement document—

(a) is delivered to him within 14 days after the service of the notice, and

(b) complies with the requirements of this section (or section 706) or is not rejected by him for failure to comply with those requirements,

the original document shall be deemed not to have been delivered to him.

But for the purposes of any enactment imposing a penalty for failure to deliver, so far as it imposes a penalty for continued contravention, no account shall be taken of the period between the delivery of the original document and the end of the period of 14 days after service of the registrar's notice.

(7) The Secretary of State may by regulations make further provision with respect to the application of this section in relation to instantaneous forms of communication.

(8) Regulations made for the purposes of this section may make different provision with respect to different descriptions of document and different forms of communication, and as respects delivery to the registrar for England and Wales and delivery to the registrar for Scotland."

126. Keeping and inspection of company records

—(1) In Part XXIV of the [1985 c. 6.] Companies Act 1985 (the registrar of companies, his functions and offices), after the sections inserted by section 125 above, insert—

"The keeping of company records by the registrar.

707A.—(1) The information contained in a document delivered to the registrar under the Companies Acts may be recorded and kept by him in any form he thinks fit, provided it is possible to inspect the information and to produce a copy of it in legible form.

This is sufficient compliance with any duty of his to keep, file or register the document.

(2) The originals of documents delivered to the registrar in legible form shall be kept by him for ten years, after which they may be destroyed.

(3) Where a company has been dissolved, the registrar may, at any time after the expiration of two years from the date of the dissolution, direct that any records in his custody relating to the company may be removed to the Public Record Office; and records in respect of which such a direction is given shall be disposed of in accordance with the enactments relating to that Office and the rules made under

them.

This subsection does not extend to Scotland.

(4) In subsection (3) "company" includes a company provisionally or completely registered under the Joint Stock Companies Act 1844."

(2) For sections 709 and 710 of the [1985 c. 6.] Companies Act 1985 (inspection of documents kept by the registrar) substitute—

"Inspection, &c. of records kept by the registrar.

709.—(1) Any person may inspect any records kept by the registrar for the purposes of the Companies Acts and may require—

(a) a copy, in such form as the registrar considers appropriate, of any information contained in those records, or

(b) a certified copy of, or extract from, any such record.

(2) The right of inspection extends to the originals of documents delivered to the registrar in legible form only where the record kept by the registrar of the contents of the document is illegible or unavailable.

(3) A copy of or extract from a record kept at any of the offices for the registration of companies in England and Wales or Scotland, certified in writing by the registrar (whose official position it is unnecessary to prove) to be an accurate record of the contents of any document delivered to him under the Companies Acts, is in all legal proceedings admissible in evidence as of equal validity with the original document and as evidence of any fact stated therein of which direct oral evidence would be admissible.

In England and Wales this is subject to compliance with any applicable rules of court under section 5 of the Civil Evidence Act 1968 or section 69(2) of the Police and Criminal Evidence Act 1984 (which relate to evidence from computer records).

(4) Copies of or extracts from records furnished by the registrar may, instead of being certified by him in writing to be an accurate record, be sealed with his official seal.

(5) No process for compelling the production of a record kept by the registrar shall issue from any court except with the leave of the court; and any such process shall bear on it a statement that it is issued with the leave of the court.

Certificate of incorporation.

710. Any person may require a certificate of the incorporation of a company, signed by the registrar or authenticated by his official seal.

Provision and authentication by registrar of documents in non-legible form.	**710A.**—(1) Any requirement of the Companies Acts as to the supply by the registrar of a document may, if the registrar thinks fit, be satisfied by the communication by the registrar of the requisite information in any non-legible form prescribed for the purposes of this section by regulations or approved by him. (2) Where the document is required to be signed by him or sealed with his official seal, it shall instead be authenticated in such manner as may be prescribed by regulations or approved by the registrar."

127.   Supplementary provisions as to company records and related matters

—(1) In Part XXIV of the [1985 c. 6.] Companies Act 1985 (the registrar of companies, his functions and offices), after section 715 insert—

"Interpretation.	**715A.**—(1) In this Part— "document" includes information recorded in any form; and "legible", in the context of documents in legible or non-legible form, means capable of being read with the naked eye. (2) References in this Part to delivering a document include sending, forwarding, producing or (in the case of a notice) giving it."

(2) In section 708(1) of the [1985 c. 6.] Companies Act 1985 (fees)—

(a) in paragraph (a) for the words from "any notice or other document" to the end substitute "any document which under those Acts is required to be delivered to him", and

(b) in paragraph (b) omit "or other material".

(3) Omit sections 712 and 715 of the [1985 c. 6.] Companies Act 1985 (removal and destruction of old records).

(4) In section 713(1) (enforcement of duty to make returns, &c.), for the words from "file with" to "or other document" substitute "deliver a document to the registrar of companies".

(5) In section 735A(2) of the [1985 c. 6.] Companies Act 1985 (provisions applying to Insolvency Act 1986 and [1986 c. 46.] Company Directors Disqualification Act 1986 as to the Companies Acts)—

(a) after "707(1)," insert "707A(1),",

(b) after "708(1)(a) and (4)," insert "709(1) and (3),", and

(c) for "710(5)" substitute "710A".

(6) After section 735A of the [1985 c. 6.] Companies Act 1985 insert—

"Relationship of this Act to Parts IV and V of the Financial Services Act 1986.

735B. In sections 704(5), 706(1), 707(1), 707A(1), 708(1)(a) and (4), 709(1) and (3), 710A and 713(1) references to the Companies Acts include Parts IV and V of the Financial Services Act 1986.".

(7) In Schedule 22 to the [1985 c. 6.] Companies Act 1985 (unregistered companies), in the entry for Part XXIV for "sections 706, 708 to 710, 712 and 713" substitute "sections 706 to 710A, 713 and 715A".

Miscellaneous

128. Form of articles for partnership company

In Chapter I of Part I of the [1985 c. 6.] Companies Act 1985 (company formation), after section 8 (Tables A, C, D and E) insert—

"Table G.

8A.—(1) The Secretary of State may by regulations prescribe a Table G containing articles of association appropriate for a partnership company, that is, a company limited by shares whose shares are intended to be held to a substantial extent by or on behalf of its employees.

(2) A company limited by shares may for its articles adopt the whole or any part of that Table.

(3) If in consequence of regulations under this section Table G is altered, the alteration does not affect a company registered before the alteration takes effect, or repeal as respects that company any portion of the Table.

(4) Regulations under this section shall be made by statutory instrument which shall be subject to annulment in pursuance of a resolution of either House of Parliament."

129. Membership of holding company

—(1) In Chapter I of Part I of the Companies Act [1985 c. 6.] 1985 (company formation), for section 23 (membership of holding company) substitute—

"Membership of holding company.

23.—(1) Except as mentioned in this section, a body corporate cannot be a member of a company which is its holding company and any allotment or transfer of shares in a company to its subsidiary is void.

(2) The prohibition does not apply where the subsidiary is concerned only as personal representative or trustee unless, in the latter case, the holding company or a subsidiary of it is beneficially interested under the trust.

For the purpose of ascertaining whether the holding company or a subsidiary is so interested, there shall be disregarded—

    (a) any interest held only by way of security for the purposes of a transaction entered into by the holding company or subsidiary in the ordinary course of a business which includes the lending of money;

    (b) any such interest as is mentioned in Part I of Schedule 2.

(3) The prohibition does not apply where the subsidiary is concerned only as a market maker.

For this purpose a person is a market maker if—

    (a) he holds himself out at all normal times in compliance with the rules of a recognised investment exchange other than an overseas investment exchange (within the meaning of the Financial Services Act 1986) as willing to buy and sell securities at prices specified by him, and

    (b) he is recognised as so doing by that investment exchange.

(4) Where a body corporate became a holder of shares in a company—

    (a) before 1st July 1948, or

    (b) on or after that date and before the commencement of section 129 of the Companies Act 1989, in circumstances in which this section as it then had effect did not apply,

but at any time after the commencement of that section falls within the prohibition in subsection (1) above in respect of those shares, it may continue to be a member of that company; but for so long as that prohibition would apply, apart from this subsection, it has no right to vote in respect of those shares at meetings of the company or of any class of its members.

(5) Where a body corporate becomes a holder of shares in a company after the commencement of that section in circumstances in which the prohibition in subsection (1) does not apply, but subsequently falls within that prohibition in respect of those shares, it may continue to be a member of that company; but for so long as that prohibition would apply, apart from this subsection, it has no right to vote in respect of those shares at meetings of the company or of any class of its members.

(6) Where a body corporate is permitted to continue as a member of a company by virtue of subsection (4) or (5), an allotment to it of fully paid shares in the company may be validly made by way of capitalisation of reserves of the company; but for so long as the prohibition in subsection (1) would apply, apart from subsection (4) or (5), it has no right to vote in respect of those shares at meetings of the company or of any class of its members.

(7) The provisions of this section apply to a nominee acting on behalf of a subsidiary as to the subsidiary itself.

(8) In relation to a company other than a company limited by shares, the references in this section to shares shall be construed as references to the interest of its members as such, whatever the form of that interest."

(2) In Schedule 2 to the [1985 c. 6.] Companies Act 1985 (interpretation of references to "beneficial interest"), in paragraphs 1(1), 3(1) and 4(2) for "as respects section 23(4)" substitute "as this paragraph applies for the purposes of section 23(2)"

130. Company contracts and execution of documents by companies

—(1) In Chapter III of Part I of the [1985 c. 6.] Companies Act 1985 (a company's capacity; the formalities of carrying on business), for section 36 (form of company contracts) substitute—

"Company contracts: England and Wales.

36. Under the law of England and Wales a contract may be made—

(a) by a company, by writing under its common seal, or

(b) on behalf of a company, by any person acting under its authority, express or implied;

and any formalities required by law in the case of a contract made by an individual also apply, unless a contrary intention appears, to a contract made by or on behalf of a company." .

(2) After that section insert—

"Execution of documents: England and Wales.

36A.—(1) Under the law of England and Wales the following provisions have effect with respect to the execution of documents by a company.

(2) A document is executed by a company by the affixing of its common seal.

(3) A company need not have a common seal, however, and the following subsections apply whether it does or not.

(4) A document signed by a director and the secretary of a company, or by two directors of a company, and expressed (in whatever form of words) to be executed by the company has the same effect as if executed under the common seal of the

company.

(5) A document executed by a company which makes it clear on its face that it is intended by the person or persons making it to be a deed has effect, upon delivery, as a deed; and it shall be presumed, unless a contrary intention is proved, to be delivered upon its being so executed.

(6) In favour of a purchaser a document shall be deemed to have been duly executed by a company if it purports to be signed by a director and the secretary of the company, or by two directors of the company, and, where it makes it clear on its face that it is intended by the person or persons making it to be a deed, to have been delivered upon its being executed.

A "purchaser" means a purchaser in good faith for valuable consideration and includes a lessee, mortgagee or other person who for valuable consideration acquires an interest in property.

"

(3) After the section inserted by subsection (2) insert—

"Execution of documents: Scotland.

36B.—(1) Under the law of Scotland the following provisions have effect with respect to the execution of documents by a company.

(2) A document—

(a) is signed by a company if it is signed on its behalf by a director, or by the secretary, of the company or by a person authorised to sign the document on its behalf, and

(b) is subscribed by a company if it is subscribed on its behalf by being signed in accordance with the provisions of paragraph (a) at the end of the last page.

(3) A document shall be presumed, unless the contrary is shown, to have been subscribed by a company in accordance with subsection (2) if—

(a) it bears to have been subscribed on behalf of the company by a director, or by the secretary, of the company or by a person bearing to have been authorised to subscribe the document on its behalf; and

(b) it bears—

(i) to have been signed by a person as a witness of the subscription of the director, secretary or other person subscribing on behalf of the company; or

(ii) (if the subscription is not so witnessed) to have been sealed with the common seal of the company.

(4) A presumption under subsection (3) as to subscription of a document does not include a presumption—

(a) that a person bearing to subscribe the document as a director or the secretary of the company was such director or secretary; or

(b) that a person subscribing the document on behalf of the company bearing to have been authorised to do so was authorised to do so.

(5) Notwithstanding subsection (3)(b)(ii), a company need not have a common seal.

(6) Any reference in any enactment (including an enactment contained in a subordinate instrument) to a probative document shall, in relation to a document executed by a company after the commencement of section 130 of the Companies Act 1989, be construed as a reference to a document which is presumed under subsection (3) above to be subscribed by the company.

(7) Subsections (1) to (4) above do not apply where an enactment (including an enactment contained in a subordinate instrument) provides otherwise."

(4) After the section inserted by subsection (3) insert—

"Pre-incorporation contracts, deeds and obligations.

36C.—(1) A contract which purports to be made by or on behalf of a company at a time when the company has not been formed has effect, subject to any agreement to the contrary, as one made with the person purporting to act for the company or as agent for it, and he is personally liable on the contract accordingly.

(2) Subsection (1) applies—

(a) to the making of a deed under the law of England and Wales, and

(b) to the undertaking of an obligation under the law of Scotland,

as it applies to the making of a contract."

(5) In Schedule 22 of the [1985 c. 6.] Companies Act 1985 (provisions applying to unregistered companies), at the appropriate place insert—

Section 36	Company contracts.	Subject to section 718(3).
Sections 36A and 36B	Execution of documents.	Subject to section 718(3).
Section 36C	Pre-incorporation contracts, deeds and obligations.	Subject to section 718(3).

(6) The Secretary of State may make provision by regulations applying sections 36 to 36C of the [1985 c. 6.] Companies Act 1985 (company contracts; execution of documents; pre-incorporation contracts, deeds and obligations) to companies incorporated outside Great Britain, subject to such exceptions, adaptations or modifications as may be specified in the regulations.

Regulations under this subsection shall be made by statutory instrument which shall be subject to annulment in pursuance of a resolution of either House of Parliament.

(7) Schedule 17 contains further minor and consequential amendments relating to company contracts, the execution of documents by companies and related matters.

131. Members' rights to damages, &c

—(1) In Part IV of the [1985 c. 6.] Companies Act 1985 (allotment of shares and debentures), before section 112 and after the heading "*Other matters arising out of allotment &c*.", insert—

"Right to damages, &c. not affected. 111A. A person is not debarred from obtaining damages or other compensation from a company by reason only of his holding or having held shares in the company or any right to apply or subscribe for shares or to be included in the company's register in respect of shares." .

(2) In section 116 of the [1985 c. 6.] Companies Act 1985 (extended operation of certain provisions applying to public companies) for "and 110 to 115" substitute ", 110, 111 and 112 to 115".

132. Financial assistance for purposes of employees' share scheme

In Chapter VI of Part V of the [1985 c. 6.] Companies Act 1985 (financial assistance by company for purchase of its own shares), in section 153 (transactions not prohibited), for subsection (4)(b) (provision of money in accordance with employees' share scheme) substitute—

"(b) the provision by a company, in good faith in the interests of the company, of financial assistance for the purposes of an employees' share scheme," .

133. Issue of redeemable shares

—(1) In Part V of the [1985 c. 6.] Companies Act 1985 (share capital, its increase, maintenance and reduction), Chapter III (redeemable shares, purchase by a company of its own shares) is amended as follows.

(2) After section 159 (power to issue redeemable shares) insert—

"Terms and manner of redemption.

159A.—(1) Redeemable shares may not be issued unless the following conditions are satisfied as regards the terms and manner of redemption.

(2) The date on or by which, or dates between which, the shares are to be or may be redeemed must be specified in the company's articles or, if the articles so provide, fixed by the directors, and in the latter case the date or dates must be fixed before the shares are issued.

(3) Any other circumstances in which the shares are to be or may be redeemed must be specified in the company's articles.

(4) The amount payable on redemption must be specified in, or determined in accordance with, the company's articles, and in the latter case the articles must not provide for the amount to be determined by reference to any person's discretion or opinion.

(5) Any other terms and conditions of redemption shall be specified in the company's articles.

(6) Nothing in this section shall be construed as requiring a company to provide in its articles for any matter for which provision is made by this Act."

(3) In section 160 (financing, &c. of redemption)—

(a) omit subsection (3) (which is superseded by the new section 159A), and

(b) in subsection (4) (cancellation of shares on redemption) for "redeemed under this section" substitute "redeemed under this Chapter".

(4) In section 162 (power of company to purchase own shares), for subsection (2) (application of provisions relating to redeemable shares) substitute—

"(2) Sections 159, 160 and 161 apply to the purchase by a company under this section of its own shares as they apply to the redemption of redeemable shares." .

134. Disclosure of interests in shares

—(1) Part VI of the [1985 c. 6.] Companies Act 1985 (disclosure of interests in shares) is amended as follows.

(2) In section 199(2) (notifiable interests), for the words from "the percentage" to the end substitute "3 per cent. of the nominal value of that share capital".

The order bringing the above amendment into force may make such provision as appears to the Secretary of State appropriate as to the obligations of a person whose interest in a company's shares becomes notifiable by virtue of the amendment coming into force.

(3) In sections 202(1) and (4) and 206(8) (which require notification of certain matters within a specified period) for "5 days" substitute "2 days".

(4) In section 202 (particulars to be contained in notification), for subsection (3) substitute—

"(3) A notification (other than one stating that a person no longer has a notifiable interest) shall include the following particulars, so far as known to the person making the notification at the date when it is made—

(a) the identity of each registered holder of shares to which the notification relates and the number of such shares held by each of them, and

(b) the number of such shares in which the interest of the person giving the notification is such an interest as is mentioned in section 208(5)."

(5) After section 210 insert—

"Power to make further provision by regulations.

210A.—(1) The Secretary of State may by regulations amend—

(a) the definition of "relevant share capital" (section 198(2)),

(b) the percentage giving rise to a "notifiable interest" (section 199(2)),
(c) the periods within which an obligation of disclosure must be fulfilled or a notice must be given (sections 202(1) and (4) and 206(8)),

(d) the provisions as to what is taken to be an interest in shares (section 208) and what interests are to be disregarded (section 209), and

(e) the provisions as to company investigations (section 212);

and the regulations may amend, replace or repeal the provisions referred to above and make such other consequential amendments or repeals of provisions of this Part as appear to the Secretary of State to be appropriate.

(2) The regulations may in any case make different provision for different descriptions of company; and regulations under subsection (1)(b), (c) or (d) may make different provision for different descriptions of person, interest or share capital.

(3) The regulations may contain such transitional and other supplementary and incidental provisions as appear to the Secretary of State to be appropriate, and may

in particular make provision as to the obligations of a person whose interest in a company's shares becomes or ceases to be notifiable by virtue of the regulations.

(4) Regulations under this section shall be made by statutory instrument.

(5) No regulations shall be made under this section unless a draft of the regulations has been laid before and approved by a resolution of each House of Parliament."

(6) Any regulations made under section 209(1)(j) which are in force immediately before the repeal of that paragraph by this Act shall have effect as if made under section 210A(1)(d) as inserted by subsection (5) above.

135. Orders imposing restrictions on shares

—(1) The Secretary of State may by regulations made by statutory instrument make such amendments of the provisions of the [1985 c. 6.] Companies Act 1985 relating to orders imposing restrictions on shares as appear to him necessary or expedient—

 (a) for enabling orders to be made in a form protecting the rights of third parties;

 (b) with respect to the circumstances in which restrictions may be relaxed or removed;

 (c) with respect to the making of interim orders by a court.

(2) The provisions referred to in subsection (1) are section 210(5), section 216(1) and (2), section 445 and Part XV of the [1985 c. 6.] Companies Act 1985.

(3) The regulations may make different provision for different cases and may contain such transitional and other supplementary and incidental provisions as appear to the Secretary of State to be appropriate.

(4) Regulations under this section shall not be made unless a draft of the regulations has been laid before Parliament and approved by resolution of each House of Parliament.

136. A company's registered office

For section 287 of the [1985 c. 6.] Companies Act 1985 (registered office) substitute—

"Registered office. **287.**—(1) A company shall at all times have a registered office to which all communications and notices may be addressed.

 (2) On incorporation the situation of the company's registered office is that specified in the statement sent to the registrar under section 10.

 (3) The company may change the situation of its registered office from time to time by giving notice in the prescribed form to the registrar.

(4) The change takes effect upon the notice being registered by the registrar, but until the end of the period of 14 days beginning with the date on which it is registered a person may validly serve any document on the company at its previous registered office.

(5) For the purposes of any duty of a company—

(a) to keep at its registered office, or make available for public inspection there, any register, index or other document, or

(b) to mention the address of its registered office in any document,

a company which has given notice to the registrar of a change in the situation of its registered office may act on the change as from such date, not more than 14 days after the notice is given, as it may determine.

(6) Where a company unavoidably ceases to perform at its registered office any such duty as is mentioned in subsection (5)(a) in circumstances in which it was not practicable to give prior notice to the registrar of a change in the situation of its registered office, but—

(a) resumes performance of that duty at other premises as soon as practicable, and

(b) gives notice accordingly to the registrar of a change in the situation of its registered office within 14 days of doing so,

it shall not be treated as having failed to comply with that duty.

(7) In proceedings for an offence of failing to comply with any such duty as is mentioned in subsection (5), it is for the person charged to show that by reason of the matters referred to in that subsection or subsection (6) no offence was committed."

137. Effecting of insurance for officers and auditors of company

—(1) In section 310 of the [1985 c. 6.] Companies Act 1985 (provisions exempting officers and auditors from liability), for subsection (3) (permitted provisions) substitute—

"(3) This section does not prevent a company—

(a) from purchasing and maintaining for any such officer or auditor insurance against any such liability, or

(b) from indemnifying any such officer or auditor against any liability incurred by him—

(i) in defending any proceedings (whether civil or criminal) in which judgment is given in his favour or he is acquitted, or

(ii) in connection with any application under section 144(3) or (4) (acquisition of shares by innocent nominee) or section 727 (general power to grant relief in case of honest and reasonable conduct) in which relief is granted to him by the court."

(2) In Part I of Schedule 7 to the [1985 c. 6.] Companies Act 1985 (general matters to be dealt with in directors' report), after paragraph 5 insert—

"**5A.** Where in the financial year the company has purchased or maintained any such insurance as is mentioned in section 310(3)(a) (insurance of officers or auditors against liabilities in relation to the company), that fact shall be stated in the report."

138. Increase of limits on certain exemptions

Part X of the [1985 c. 6.] Companies Act 1985 (enforcement of fair dealing by directors) is amended as follows—

(a) in section 332(1)(b) (short-term quasi-loans) for "£1,000" substitute "£5,000";

(b) in section 334 (loans of small amounts) for "£2,500" substitute "£5,000";

(c) in section 338(4) and (6) (loans or quasi-loans by money-lending company) for "£50,000" substitute "£100,000".

139. Annual returns

—(1) In Part XI of the [1985 c. 6.] Companies Act 1985 (company administration and procedure), for Chapter III (annual return) substitute—

"Chapter III

Annual Return

"Duty to deliver annual returns.

363.—(1) Every company shall deliver to the registrar successive annual returns each of which is made up to a date not later than the date which is from time to time the company's "return date", that is—

(a) the anniversary of the company's incorporation, or

(b) if the company's last return delivered in accordance with this Chapter was made up to a different date, the anniversary of that date.

(2) Each return shall—

(a) be in the prescribed form,

(b) contain the information required by or under the following provisions of this Chapter, and

(c) be signed by a director or the secretary of the company;

and it shall be delivered to the registrar within 28 days after the date to which it is made up.

(3) If a company fails to deliver an annual return in accordance with this Chapter before the end of the period of 28 days after a return date, the company is guilty of an offence and liable to a fine and, in the case of continued contravention, to a daily default fine.

The contravention continues until such time as an annual return made up to that return date and complying with the requirements of subsection (2) (except as to date of delivery) is delivered by the company to the registrar.

(4) Where a company is guilty of an offence under subsection (3), every director or secretary of the company is similarly liable unless he shows that he took all reasonable steps to avoid the commission or continuation of the offence.

(5) The references in this section to a return being delivered "in accordance with this Chapter" are—

(a) in relation to a return made after the commencement of section 139 of the Companies Act 1989, to a return with respect to which all the requirements of subsection (2) are complied with;

(b) in relation to a return made before that commencement, to a return with respect to which the formal and substantive requirements of this Chapter as it then had effect were complied with, whether or not the return was delivered in time.

"Contents of annual return: general.

364.—(1) Every annual return shall state the date to which it is made up and shall contain the following information—

(a) the address of the company's registered office;

(b) the type of company it is and its principal business activities;

(c) the name and address of the company secretary;

(d) the name and address of every director of the company;

(e) in the case of each individual director—

>(i) his nationality, date of birth and business occupation, and

>(ii) such particulars of other directorships and former names as are required to be contained in the company's register of directors;

(f) in the case of any corporate director, such particulars of other directorships as would be required to be contained in that register in the case of an individual;

(g) if the register of members is not kept at the company's registered office, the address of the place where it is kept;

(h) if any register of debenture holders (or a duplicate of any such register or a part of it) is not kept at the company's registered office, the address of the place where it is kept;

(i) if the company has elected—

>(i) to dispense under section 252 with the laying of accounts and reports before the company in general meeting, or

>(ii) to dispense under section 366A with the holding of annual general meetings,

a statement to that effect.

(2) The information as to the company's type shall be given by reference to the classification scheme prescribed for the purposes of this section.

(3) The information as to the company's principal business activities may

be given by reference to one or more categories of any prescribed system of classifying business activities.

(4) A person's "name" and "address" mean, respectively—

(a) in the case of an individual, his Christian name (or other forename) and surname and his usual residential address;

(b) in the case of a corporation or Scottish firm, its corporate or firm name and its registered or principal office.

(5) In the case of a peer, or an individual usually known by a title, the title may be stated instead of his Christian name (or other forename) and surname or in addition to either or both of them.

(6) Where all the partners in a firm are joint secretaries, the name and principal office of the firm may be stated instead of the names and addresses of the partners.

"Contents of annual return: particulars of share capital and shareholders.

364A.—(1) The annual return of a company having a share capital shall contain the following information with respect to its share capital and members.

(2) The return shall state the total number of issued shares of the company at the date to which the return is made up and the aggregate nominal value of those shares.

(3) The return shall state with respect to each class of shares in the company—

(a) the nature of the class, and

(b) the total number and aggregate nominal value of issued shares of that class at the date to which the return is made up.

(4) The return shall contain a list of the names and addresses of every person who—

(a) is a member of the company on the date to which the return is made up, or

(b) has ceased to be a member of the company since the date to which the last return was made up (or, in the case of the first return, since the incorporation of the company);

and if the names are not arranged in alphabetical order the return shall have annexed to it an index sufficient to enable the name of any person in the list to be easily found.

(5) The return shall also state—

(a) the number of shares of each class held by each member of the company at the date to which the return is made up, and

(b) the number of shares of each class transferred since the date to which the last return was made up (or, in the case of the first return, since the incorporation of the company) by each member or person who has ceased to be a member, and the dates of registration of the transfers.

(6) The return may, if either of the two immediately preceding returns has given the full particulars required by subsections (4) and (5), give only such particulars as relate to persons ceasing to be or becoming members since the date of the last return and to shares transferred since that date.

(7) Subsections (4) and (5) do not require the inclusion of particulars entered in an overseas branch register if copies of those entries have not been received at the company's registered office by the date to which the return is made up.

Those particulars shall be included in the company's next annual return after they are received.

(8) Where the company has converted any of its shares into stock, the return shall give the corresponding information in relation to that stock, stating the amount of stock instead of the number or nominal value of shares.

"Supplementary provisions: regulations and interpretation.

365.—(1) The Secretary of State may by regulations make further provision as to the information to be given in a company's annual return, which may amend or repeal the provisions of sections 364 and 364A.

(2) Regulations under this section shall be made by statutory instrument which shall be subject to annulment in pursuance of a resolution of either House of Parliament.

(3) For the purposes of this Chapter, except section 363(2)(c) (signature of annual return), a shadow director shall be deemed to be a director.

(2) Where a company was, immediately before the commencement of this section, in default with respect to the delivery of one or more annual returns, this section does not affect its obligation to make such a return (in accordance with Chapter III of Part XI of the [1985 c. 6.] Companies Act 1985 as it then had effect) or any liability arising from failure to do so.

(3) In Schedule 24 to the [1985 c. 6.] Companies Act 1985 (punishment of offences) in the entry relating to section 363(7), in the first column for "363(7)" substitute "363(3)".

(4) In Schedule 1 to the [1986 c. 46.] Company Directors Disqualification Act 1986 (matters relevant to determining unfitness of directors), in paragraph 4 (failure of company to comply with certain provisions), for sub-paragraphs (f) and (g) substitute—

"(f) section 363 (duty of company to make annual returns);".

(5) In section 565(6) of the [1988 c. 1.] Income and Corporation Taxes Act 1988 (conditions for exemption from provisions relating to sub-contractors in construction industry: compliance with requirements of [1985 c. 6.] Companies Act 1985), in paragraph (d) for "sections 363, 364 and 365" substitute "sections 363 to 365".

140. Floating charges (Scotland)

—(1) In section 463 of the [1985 c. 6.] Companies Act 1985 (effect of floating charge on winding up), in subsection (1) for the words "On the commencement of the winding up of a company," there shall be substituted the words "Where a company goes into liquidation within the meaning of section 247(2) of the Insolvency Act 1986,".

(2) Section 464 of the [1985 c. 6.] Companies Act 1985 (ranking of floating charges) is amended as follows.

(3) In subsection (1)(b) at the beginning there shall be inserted the words "with the consent of the holder of any subsisting floating charge or fixed security which would be adversely affected,".

(4) After subsection (1) there shall be inserted the following subsection—

"(1A) Where an instrument creating a floating charge contains any such provision as is mentioned in subsection (1)(a), that provision shall be effective to confer priority on the floating charge over any fixed security or floating charge created after the date of the instrument.".

(5) For subsection (3) there shall be substituted—

"(3) The order of ranking of the floating charge with any other subsisting or future floating charges or fixed securities over all or any part of the company's property is determined in accordance with the provisions of subsections (4) and (5) except where it is determined in accordance with any provision such as is mentioned in paragraph (a) or (b) of subsection (1).".

(6) In subsection (5) at the end there shall be added the following paragraph—

"; and

(e) (in the case of a floating charge to secure a contingent liability other than a liability arising under any further advances made from time to time) the maximum sum to which that contingent liability is capable of amounting whether or not it is contractually limited.".

(7) In subsection (6) after the words "subject to" there shall be inserted the words "Part XII and to".

(8) In section 466 of the [1985 c. 6.] Companies Act 1985 (alteration of floating charges), subsections (4) and (5) and in subsection (6) the words "falling under subsection (4) of this section" shall cease to have effect.

141. Application to declare dissolution of company void

—(1) Section 651 of the [1985 c. 6.] Companies Act 1985 (power of court to declare dissolution of company void) is amended as follows.

(2) In subsection (1) omit the words "at any time within 2 years of the date of the dissolution".

(3) After subsection (3) add—

"(4) Subject to the following provisions, an application under this section may not be made after the end of the period of two years from the date of the dissolution of the company.

(5) An application for the purpose of bringing proceedings against the company—

(a) for damages in respect of personal injuries (including any sum claimed by virtue of section 1(2)(c) of the Law Reform (Miscellaneous Provisions) Act 1934 (funeral expenses)), or

(b) for damages under the Fatal Accidents Act 1976 or the Damages (Scotland) Act 1976,

may be made at any time; but no order shall be made on such an application if it appears to the court that the proceedings would fail by virtue of any enactment as to the time within which proceedings must be brought.

(6) Nothing in subsection (5) affects the power of the court on making an order under this section to direct that the period between the dissolution of the company and the making of the order shall not count for the purposes of any such enactment.

(7) In subsection (5)(a) "personal injuries" includes any disease and any impairment of a person's physical or mental condition." .

(4) An application may be made under section 651(5) of the [1985 c. 6.] Companies Act 1985 as inserted by subsection (3) above (proceedings for damages for personal injury, &c.) in relation to a company dissolved before the commencement of this section notwithstanding that the time within which the dissolution might formerly have been declared void under that section had expired before commencement.

But no such application shall be made in relation to a company dissolved more than twenty years before the commencement of this section.

(5) Except as provided by subsection (4), the amendments made by this section do not apply in relation to a company which was dissolved more than two years before the commencement of this

section.

142. Abolition of doctrine of deemed notice

—(1) In Part XXIV of the [1985 c. 6.] Companies Act 1985 (the registrar of companies, his functions and offices), after section 711 insert—

"Exclusion of deemed notice.

711A.—(1) A person shall not be taken to have notice of any matter merely because of its being disclosed in any document kept by the registrar of companies (and thus available for inspection) or made available by the company for inspection.

(2) This does not affect the question whether a person is affected by notice of any matter by reason of a failure to make such inquiries as ought reasonably to be made.

(3) In this section "document" includes any material which contains information.

(4) Nothing in this section affects the operation of—

(a) section 416 of this Act (under which a person taking a charge over a company's property is deemed to have notice of matters disclosed on the companies charges register), or

(b) section 198 of the Law of Property Act 1925 as it applies by virtue of section 3(7) of the Land Charges Act 1972 (under which the registration of certain land charges under Part XII, or Chapter III of Part XXIII, of this Act is deemed to constitute actual notice for all purposes connected with the land affected)."

(2) In Schedule 22 to the [1985 c. 6.] Companies Act 1985 (unregistered companies), in the entry for Part XXIV at the appropriate place insert—

"

| Section 711A | Abolition of doctrine of deemed notice. | Subject to section 718(3). |

"

143. Rights of inspection and related matters

—(1) In Part XXV of the [1985 c. 6.] Companies Act 1985 (miscellaneous and supplementary provisions), after section 723 insert—

"Obligations of company as to inspection of

723A.—(1) The Secretary of State may make provision by regulations as to the obligations of a company which is required by any provision of this Act—

registers, &c.

    (a) to make available for inspection any register, index or document, or

    (b) to provide copies of any such register, index or document, or part of it;

and a company which fails to comply with the regulations shall be deemed to have refused inspection or, as the case may be, to have failed to provide a copy.

(2) The regulations may make provision as to the time, duration and manner of inspection, including the circumstances in which and extent to which the copying of information is permitted in the course of inspection.

(3) The regulations may define what may be required of the company as regards the nature, extent and manner of extracting or presenting any information for the purposes of inspection or the provision of copies.

(4) Where there is power to charge a fee, the regulations may make provision as to the amount of the fee and the basis of its calculation.

(5) Regulations under this section may make different provision for different classes of case.

(6) Nothing in any provision of this Act or in the regulations shall be construed as preventing a company from affording more extensive facilities than are required by the regulations or, where a fee may be charged, from charging a lesser fee than that prescribed or no fee at all.

(7) Regulations under this section shall be made by statutory instrument which shall be subject to annulment in pursuance of a resolution of either House of Parliament."

(2) In section 169(5) of the [1985 c. 6.] Companies Act 1985 (contract for purchase by company of its own shares), omit the words from ", during business hours" to "for inspection)".

(3) In section 175(6) of the [1985 c. 6.] Companies Act 1985 (statutory declaration and auditors' report relating to payment out of capital), in paragraph (b) omit the words from "during business hours" to "period".

(4) In section 191 of the [1985 c. 6.] Companies Act 1985 (register of debenture holders)—

    (a) in subsection (1), omit the words from "(but" to "for inspection)" and for the words from "a fee of 5 pence" to the end substitute "such fee as may be prescribed";

    (b) in subsection (2) for the words from "10 pence" to the end substitute "such fee as may be prescribed"; and

    (c) in subsection (3), after "on payment" insert "of such fee as may be prescribed" and omit paragraphs (a) and (b).

(5) In section 219 of the [1985 c. 6.] Companies Act 1985 (register of interests in shares, &c.)—

    (a) in subsection (1), omit the words from "during" to "for inspection)"; and

    (b) in subsection (2) for the words from "10 pence" to "required to be copied" substitute "such fee as may be prescribed".

(6) In section 288 of the [1985 c. 6.] Companies Act 1985 (register of directors and secretaries), in subsection (3), omit the words from "during" to "for inspection)" and for the words from ".5 pence" to the end substitute "such fee as may be prescribed".

(7) In section 318 of the [1985 c. 6.] Companies Act 1985 (directors' service contracts), in subsection (7) omit the words from ", during business hours" to "for inspection)".

(8) In section 356 of the [1985 c. 6.] Companies Act 1985 (register and index of members' names)—

    (a) in subsection (1), omit "during business hours" and for "the appropriate charge" substitute "such fee as may be prescribed";

    (b) omit subsection (2);

    (c) in subsection (3) for "the appropriate charge" substitute "such fee as may be prescribed"; and

    (d) omit subsection (4).

(9) In section 383 of the [1985 c. 6.] Companies Act 1985 (minutes of proceedings of general meetings)—

    (a) in subsection (1), omit "during business hours";

    (b) omit subsection (2); and

    (c) in subsection (3), after "entitled" insert "on payment of such fee as may be prescribed" and omit the words from "at a charge" to the end.

(10) In Part IV of Schedule 13 to the [1985 c. 6.] Companies Act 1985 (register of directors' interests)—

    (a) in paragraph 25, omit the words from "during" to "for inspection)" and for the words from ".5 pence" to the end substitute "such fee as may be prescribed"; and

    (b) in paragraph 26(1), for the words from "10 pence" to the end substitute "such fee as may be prescribed".

(11) In Schedule 22 to the [1985 c. 6.] Companies Act 1985 (provisions applying to unregistered companies), in the entry relating to Part XXV at the appropriate place insert—

| Section 723A | Rights of inspection and related matters. | To apply only so far as this provision has effect in relation to provisions applying by virtue of the foregoing provisions of this Schedule. |

144. "Subsidiary", "holding company" and "wholly-owned subsidiary"

—(1) In Part XXVI of the [1985 c. 6.] Companies Act 1985 (general interpretation provisions), for section 736 substitute—

"Subsidiary", "holding company" and "wholly-owned subsidiary".

736.—(1) A company is a "subsidiary" of another company, its "holding company", if that other company—

(a) holds a majority of the voting rights in it, or

(b) is a member of it and has the right to appoint or remove a majority of its board of directors, or

(c) is a member of it and controls alone, pursuant to an agreement with other shareholders or members, a majority of the voting rights in it,

or if it is a subsidiary of a company which is itself a subsidiary of that other company.

(2) A company is a "wholly-owned subsidiary" of another company if it has no members except that other and that other's wholly-owned subsidiaries or persons acting on behalf of that other or its wholly-owned subsidiaries.

(3) In this section "company" includes any body corporate.

Provisions supplementing s. 736.

736A.—(1) The provisions of this section explain expressions used in section 736 and otherwise supplement that section.

(2) In section 736(1)(a) and (c) the references to the voting rights in a company are to the rights conferred on shareholders in respect of their shares or, in the case of a company not having a share capital, on members, to vote at general meetings of the company on all, or substantially all, matters.

(3) In section 736(1)(b) the reference to the right to appoint or remove a majority of the board of directors is to the right to appoint or remove directors holding a majority of the voting rights at meetings of the board on all, or substantially all, matters; and for the purposes of that provision—

(a) a company shall be treated as having the right to appoint to a directorship if—

    (i) a person's appointment to it follows necessarily from his appointment as director of the company, or

    (ii) the directorship is held by the company itself; and

(b) a right to appoint or remove which is exercisable only with the consent or concurrence of another person shall be left out of account unless no other person has a right to appoint or, as the case may be, remove in relation to that directorship.

(4) Rights which are exercisable only in certain circumstances shall be taken into account only—

    (a) when the circumstances have arisen, and for so long as they continue to obtain, or

    (b) when the circumstances are within the control of the person having the rights;

and rights which are normally exercisable but are temporarily incapable of exercise shall continue to be taken into account.

(5) Rights held by a person in a fiduciary capacity shall be treated as not held by him.

(6) Rights held by a person as nominee for another shall be treated as held by the other; and rights shall be regarded as held as nominee for another if they are exercisable only on his instructions or with his consent or concurrence.

(7) Rights attached to shares held by way of security shall be treated as held by the person providing the security—

    (a) where apart from the right to exercise them for the purpose of preserving the value of the security, or of realising it, the rights are exercisable only in accordance with his instructions;

    (b) where the shares are held in connection with the granting of loans as part of normal business activities and apart from the right to exercise them for the purpose of preserving the value of the security, or of realising it, the rights are exercisable only in his interests.

(8) Rights shall be treated as held by a company if they are held by any of its subsidiaries; and nothing in subsection (6) or (7) shall be construed as requiring rights held by a company to be treated as held by any of its subsidiaries.

(9) For the purposes of subsection (7) rights shall be treated as being exercisable in accordance with the instructions or in the interests of a company if they

are exercisable in accordance with the instructions of or, as the case may be, in the interests of—

    (a) any subsidiary or holding company of that company, or

    (b) any subsidiary of a holding company of that company.

(10) The voting rights in a company shall be reduced by any rights held by the company itself.

(11) References in any provision of subsections (5) to (10) to rights held by a person include rights falling to be treated as held by him by virtue of any other provision of those subsections but not rights which by virtue of any such provision are to be treated as not held by him.

(12) In this section "company" includes any body corporate."

(2) Any reference in any enactment (including any enactment contained in subordinate legislation within the meaning of the [1978 c. 30.] Interpretation Act 1978) to a "subsidiary" or "holding company" within the meaning of section 736 of the [1985 c. 6.] Companies Act 1985 shall, subject to any express amendment or saving made by or under this Act, be read as referring to a subsidiary or holding company as defined in section 736 as substituted by subsection (1) above.

This applies whether the reference is specific or general, or express or implied.

(3) In Part XXVI of the [1985 c. 6.] Companies Act 1985 (general interpretation provisions), after section 736A insert—

"Power to amend ss. 736 and 736A.

736B.—(1) The Secretary of State may by regulations amend sections 736 and 736A so as to alter the meaning of the expressions "holding company", "subsidiary" or "wholly-owned subsidiary".

(2) The regulations may make different provision for different cases or classes of case and may contain such incidental and supplementary provisions as the Secretary of State thinks fit.

(3) Regulations under this section shall be made by statutory instrument which shall be subject to annulment in pursuance of a resolution of either House of Parliament.

(4) Any amendment made by regulations under this section does not apply for the purposes of enactments outside the Companies Acts unless the regulations so provide.

(5) So much of section 23(3) of the Interpretation Act 1978 as applies section 17(2)(a) of that Act (effect of repeal and re-enactment) to deeds, instruments and documents other than enactments shall not apply in relation to any repeal and re-enactment effected by regulations made under this section."

(4) Schedule 18 contains amendments and savings consequential on the amendments made by this section; and the Secretary of State may by regulations make such further amendments or savings as appear to him to be necessary or expedient.

(5) Regulations under this section shall be made by statutory instrument which shall be subject to annulment in pursuance of a resolution of either House of Parliament.

(6) So much of section 23(3) of the [1978 c. 30.] Interpretation Act 1978 as applies section 17(2)(a) of that Act (presumption as to meaning of references to enactments repealed and re-enacted) to deeds or other instruments or documents does not apply in relation to the repeal and re-enactment by this section of section 736 of the [1985 c. 6.] Companies Act 1985.

145.   Minor amendments

The [1985 c. 6.] Companies Act 1985 has effect with the further amendments specified in Schedule 19.

Part VI: Mergers and Related Matters

146.   Restriction on references where prior notice given

After section 75 of the [1973 c. 41.] Fair Trading Act 1973 there is inserted—

"Restriction on power to make merger reference where prior notice has been given

General rule where notice given by acquirer and no reference made within period for considering notice.

75A.—(1) Notice may be given to the Director by a person authorised by regulations to do so of proposed arrangements which might result in the creation of a merger situation qualifying for investigation.

(2) The notice must be in the prescribed form and state that the existence of the proposal has been made public.

(3) If the period for considering the notice expires without any reference being made to the Commission with respect to the notified arrangements, no reference may be made under this Part of this Act to the Commission with respect to those arrangements or to the creation or possible creation of any merger situation qualifying for investigation which is created in consequence of carrying those arrangements into effect.

(4) Subsection (3) of this section is subject to sections 75B(5) and 75C of this Act.

(5) A notice under subsection (1) of this section is referred to in sections 75B to 75F of this Act as a "merger notice".

The role of the Director.

75B.—(1) The Director shall, when the period for considering any merger notice begins, take such action as he considers appropriate to bring the existence of the proposal, the fact that the merger notice has been given and the date on which the period for considering the notice may expire to the attention of those who in his opinion would be affected if the arrangements were carried into effect.

(2) The period for considering a merger notice is the period of twenty days, determined in accordance with subsection (9) of this section, beginning with the first day after—

> (a) the notice has been received by the Director, and

> (b) any fee payable to the Director in respect of the notice has been paid.

(3) The Director may, and shall if required to do so by the Secretary of State, by notice to the person who gave the merger notice—

> (a) extend the period mentioned in subsection (2) of this section by a further ten days, and

> (b) extend that period as extended under paragraph (a) of this subsection by a further fifteen days.

(4) The Director may by notice to the person who gave the merger notice request him to provide the Director within such period as may be specified in the notice with such information as may be so specified.

(5) If the Director gives to the person who gave the merger notice (in this subsection referred to as "the relevant person") a notice stating that the Secretary of State is seeking undertakings under section 75G of this Act, section 75A(3) of this Act does not prevent a reference being made to the Commission unless—

> (a) after the Director has given that notice, the relevant person has given a notice to the Director stating that he does not intend to give such undertakings, and

> (b) the period of ten days beginning with the first day after the notice under paragraph (a) of this subsection was received by the Director has expired.

(6) A notice by the Director under subsection (3), (4) or (5) of this section must either be given to the person who gave the merger notice before the period for considering the merger notice expires or be sent in a properly addressed and pre-paid letter posted to him at such time that, in the ordinary course of post, it would be delivered to him before that period expires.

(7) The Director may, at any time before the period for considering any merger notice expires, reject the notice if—

(a) he suspects that any information given in respect of the notified arrangements, whether in the merger notice or otherwise, by the person who gave the notice or any connected person is in any material respect false or misleading,

(b) he suspects that it is not proposed to carry the notified arrangements into effect, or

(c) any prescribed information is not given in the merger notice or any information requested by notice under subsection (4) of this section is not provided within the period specified in the notice.

(8) If—

(a) under subsection (3)(b) of this section the period for considering a merger notice has been extended by a further fifteen days, but

(b) the Director has not made any recommendation to the Secretary of State under section 76(b) of this Act as to whether or not it would in the Director's opinion be expedient for the Secretary of State to make a reference to the Commission with respect to the notified arrangements,

then, during the last five of those fifteen days, the power of the Secretary of State to make a reference to the Commission with respect to the notified arrangements is not affected by the absence of any such recommendation.

(9) In determining any period for the purposes of subsections (2), (3) and (5) of this section no account shall be taken of—

(a) Saturday, Sunday, Good Friday and Christmas Day, and

(b) any day which is a bank holiday in England and Wales.

Cases where power to refer unaffected.

75C.—(1) Section 75A(3) of this Act does not prevent any reference being made to the Commission if—

(a) before the end of the period for considering the merger notice, it is rejected by the Director under section 75B(7) of this Act,

(b) before the end of that period, any of the enterprises to which the notified arrangements relate cease to be distinct from each other,

(c) any information (whether prescribed information or not) that—

(i) is, or ought to be, known to the person who gave the merger notice or any connected person, and

(ii) is material to the notified arrangements;

is not disclosed to the Secretary of State or the Director by such time before the end of that period as may be specified in regulations,

(d) at any time after the merger notice is given but before the enterprises to which the notified arrangements relate cease to be distinct from each other, any of those enterprises ceases to be distinct from any enterprise other than an enterprise to which those arrangements relate,

(e) the six months beginning with the end of the period for considering the merger notice expires without the enterprises to which the notified arrangements relate ceasing to be distinct from each other,

(f) the merger notice is withdrawn, or

(g) any information given in respect of the notified arrangements, whether in the merger notice or otherwise, by the person who gave the notice or any connected person is in any material respect false or misleading.

(2) Where—

(a) two or more transactions which have occurred or, if any arrangements are carried into effect, will occur may be treated for the purposes of a merger reference as having occurred simultaneously on a particular date, and

(b) subsection (3) of section 75A of this Act does not prevent such a reference with respect to the last of those transactions,

that subsection does not prevent such a reference with respect to any of those transactions which actually occurred less than six months before—

(i) that date, or

(ii) the actual occurrence of another of those transactions with respect to which such a reference may be made (whether or not by virtue of this subsection).

(3) In determining for the purposes of subsection (2) of this section the time at which any transaction actually occurred, no account shall be taken of any option or other conditional right until the option is exercised or the condition is satisfied.

Regulations.   **75D.**–(1) The Secretary of State may make regulations for the purposes of sections 75A to 75C of this Act.

(2) The regulations may, in particular—

(a) provide for section 75B(2) or (3) or section 75C(1)(e) of this Act to apply as if any reference to a period of days or months were a reference to a period specified in the regulations for the purposes of the provision in question,

(b) provide for the manner in which any merger notice is authorised or required to be given, rejected or withdrawn, and the time at which any merger notice is to be treated as received or rejected,

(c) provide for the manner in which any information requested by the Director or any other material information is authorised or required to be provided or disclosed, and the time at which such information is to be treated as provided or disclosed,

(d) provide for the manner in which any notice under section 75B of this Act is authorised or required to be given,

(e) provide for the time at which any notice under section 75B(5)(a) of this Act is to be treated as received,

(f) provide for the address which is to be treated for the purposes of section 75B(6) of this Act and of the regulations as a person's proper address,

(g) provide for the time at which any fee is to be treated as paid, and

(h) provide that a person is, or is not, to be treated, in such circumstances as may be specified in the regulations, as acting on behalf of a person authorised by regulations to give a merger notice or a person who has given such a notice.

(3) The regulations may make different provision for different cases.

(4) Regulations under this section shall be made by statutory instrument.

Interpretation of sections 75A to 75D.

75E. In this section and sections 75A to 75D of this Act—

"connected person", in relation to the person who gave a merger notice, means—

(a) any person who, for the purposes of section 77 of this Act, is associated with him, or

(b) any subsidiary of the person who gave the merger notice or of any person so associated with him,

"merger notice" is to be interpreted in accordance with section 75A(5) of this Act,

"notified arrangements" means the arrangements mentioned in the merger notice or arrangements not differing from them in any material respect,

"prescribed" means prescribed by the Director by notice having effect for the time being and published in the London, Edinburgh and Belfast Gazettes,

"regulations" means regulations under section 75D of this Act, and

"subsidiary" has the meaning given by section 75(4K) of this Act,

and references to the enterprises to which the notified arrangements relate are references to those enterprises that would have ceased to be distinct from one another if the arrangements mentioned in the merger notice in question had been carried into effect at the time when the notice was given.

Power to amend sections 75B to 75D.

75F.—(1) The Secretary of State may, for the purpose of determining the effect of giving a merger notice and the steps which may be or are to be taken by any person in connection with such a notice, by regulations made by statutory instrument amend sections 75B to 75D of this Act.

(2) The regulations may make different provision for different cases and may contain such incidental and supplementary provisions as the Secretary of

State thinks fit.

(3) No regulations shall be made under this section unless a draft of the regulations has been laid before and approved by resolution of each House of Parliament."

147.   Undertakings as alternative to merger reference

In Part V of the [1973 c. 41.] Fair Trading Act 1973 after the sections inserted by section 146 of this Act there is inserted—

'Undertakings as alternative to merger reference

Acceptance of undertakings.

75G.—(1) Where—

(a) the Secretary of State has power to make a merger reference to the Commission under section 64 or 75 of this Act,

(b) the Director has made a recommendation to the Secretary of State under section 76 of this Act that such a reference should be made, and

(c) the Director has (in making that recommendation or subsequently) given advice to the Secretary of State specifying particular effects adverse to the public interest which in his opinion the creation of the merger situation qualifying for investigation may have or might be expected to have,

the Secretary of State may, instead of making a merger reference to the Commission, accept from such of the parties concerned as he considers appropriate undertakings complying with subsections (2) and (3) of this section to take specified action which the Secretary of State considers appropriate to remedy or prevent the effects adverse to the public interest specified in the advice.

(2) The undertakings must provide for one or more of the following—

(a) the division of a business by the sale of any part of the undertaking or assets or otherwise (for which purpose all the activities carried on by way of business by any one person or by any two or more interconnected bodies corporate may be treated as a single business),

(b) the division of a group of interconnected bodies corporate, and

(c) the separation, by the sale of any part of the undertaking or assets concerned or other means, of enterprises which are under common control otherwise than by reason of their being enterprises of interconnected bodies corporate.

(3) The undertakings may also contain provision—

    (a) preventing or restricting the doing of things which might prevent or impede the division or separation,

    (b) as to the carrying on of any activities or the safeguarding of any assets until the division or separation is effected,

    (c) for any matters necessary to effect or take account of the division or separation, and

    (d) for enabling the Secretary of State to ascertain whether the undertakings are being fulfilled.

(4) If the Secretary of State has accepted one or more undertakings under this section, no reference may be made to the Commission with respect to the creation or possible creation of the merger situation qualifying for investigation by reference to which the undertakings were accepted, except in a case falling within subsection (5) of this section.

(5) Subsection (4) of this section does not prevent a reference being made to the Commission if material facts about the arrangements or transactions, or proposed arrangements or transactions, in consequence of which the enterprises concerned ceased or may cease to be distinct enterprises were not—

    (a) notified to the Secretary of State or the Director, or

    (b) made public,

before the undertakings were accepted.

(6) In subsection (5) of this section "made public" has the same meaning as in section 64 of this Act.

Publication of undertakings.

75H.—(1) The Secretary of State shall arrange for—

    (a) any undertaking accepted by him under section 75G of this Act,

    (b) the advice given by the Director for the purposes of subsection (1)(c) of that section in any case where such an undertaking has been accepted, and

(c) any variation or release of such an undertaking,

to be published in such manner as he may consider appropriate.

(2) In giving advice for the purposes of section 75G(1)(c) of this Act the Director shall have regard to the need for excluding, so far as practicable, any matter to which subsection (4) of this section applies.

(3) The Secretary of State shall exclude from any such advice as published under this section—

(a) any matter to which subsection (4) of this section applies and in relation to which he is satisfied that its publication in the advice would not be in the public interest, and

(b) any other matter in relation to which he is satisfied that its publication in the advice would be against the public interest.

(4) This subsection applies to—

(a) any matter which relates to the private affairs of an individual, where publication of that matter would or might, in the opinion of the Director or the Secretary of State, as the case may be, seriously and prejudicially affect the interests of that individual, and

(b) any matter which relates specifically to the affairs of a particular body of persons, whether corporate or unincorporate, where publication of that matter would or might, in the opinion of the Director or the Secretary of State, as the case may be, seriously and prejudicially affect the interests of that body, unless in his opinion the inclusion of that matter relating specifically to that body is necessary for the purposes of the advice.

(5) For the purposes of the law relating to defamation, absolute privilege shall attach to any advice given by the Director for the purposes of section 75G(1)(c) of this Act.

Review of undertakings.

75J. Where an undertaking has been accepted by the Secretary of State under section 75G of this Act, it shall be the duty of the Director—

(a) to keep under review the carrying out of that undertaking, and from time to time consider whether, by reason of any change of circumstances, the undertaking is no longer appropriate and either—

(i) one or more of the parties to it can be released from it, or

(ii) it needs to be varied or to be superseded by a new undertaking, and

(b) if it appears to him that the undertaking has not been or is not being fulfilled, that any person can be so released or that the undertaking needs to be varied or superseded, to give such advice to the Secretary of State as he may think proper in the circumstances.

Order of Secretary of State where undertaking not fulfilled.

75K.—(1) The provisions of this section shall have effect where it appears to the Secretary of State that an undertaking accepted by him under section 75G of this Act has not been, is not being or will not be fulfilled.

(2) The Secretary of State may by order made by statutory instrument exercise such one or more of the powers specified in paragraphs 9A and 12 to 12C and Part II of Schedule 8 to this Act as he may consider it requisite to exercise for the purpose of remedying or preventing the adverse effects specified in the advice given by the Director for the purposes of section 75G(1)(c) of this Act; and those powers may be so exercised to such extent and in such manner as the Secretary of State considers requisite for that purpose.

(3) In determining whether, or to what extent or in what manner, to exercise any of those powers, the Secretary of State shall take into account any advice given by the Director under section 75J(b) of this Act.

(4) The provision contained in an order under this section may be different from that contained in the undertaking.

(5) On the making of an order under this section, the undertaking and any other undertaking accepted under section 75G of this Act by reference to the same merger situation qualifying for investigation are released by virtue of this section."

148. Enforcement of undertakings

After section 93 of the [1973 c. 41.] Fair Trading Act 1973 there is inserted—

"Enforcement of undertakings.

93A.—(1) This section applies where a person (in this section referred to as "the responsible person") has given an undertaking which—

(a) has been accepted by the Secretary of State under section 75G of this Act,

(b) has been accepted by the appropriate Minister or Ministers under section 88 of this Act after the commencement of this section, or

(c) has been accepted by the Director under section 4 or 9 of the Competition Act 1980 after that time.

(2) Any person may bring civil proceedings in respect of any failure, or appre-

hended failure, of the responsible person to fulfil the undertaking, as if the obligations imposed by the undertaking on the responsible person had been imposed by an order to which section 90 of this Act applies."

149.   Temporary restrictions on share dealings

—(1) In section 75 of the [1973 c. 41.] Fair Trading Act 1973 (reference in anticipation of merger), after subsection (4) there is inserted—

"(4A) Where a merger reference is made under this section, it shall be unlawful, except with the consent of the Secretary of State under subsection (4C) of this section—

(a) for any person carrying on any enterprise to which the reference relates or having control of any such enterprise or for any subsidiary of his, or

(b) for any person associated with him or for any subsidiary of such a person,

directly or indirectly to acquire, at any time during the period mentioned in subsection (4B) of this section, an interest in shares in a company if any enterprise to which the reference relates is carried on by or under the control of that company.

(4B) The period referred to in subsection (4A) of this section is the period beginning with the announcement by the Secretary of State of the making of the merger reference concerned and ending—

(a) where the reference is laid aside at any time, at that time,

(b) where the time (including any further period) allowed to the Commission for making a report on the reference expires without their having made such a report, on the expiration of that time,

(c) where a report of the Commission on the reference not including such conclusions as are referred to in section 73(1)(b) of this Act is laid before Parliament, at the end of the day on which the report is so laid,

(d) where a report of the Commission on the reference including such conclusions is laid before Parliament, at the end of the period of forty days beginning with the day on which the report is so laid,

and where such a report is laid before each House on different days, it is to be treated for the purposes of this subsection as laid on the earlier day.

(4C) The consent of the Secretary of State—

>
> (a) may be either general or special,
>
> (b) may be revoked by the Secretary of State, and
>
> (c) shall be published in such way as, in the opinion of the Secretary of State, to give any person entitled to the benefit of it an adequate opportunity of getting to know of it, unless in the Secretary of State's opinion publication is not necessary for that purpose.

(4D) Section 93 of this Act applies to any contravention or apprehended contravention of subsection (4A) of this section as it applies to a contravention or apprehended contravention of an order to which section 90 of this Act applies.

(4E) Subsections (4F) to (4K) of this section apply for the interpretation of subsection (4A).

(4F) The circumstances in which a person acquires an interest in shares include those where—

> (a) he enters into a contract to acquire the shares (whether or not for cash),
>
> (b) not being the registered holder, he acquires a right to exercise, or to control the exercise of, any right conferred by the holding of the shares, or
>
> (c) he acquires a right to call for delivery of the shares to himself or to his order or to acquire an interest in the shares or assumes an obligation to acquire such an interest,

but does not include those where he acquires an interest in pursuance of an obligation assumed before the announcement by the Secretary of State of the making of the merger reference concerned.

(4G) The circumstances in which a person acquires a right mentioned in subsection (4F) of this section—

> (a) include those where he acquires a right or assumes an obligation the exercise or fulfilment of which would give him that right, but
>
> (b) does not include those where he is appointed as proxy to vote at a specified meeting of a company or of any class of its members or at any adjournment of the meeting or he is appointed by a corporation to act as its representative at any meeting of the company or of any class of its members,

and references to rights and obligations in this subsection and subsection (4F) of this section include conditional rights and conditional obligations.

(4H) Any reference to a person carrying on or having control of any enterprise includes a group of persons carrying on or having control of an enterprise and any member of such a group.

(4J) Sections 65(2) to (4) and 77(1) and (4) to (6) of this Act apply to determine whether any person or group of persons has control of any enterprise and whether persons are associated as they apply for the purposes of section 65 of this Act to determine whether enterprises are brought under common control.

(4K) "Subsidiary" has the meaning given by section 736 of the [1985 c. 6.] Companies Act 1985, but that section and section 736A of that Act also apply to determine whether a company is a subsidiary of an individual or of a group of persons as they apply to determine whether it is a subsidiary of a company and references to a subsidiary in subsections (8) and (9) of section 736A as so applied are to be read accordingly.

(4L) In this section—

"company" includes any body corporate, and

"share" means share in the capital of a company, and includes stock.

(4M) Nothing in subsection (4A) of this section makes anything done by a person outside the United Kingdom unlawful unless he is—

(a) a British citizen, a British Dependent Territories citizen, a British Overseas citizen or a British National (Overseas),

(b) a body corporate incorporated under the law of the United Kingdom or of a part of the United Kingdom, or

(c) a person carrying on business in the United Kingdom, either alone or in partnership with one or more other persons."

(2) This section does not apply in relation to any merger reference made before the passing of this Act.

150. Obtaining control by stages

—(1) After section 66 of the [1973 c. 41.] Fair Trading Act 1973 there is inserted—

"Obtaining control by stages.

66A.—(1) Where an enterprise is brought under the control of a person or group of persons in the course of two or more transactions (referred to in this section as a "series of transactions") falling within subsection (2) of this section, those transactions may, if the Secretary of State or, as the case may be, the Commission thinks fit, be treated for the purposes of a merger reference as having occurred simultaneously on the date on which the latest of them occurred.

(2) The transactions falling within this subsection are—

  (a) any transaction which—

    (i) enables that person or group of persons directly or indirectly to control or materially to influence the policy of any person carrying on the enterprise,

    (ii) enables that person or group of persons to do so to a greater degree, or

    (iii) is a step (whether direct or indirect) towards enabling that person or group of persons to do so, and

  (b) any transaction whereby that person or group of persons acquires a controlling interest in the enterprise or, where the enterprise is carried on by a body corporate, in that body corporate.

(3) Where a series of transactions includes a transaction falling within subsection (2)(b) of this section, any transaction occurring after the occurrence of that transaction is to be disregarded for the purposes of subsection (1) of this section.

(4) Where the period within which a series of transactions occurs exceeds two years, the transactions that may be treated as mentioned in subsection (1) of this section are any of those transactions that occur within a period of two years.

(5) Sections 65(2) to (4) and 77(1) and (4) to (6) of this Act apply for the purposes of this section to determine whether an enterprise is brought under the control of a person or group of persons and whether a transaction falls within subsection (2) of this section as they apply for the purposes of section 65 of this Act to determine whether enterprises are brought under common control.

(6) In determining for the purposes of this section the time at which any transaction occurs, no account shall be taken of any option or other conditional right until the option is exercised or the condition is satisfied."

(2) This section does not apply in relation to any merger reference made before the passing of this Act.

151. False or misleading information

At the end of Part VIII of the [1973 c. 41.] Fair Trading Act 1973 there is inserted—

"False or misleading information.

93B.—(1) If a person furnishes any information—

  (a) to the Secretary of State, the Director or the Commission in connection with any of their functions under Parts IV, V, VI or this Part of this Act or under the Competition Act 1980, or

(b) to the Commission in connection with the functions of the Commission under the Telecommunications Act 1984 or the Airports Act 1986,

and either he knows the information to be false or misleading in a material particular, or he furnishes the information recklessly and it is false or misleading in a material particular, he is guilty of an offence.

(2) A person who—

(a) furnishes any information to another which he knows to be false or misleading in a material particular, or

(b) recklessly furnishes any information to another which is false or misleading in a material particular,

knowing that the information is to be used for the purpose of furnishing information as mentioned in subsection (1)(a) or (b) of this section, is guilty of an offence.

(3) A person guilty of an offence under subsection (1) or (2) of this section is liable—

(a) on summary conviction, to a fine not exceeding the statutory maximum, and

(b) on conviction on indictment, to imprisonment for a term not exceeding two years or to a fine or to both.

(4) Section 129(1) of this Act does not apply to an offence under this section."

152. Fees

—(1) The Secretary of State may by regulations made by statutory instrument require the payment to him or to the Director of such fees as may be prescribed by the regulations in connection with the exercise by the Secretary of State, the Director and the Commission of their functions under Part V of the [1973 c. 41.] Fair Trading Act 1973.

(2) The regulations may provide for fees to be payable—

(a) in respect of—

(i) an application for the consent of the Secretary of State under section 58(1) of the Fair Trading Act 1973 to the transfer of a newspaper or of newspaper assets, and

(ii) a notice under section 75A(1) of that Act, and

(b) on the occurrence of any event specified in the regulations.

(3) The events that may be specified in the regulations by virtue of subsection (2)(b) above include—

(a) the making by the Secretary of State of a merger reference to the Commission under section 64 or 75 of the Fair Trading Act 1973,

(b) the announcement by the Secretary of State of his decision not to make a merger reference in any case where, at the time the announcement is made, he would under one of those sections have power to make a such a reference.

(4) The regulations may also contain provision—

(a) for ascertaining the persons by whom fees are payable,

(b) specifying whether any fee is payable to the Secretary of State or to the Director,

(c) for the amount of any fee to be calculated by reference to matters which may include—

(i) in a case involving functions of the Secretary of State under sections 57 to 61 of the [1973 c. 41.] Fair Trading Act 1973, the number of newspapers concerned, the number of separate editions (determined in accordance with the regulations) of each newspaper and the average circulation per day of publication (within the meaning of Part V of that Act) of each newspaper, and

(ii) in any other case, the value (determined in accordance with the regulations) of any assets concerned,

(d) as to the time when any fee is to be paid, and

(e) for the repayment by the Secretary of State or the Director of the whole or part of any fee in specified circumstances.

(5) The regulations may make different provision for different cases.

(6) Subsections (2) to (5) above do not prejudice the generality of subsection (1) above.

(7) In determining the amount of any fees to be prescribed by the regulations, the Secretary of State may take into account all costs incurred by him and by the Director in respect of the exercise by him, by the Commission and by the Director of their respective functions—

(a) under Part V of the Fair Trading Act 1973, and

(b) under Parts I, VII and VIII of that Act in relation to merger references or other matters arising under Part V.

(8) A statutory instrument containing regulations under this section shall be subject to annulment in pursuance of a resolution of either House of Parliament.

(9) Fees paid to the Secretary of State or the Director under this section shall be paid into the Consolidated Fund.

(10) In this section—

"the Commission",

"the Director", and

"merger reference",

have the same meaning as in the Fair Trading Act 1973, and "newspaper" has the same meaning as in Part V of that Act.

(11) References in this section to Part V of the [1973 c. 41.] Fair Trading Act 1973 and to merger references under section 64 or 75 of that Act or under that Part include sections 29 and 30 of the Water Act 1989 and any reference under section 29 of that Act.

153. Other amendments about mergers and related matters

Schedule 20 to this Act has effect.

Part VII: Financial Markets and Insolvency

154. Introduction

This Part has effect for the purposes of safeguarding the operation of certain financial markets by provisions with respect to—

(a) the insolvency, winding up or default of a person party to transactions in the market (sections 155 to 172),

(b) the effectiveness or enforcement of certain charges given to secure obligations in connection with such transactions (sections 173 to 176), and

(c) rights and remedies in relation to certain property provided as cover for margin in relation to such transactions or subject to such a charge (sections 177 to 181).

Recognised investment exchanges and clearing houses

155. Market contracts

—(1) This Part applies to the following descriptions of contract connected with a recognised investment exchange or recognised clearing house.

The contracts are referred to in this Part as "market contracts".

(2) In relation to a recognised investment exchange, this Part applies to—

(a) contracts entered into by a member or designated non-member of the exchange which are made on or otherwise subject to the rules of the exchange; and

(b) contracts subject to the rules of the exchange entered into by the exchange for the purposes of or in connection with the provision of clearing services.

A "designated non-member" means a person in respect of whom action may be taken under the default rules of the exchange but who is not a member of the exchange.

(3) In relation to a recognised clearing house, this Part applies to contracts subject to the rules of the clearing house entered into by the clearing house for the purposes of or in connection with the provision of clearing services for a recognised investment exchange.

(4) The Secretary of State may by regulations make further provision as to the contracts to be treated as "market contracts", for the purposes of this Part, in relation to a recognised investment exchange or recognised clearing house.

(5) The regulations may add to, amend or repeal the provisions of subsections (2) and (3) above.

156. Additional requirements for recognition: default rules, &c

—(1) The [1986 c. 60.] Financial Services Act 1986 shall have effect as if the requirements set out in Schedule 21 to this Act (the "additional requirements") were among those specified in that Act for recognition of an investment exchange or clearing house.

(2) In particular, that Act shall have effect—

(a) as if the requirements set out in Part I of that Schedule were among those specified in Schedule 4 to that Act (requirements for recognition of UK investment exchange),

(b) as if the requirements set out in Part II of that Schedule were among those specified in section 39(4) of that Act (requirements for recognition of UK clearing house), and

(c) as if the requirement set out in Part III of that Schedule was among those specified in section 40(2) of that Act (requirements for recognition of overseas investment exchange or clearing house).

(3) The additional requirements do not affect the status of an investment exchange or clearing house recognised before the commencement of this section, but if the Secretary of State is of the opinion that any of those requirements is not met in the case of such a body, he shall within one month of commencement give notice to the body stating his opinion.

(4) Where the Secretary of State gives such a notice, he shall not—

(a) take action to revoke the recognition of such a body on the ground that any of the additional requirements is not met, unless he considers it essential to do so in the interests of investors, or

(b) apply on any such ground for a compliance order under section 12 of the Financial Services Act 1986,

until after the end of the period of six months beginning with the date on which the notice was given.

(5) The Secretary of State may extend, or further extend, that period if he considers there is good reason to do so.

157. Changes in default rules

—(1) A recognised UK investment exchange or recognised UK clearing house shall give the Secretary of State at least 14 days' notice of any proposal to amend, revoke or add to its default rules; and the Secretary of State may within 14 days from receipt of the notice direct the exchange or clearing house not to proceed with the proposal, in whole or in part.

(2) A direction under this section may be varied or revoked.

(3) Any amendment or revocation of, or addition to, the default rules of an exchange or clearing house in breach of a direction under this section is ineffective.

158. Modifications of the law of insolvency

—(1) The general law of insolvency has effect in relation to market contracts, and action taken under the rules of a recognised investment exchange or recognised clearing house with respect to such contracts, subject to the provisions of sections 159 to 165.(2) So far as those provisions relate to insolvency proceedings in respect of a person other than a defaulter, they apply in relation to—

(a) proceedings in respect of a member or designated non-member of a recognised investment exchange or a member of a recognised clearing house, and

(b) proceedings in respect of a party to a market contract begun after a recognised investment exchange or recognised clearing house has taken action under its default rules in relation to a person party to the contract as principal,

but not in relation to any other insolvency proceedings, notwithstanding that rights or liabilities arising from market contracts fall to be dealt with in the proceedings.

(3) The reference in subsection (2)(b) to the beginning of insolvency proceedings is to—

(a) the presentation of a bankruptcy petition or a petition for sequestration of a person's estate, or

(b) the presentation of a petition for an administration order or a winding-up petition or the passing of a resolution for voluntary winding up, or

(c) the appointment of an administrative receiver.

(4) The Secretary of State may make further provision by regulations modifying the law of insolvency in relation to the matters mentioned in subsection (1).

(5) The regulations may add to, amend or repeal the provisions mentioned in subsection (1), and any other provision of this Part as it applies for the purposes of those provisions, or provide that those provisions have effect subject to such additions, exceptions or adaptations as are specified in the regulations.

159. Proceedings of exchange or clearing house take precedence over insolvency procedures

—(1) None of the following shall be regarded as to any extent invalid at law on the ground of inconsistency with the law relating to the distribution of the assets of a person on bankruptcy, winding up or sequestration, or in the administration of an insolvent estate—

(a) a market contract,

(b) the default rules of a recognised investment exchange or recognised clearing house,

(c) the rules of a recognised investment exchange or recognised clearing house as to the settlement of market contracts not dealt with under its default rules.

(2) The powers of a relevant office-holder in his capacity as such, and the powers of the court under the [1986 c. 45.] Insolvency Act 1986 or the [1985 c. 66.] Bankruptcy (Scotland) Act 1985 shall not be exercised in such a way as to prevent or interfere with—

(a) the settlement in accordance with the rules of a recognised investment exchange or recognised clearing house of a market contract not dealt with under its default rules, or

(b) any action taken under the default rules of such an exchange or clearing house.

This does not prevent a relevant office-holder from afterwards seeking to recover any amount under section 163(4) or 164(4) or prevent the court from afterwards making any such order or decree as is mentioned in section 165(1) or (2) (but subject to subsections (3) and (4) of that section).

(3) Nothing in the following provisions of this Part shall be construed as affecting the generality of the above provisions.

(4) A debt or other liability arising out of a market contract which is the subject of default proceedings may not be proved in a winding up or bankruptcy, or in Scotland claimed in a winding up or sequestration, until the completion of the default proceedings.

A debt or other liability which by virtue of this subsection may not be proved or claimed shall not be taken into account for the purposes of any set-off until the completion of the default proceedings.

(5) For the purposes of subsection (4) the default proceedings shall be taken to be completed in relation to a person when a report is made under section 162 stating the sum (if any) certified to be due to or from him.

160. Duty to give assistance for purposes of default proceedings

—(1) It is the duty of—

(a) any person who has or had control of any assets of a defaulter, and

(b) any person who has or had control of any documents of or relating to a defaulter,

to give a recognised investment exchange or recognised clearing house such assistance as it may reasonably require for the purposes of its default proceedings.

This applies notwithstanding any duty of that person under the enactments relating to insolvency.

(2) A person shall not under this section be required to provide any information or produce any document which he would be entitled to refuse to provide or produce on grounds of legal professional privilege in proceedings in the High Court or on grounds of confidentiality as between client and professional legal adviser in proceedings in the Court of Session.

(3) Where original documents are supplied in pursuance of this section, the exchange or clearing house shall return them forthwith after the completion of the relevant default proceedings, and shall in the meantime allow reasonable access to them to the person by whom they were supplied and to any person who would be entitled to have access to them if they were still in the control of the person by whom they were supplied.

(4) The expenses of a relevant office-holder in giving assistance under this section are recoverable as part of the expenses incurred by him in the discharge of his duties; and he shall not be required under this section to take any action which involves expenses which cannot be so recovered, unless the exchange or clearing house undertakes to meet them.

There shall be treated as expenses of his such reasonable sums as he may determine in respect of time spent in giving the assistance.

(5) The Secretary of State may by regulations make further provision as to the duties of persons to give assistance to a recognised investment exchange or recognised clearing house for the purposes of its default proceedings, and the duties of the exchange or clearing house with respect to information supplied to it.

The regulations may add to, amend or repeal the provisions of subsections (1) to (4) above.

(6) In this section "document" includes information recorded in any form.

161. Supplementary provisions as to default proceedings

—(1) If the court is satisfied on an application by a relevant office-holder that a party to a market contract with a defaulter intends to dissipate or apply his assets so as to prevent the office-holder recovering such sums as may become due upon the completion of the default proceedings, the court may grant such interlocutory relief (in Scotland, such interim order) as it thinks fit.

(2) A liquidator or trustee of a defaulter or, in Scotland, a permanent trustee on the sequestrated estate of the defaulter shall not—

    (a) declare or pay any dividend to the creditors, or

    (b) return any capital to contributories,

unless he has retained what he reasonably considers to be an adequate reserve in respect of any claims arising as a result of the default proceedings of the exchange or clearing house concerned.

(3) The court may on an application by a relevant office-holder make such order as it thinks fit altering or dispensing from compliance with such of the duties of his office as are affected by the fact that default proceedings are pending or could be taken, or have been or could have been taken.

(4) Nothing in section 10(1)(c), 11(3), 126, 128, 130, 185 or 285 of the [1986 c. 45.] Insolvency Act 1986 (which restrict the taking of certain legal proceedings and other steps), and nothing in any rule of law in Scotland to the like effect as the said section 285, in the [1985 c. 66.] Bankruptcy (Scotland) Act 1985 or in the [1987 c. 18.] Debtors (Scotland) Act 1987 as to the effect of sequestration, shall affect any action taken by an exchange or clearing house for the purpose of its default proceedings.

162. Duty to report on completion of default proceedings

—(1) A recognised investment exchange or recognised clearing house shall, on the completion of proceedings under its default rules, report to the Secretary of State on its proceedings stating in respect of each creditor or debtor the sum certified by them to be payable from or to the defaulter or, as the case may be, the fact that no sum is payable.

(2) The exchange or clearing house may make a single report or may make reports from time to time as proceedings are completed with respect to the transactions affecting particular persons.

(3) The exchange or clearing house shall supply a copy of every report under this section to the defaulter and to any relevant office-holder acting in relation to him or his estate.

(4) When a report under this section is received by the Secretary of State, he shall publish notice of that fact in such manner as he thinks appropriate for bringing it to the attention of creditors and debtors of the defaulter.

(5) An exchange or clearing house shall make available for inspection by a creditor or debtor of the defaulter so much of any report by it under this section as relates to the sum (if any) certified to be due to or from him or to the method by which that sum was determined.

(6) Any such person may require the exchange or clearing house, on payment of such reasonable fee as the exchange or clearing house may determine, to provide him with a copy of any part of a report which he is entitled to inspect.

163. Net sum payable on completion of default proceedings

—(1) The following provisions apply with respect to the net sum certified by a recognised investment exchange or recognised clearing house, upon proceedings under its default rules being duly completed in accordance with this Part, to be payable by or to a defaulter.

(2) If, in England and Wales, a bankruptcy or winding-up order has been made, or a resolution for voluntary winding up has been passed, the debt—

    (a) is provable in the bankruptcy or winding up or, as the case may be, is payable to the relevant office-holder, and

    (b) shall be taken into account, where appropriate, under section 323 of the [1986 c. 45.] Insolvency Act 1986 (mutual dealings and set-off) or the corresponding provision applicable in the case of winding up,

in the same way as a debt due before the commencement of the bankruptcy, the date on which the body corporate goes into liquidation (within the meaning of section 247 of the [1986 c. 45.] Insolvency Act 1986) or, in the case of a partnership, the date of the winding-up order.

(3) If, in Scotland, an award of sequestration or a winding-up order has been made, or a resolution for voluntary winding up has been passed, the debt—

    (a) may be claimed in the sequestration or winding up or, as the case may be, is payable to the relevant office-holder, and

    (b) shall be taken into account for the purposes of any rule of law relating to set-off applicable in sequestration or winding up,

in the same way as a debt due before the date of sequestration (within the meaning of section 73(1) of the [1985 c. 66.] Bankruptcy (Scotland) Act 1985) or the commencement of the winding up (within the meaning of section 129 of the [1986 c. 45.] Insolvency Act 1986).

(4) However, where (or to the extent that) a sum is taken into account by virtue of subsection (2)(b) or (3)(b) which arises from a contract entered into at a time when the creditor had notice—

(a) that a bankruptcy petition or, in Scotland, a petition for sequestration was pending, or

(b) that a meeting of creditors had been summoned under section 98 of the [1986 c. 45.] Insolvency Act 1986 or that a winding-up petition was pending,

the value of any profit to him arising from the sum being so taken into account (or being so taken into account to that extent) is recoverable from him by the relevant office-holder unless the court directs otherwise.

(5) Subsection (4) does not apply in relation to a sum arising from a contract effected under the default rules of a recognised investment exchange or recognised clearing house.

(6) Any sum recoverable by virtue of subsection (4) ranks for priority, in the event of the insolvency of the person from whom it is due, immediately before preferential or, in Scotland, preferred debts.

164. Disclaimer of property, rescission of contracts, &c

—(1) Sections 178, 186, 315 and 345 of the Insolvency Act 1986 (power to disclaim onerous property and court's power to order rescission of contracts, &c.) do not apply in relation to—

(a) a market contract, or

(b) a contract effected by the exchange or clearing house for the purpose of realising property provided as margin in relation to market contracts.

In the application of this subsection in Scotland, the reference to sections 178, 315 and 345 shall be construed as a reference to any rule of law having the like effect as those sections.

(2) In Scotland, a permanent trustee on the sequestrated estate of a defaulter or a liquidator is bound by any market contract to which that defaulter is a party and by any contract as is mentioned in subsection (1)(b) above notwithstanding section 42 of the [1985 c. 66.] Bankruptcy (Scotland) Act 1985 or any rule of law to the like effect applying in liquidations.

(3) Sections 127 and 284 of the Insolvency Act 1986 (avoidance of property dispositions effected after commencement of winding up or presentation of bankruptcy petition), and section 32(8) of the Bankruptcy (Scotland) Act 1985 (effect of dealing with debtor relating to estate vested in permanent trustee), do not apply to—

(a) a market contract, or any disposition of property in pursuance of such a contract,

(b) the provision of margin in relation to market contracts,

(c) a contract effected by the exchange or clearing house for the purpose of realising property provided as margin in relation to a market contract, or any disposition of property in pursuance of such a contract, or

(d) any disposition of property in accordance with the rules of the exchange or clearing house as to the application of property provided as margin.

(4) However, where—

(a) a market contract is entered into by a person who has notice that a petition has been presented for the winding up or bankruptcy or sequestration of the estate of the other party to the contract, or

(b) margin in relation to a market contract is accepted by a person who has notice that such a petition has been presented in relation to the person by whom or on whose behalf the margin is provided,

the value of any profit to him arising from the contract or, as the case may be, the amount or value of the margin is recoverable from him by the relevant office-holder unless the court directs otherwise.

(5) Subsection (4)(a) does not apply where the person entering into the contract is a recognised investment exchange or recognised clearing house acting in accordance with its rules, or where the contract is effected under the default rules of such an exchange or clearing house; but subsection (4)(b) applies in relation to the provision of margin in relation to such a contract.

(6) Any sum recoverable by virtue of subsection (4) ranks for priority, in the event of the insolvency of the person from whom it is due, immediately before preferential or, in Scotland, preferred debts.

165. Adjustment of prior transactions

—(1) No order shall be made in relation to a transaction to which this section applies under—

(a) section 238 or 339 of the [1986 c. 45.] Insolvency Act 1986 (transactions at an undervalue),

(b) section 239 or 340 of that Act (preferences), or

(c) section 423 of that Act (transactions defrauding creditors).

(2) As respects Scotland, no decree shall be granted in relation to any such transaction—

(a) under section 34 or 36 of the [1985 c. 66.] Bankruptcy (Scotland) Act 1985 or section 242 or 243 of the Insolvency Act 1986 (gratuitous alienations and unfair preferences), or

(b) at common law on grounds of gratuitous alienations or fraudulent preferences.

(3) This section applies to—

(a) a market contract to which a recognised investment exchange or recognised clearing house is a party or which is entered into under its default rules, and

(b) a disposition of property in pursuance of such a market contract.

(4) Where margin is provided in relation to a market contract and (by virtue of subsection (3)(a) or otherwise) no such order or decree as is mentioned in subsection (1) or (2) has been, or could be, made in relation to that contract, this section applies to—

(a) the provision of the margin,

(b) any contract effected by the exchange or clearing house in question for the purpose of realising the property provided as margin, and

(c) any disposition of property in accordance with the rules of the exchange or clearing house as to the application of property provided as margin.

166. Powers of Secretary of State to give directions

—(1) The powers conferred by this section are exercisable in relation to a recognised UK investment exchange or recognised UK clearing house.

(2) Where in any case an exchange or clearing house has not taken action under its default rules—

(a) if it appears to the Secretary of State that it could take action, he may direct it to do so, and

(b) if it appears to the Secretary of State that it is proposing to take or may take action, he may direct it not to do so.

(3) Before giving such a direction the Secretary of State shall consult the exchange or clearing house in question; and he shall not give a direction unless he is satisfied, in the light of that consultation—

(a) in the case of a direction to take action, that failure to take action would involve undue risk to investors or other participants in the market, or

(b) in the case of a direction not to take action, that the taking of action would be premature or otherwise undesirable in the interests of investors or other participants in the market.

(4) A direction shall specify the grounds on which it is given.

(5) A direction not to take action may be expressed to have effect until the giving of a further direction (which may be a direction to take action or simply revoking the earlier direction).

(6) No direction shall be given not to take action if, in relation to the person in question—

(a) a bankruptcy order or an award of sequestration of his estate has been made, or an interim receiver or interim trustee has been appointed, or

(b) a winding up order has been made, a resolution for voluntary winding up has been passed or an administrator, administrative receiver or provisional liquidator has been appointed;

and any previous direction not to take action shall cease to have effect on the making or passing of any such order, award or appointment.

(7) Where an exchange or clearing house has taken or been directed to take action under its default rules, the Secretary of State may direct it to do or not to do such things (being things which it has power to do under its default rules) as are specified in the direction.

The Secretary of State shall not give such a direction unless he is satisfied that it will not impede or frustrate the proper and efficient conduct of the default proceedings.

(8) A direction under this section is enforceable, on the application of the Secretary of State, by injunction or, in Scotland, by an order under section 45 of the [1988 c. 36.] Court of Session Act 1988; and where an exchange or clearing house has not complied with a direction, the court may make such order as it thinks fit for restoring the position to what it would have been if the direction had been complied with.

167. Application to determine whether default proceedings to be taken

—(1) Where there has been made or passed in relation to a member or designated non-member of a recognised investment exchange or a member of a recognised clearing house—

(a) a bankruptcy order or an award of sequestration of his estate, or an order appointing an interim receiver of his property, or

(b) an administration or winding up order, a resolution for voluntary winding up or an order appointing a provisional liquidator,

and the exchange or clearing house has not taken action under its default rules in consequence of the order, award or resolution or the matters giving rise to it, a relevant office-holder appointed by, or in consequence of or in connection with, the order, award or resolution may apply to the Secretary of State.

(2) The application shall specify the exchange or clearing house concerned and the grounds on which it is made.

(3) On receipt of the application the Secretary of State shall notify the exchange or clearing house, and unless within three business days after the day on which the notice is received the exchange or clearing house—

(a) takes action under its default rules, or

(b) notifies the Secretary of State that it proposes to do so forthwith,

then, subject as follows, the provisions of sections 158 to 165 above do not apply in relation to market contracts to which the member or designated non-member in question is a party or to anything done by the exchange or clearing house for the purposes of, or in connection with, the settlement of any such contract.

For this purpose a "business day" means any day which is not a Saturday or Sunday, Christmas Day, Good Friday or a bank holiday in any part of the United Kingdom under the [1971 c. 80.] Banking and Financial Dealings Act 1971.

(4) The provisions of sections 158 to 165 are not disapplied if before the end of the period mentioned in subsection (3) the Secretary of State gives the exchange or clearing house a direction under section 166(2)(a) (direction to take action under default rules).

No such direction may be given after the end of that period.

(5) If the exchange or clearing house notifies the Secretary of State that it proposes to take action under its default rules forthwith, it shall do so; and that duty is enforceable, on the application of the Secretary of State, by injunction or, in Scotland, by an order under section 45 of the [1988 c. 36.] Court of Session Act 1988.

168. Delegation of functions to designated agency

—(1) Section 114 of the Financial Services Act 1986 (power to transfer functions to designated agency) applies to the functions of the Secretary of State under this Part in relation to a UK investment exchange or clearing house, with the exception of his functions with respect to the making of orders and regulations.

(2) If immediately before the commencement of this section—

(a) a designated agency is exercising all functions in relation to such bodies which are capable of being transferred under that section, and

(b) no draft order is lying before Parliament resuming any of those functions,

the order bringing this section into force shall have effect as a delegation order made under that section transferring to that agency all the functions which may be transferred by virtue of this section.

(3) The Secretary of State may—

(a) in the circumstances mentioned in subsection (3), (4) or (5) of section 115 of the [1986 c. 60.] Financial Services Act 1986, or

(b) if it appears to him that a designated agency is unable or unwilling to discharge all or any of the functions under this Part which have been transferred to it,

make an order under that section resuming all functions under this Part which have been transferred to the agency.

This does not affect his power to make an order under subsection (1) or (2) of that section with respect to such functions.

169. Supplementary provisions

—(1) Section 61 of the Financial Services Act 1986 (injunctions and restitution orders) applies in relation to a contravention of any provision of the rules of a recognised investment exchange or recognised clearing house relating to the matters mentioned in Schedule 21 to this Act as it applies in relation to a contravention of any provision of such rules relating to the carrying on of investment business.

(2) The following provisions of the Financial Services Act 1986—

section 12 (compliance orders), as it applies by virtue of section 37(8) or 39(8),

section 37(7)(b) (revocation of recognition of UK investment exchange), and

section 39(7)(b) (revocation of recognition of UK clearing house),

apply in relation to a failure by a recognised investment exchange or recognised clearing house to comply with an obligation under this Part as to a failure to comply with an obligation under that Act.

(3) Where the recognition of an investment exchange or clearing house is revoked under the Financial Services Act 1986, the Secretary of State may, before or after the revocation order, give such directions as he thinks fit with respect to the continued application of the provisions of this Part, with such exceptions, additions and adaptations as may be specified in the direction, in relation to cases where a relevant event of any description specified in the directions occurred before the revocation order takes effect.

(4) The references in sections 119 and 121 of the [1986 c. 60.] Financial Services Act 1986 (competition) to what is necessary for the protection of investors shall be construed as including references to what is necessary for the purposes of this Part.

(5) Section 204 of the Financial Services Act 1986 (service of notices) applies in relation to a notice, direction or other document required or authorised by or under this Part to be given to or served on any person other than the Secretary of State.

Other exchanges and clearing houses

170. Certain overseas exchanges and clearing houses

—(1) The Secretary of State may by regulations provide that this Part applies in relation to contracts connected with an overseas investment exchange or clearing house which is approved by him in accordance with such procedures as may be specified in the regulations, as satisfying such requirements as may be so specified, as it applies in relation to contracts connected with a recognised investment exchange or clearing house.

(2) The Secretary of State shall not approve an overseas investment exchange or clearing house unless he is satisfied—

    (a) that the rules and practices of the body, together with the law of the country in which the body's head office is situated, provide adequate procedures for dealing with the default of persons party to contracts connected with the body, and

(b) that it is otherwise appropriate to approve the body.

(3) The reference in subsection (2)(a) to default is to a person being unable to meet his obligations.

(4) The regulations may apply in relation to the approval of a body under this section such of the provisions of the [1986 c. 60.] Financial Services Act 1986 as the Secretary of State considers appropriate.

(5) The Secretary of State may make regulations which, in relation to a body which is so approved—

(a) apply such of the provisions of the Financial Services Act 1986 as the Secretary of State considers appropriate, and

(b) provide that the provisions of this Part apply with such exceptions, additions and adaptations as appear to the Secretary of State to be necessary or expedient;

and different provision may be made with respect to different bodies or descriptions of body.

(6) Where the regulations apply any provisions of the Financial Services Act 1986, they may provide that those provisions apply with such exceptions, additions and adaptations as appear to the Secretary of State to be necessary or expedient.

171. Certain money market institutions

—(1) The Secretary of State may by regulations provide that this Part applies to contracts of any specified description in relation to which settlement arrangements are provided by a person for the time being included in a list maintained by the Bank of England for the purposes of this section, as it applies to contracts connected with a recognised investment exchange or recognised clearing house.

(2) The Secretary of State shall not make any such regulations unless he is satisfied, having regard to the extent to which the contracts in question—

(a) involve, or are likely to involve, investments falling within paragraph 2 of Schedule 5 to the [1986 c. 60.] Financial Services Act 1986 (money market investments), or

(b) are otherwise of a kind dealt in by persons supervised by the Bank of England,

that it is appropriate that the arrangements should be subject to the supervision of the Bank of England.

(3) The approval of the Treasury is required for—

(a) the conditions imposed by the Bank of England for admission to the list maintained by it for the purposes of this section, and

(b) the arrangements for a person's admission to and removal from the list;

and any regulations made under this section shall cease to have effect if the approval of the Treasury is withdrawn, but without prejudice to their having effect again if approval is given for fresh conditions or arrangements.

(4) The Bank of England shall publish the list as for the time being in force and provide a certified copy of it at the request of any person wishing to refer to it in legal proceedings.

A certified copy shall be evidence (in Scotland, sufficient evidence) of the contents of the list; and a copy purporting to be certified by or on behalf of the Bank shall be deemed to have been duly certified unless the contrary is shown.

(5) Regulations under this section may, in relation to a person included in the list—

（a) apply, with such exceptions, additions and adaptations as appear to the Secretary of State to be necessary or expedient, such of the provisions of the [1986 c. 60.] Financial Services Act 1986 as he considers appropriate, and

(b) provide that the provisions of this Part apply with such exceptions, additions and adaptations as appear to the Secretary of State to be necessary or expedient.

(6) Before making any regulations under this section, the Secretary of State shall consult the Treasury and the Bank of England.

(7) In section 84(1) of the [1987 c. 22.] Banking Act 1987 (disclosure of information obtained under that Act), in the Table showing the authorities to which, and functions for the purposes of which, disclosure may be made, at the end add—

"
| A person included in the list maintained by the Bank for the purposes of section 171 of the Companies Act 1989. | Functions under settlement arrangements to which regulations under that section relate. |

"

172. Settlement arrangements provided by the Bank of England

—(1) The Secretary of State may by regulations provide that this Part applies to contracts of any specified description in relation to which settlement arrangements are provided by the Bank of England, as it applies to contracts connected with a recognised investment exchange or recognised clearing house.

(2) Regulations under this section may provide that the provisions of this Part apply with such exceptions, additions and adaptations as appear to the Secretary of State to be necessary or expedient.

(3) Before making any regulations under this section, the Secretary of State shall consult the Treasury and the Bank of England.

Market charges

173. Market charges

—(1) In this Part "market charge" means a charge, whether fixed or floating, granted—

(a) in favour of a recognised investment exchange, for the purpose of securing debts or liabilities arising in connection with the settlement of market contracts,

(b) in favour of a recognised clearing house, for the purpose of securing debts or liabilities arising in connection with their ensuring the performance of market contracts, or

(c) in favour of a person who agrees to make payments as a result of the transfer of specified securities made through the medium of a computer-based system established by the Bank of England and The Stock Exchange, for the purpose of securing debts or liabilities of the transferee arising in connection therewith.

(2) Where a charge is granted partly for purposes specified in subsection (1)(a), (b) or (c) and partly for other purposes, it is a "market charge" so far as it has effect for the specified purposes.

(3) In subsection (1)(c)—

"specified securities" means securities for the time being specified in the list in Schedule 1 to the [1982 c. 41.] Stock Transfer Act 1982, and includes any right to such securities; and

"transfer", in relation to any such securities or right, means a transfer of the beneficial interest.

(4) The Secretary of State may by regulations make further provision as to the charges granted in favour of any such person as is mentioned in subsection (1)(a), (b) or (c) which are to be treated as "market charges" for the purposes of this Part; and the regulations may add to, amend or repeal the provisions of subsections (1) to (3) above.

(5) The regulations may provide that a charge shall or shall not be treated as a market charge if or to the extent that it secures obligations of a specified description, is a charge over property of a specified description or contains provisions of a specified description.

(6) Before making regulations under this section in relation to charges granted in favour of a person within subsection (1)(c), the Secretary of State shall consult the Treasury and the Bank of England.

174. Modifications of the law of insolvency

—(1) The general law of insolvency has effect in relation to market charges and action taken in enforcing them subject to the provisions of section 175.

(2) The Secretary of State may by regulations make further provision modifying the law of insolvency in relation to the matters mentioned in subsection (1).

(3) The regulations may add to, amend or repeal the provisions mentioned in subsection (1), and any other provision of this Part as it applies for the purposes of those provisions, or provide that those provisions have effect with such exceptions, additions or adaptations as are specified in the regulations.

(4) The regulations may make different provision for cases defined by reference to the nature of the charge, the nature of the property subject to it, the circumstances, nature or extent of the obligations secured by it or any other relevant factor.

(5) Before making regulations under this section in relation to charges granted in favour of a person within section 173(1)(c), the Secretary of State shall consult the Treasury and the Bank of England.

175. Administration orders, &c

—(1) The following provisions of the [1986 c. 45.] Insolvency Act 1986 (which relate to administration orders and administrators) do not apply in relation to a market charge—

(a) sections 10(1)(b) and 11(3)(c) (restriction on enforcement of security while petition for administration order pending or order in force), and

(b) section 15(1) and (2) (power of administrator to deal with charged property);

and section 11(2) of that Act (receiver to vacate office when so required by administrator) does not apply to a receiver appointed under a market charge.

(2) However, where a market charge falls to be enforced after an administration order has been made or a petition for an administration order has been presented, and there exists another charge over some or all of the same property ranking in priority to or pari passu with the market charge, the court may order that there shall be taken after enforcement of the market charge such steps as the court may direct for the purpose of ensuring that the chargee under the other charge is not prejudiced by the enforcement of the market charge.

(3) The following provisions of the Insolvency Act 1986 (which relate to the powers of receivers) do not apply in relation to a market charge—

(a) section 43 (power of administrative receiver to dispose of charged property), and

(b) section 61 (power of receiver in Scotland to dispose of an interest in property).

(4) Sections 127 and 284 of the [1986 c. 45.] Insolvency Act 1986 (avoidance of property dispositions effected after commencement of winding up or presentation of bankruptcy petition), and section 32(8) of the [1985 c. 66.] Bankruptcy (Scotland) Act 1985 (effect of dealing with debtor relating to estate vested in permanent trustee), do not apply to a disposition of property as a result of which the property becomes subject to a market charge or any transaction pursuant to which that disposition is made.

(5) However, if a person (other than the chargee under the market charge) who is party to a disposition mentioned in subsection (4) has notice at the time of the disposition that a petition has been presented for the winding up or bankruptcy or sequestration of the estate of the party making the disposition, the value of any profit to him arising from the disposition is recoverable from him by the relevant

office-holder unless the court directs otherwise.

(6) Any sum recoverable by virtue of subsection (5) ranks for priority, in the event of the insolvency of the person from whom it is due, immediately before preferential or, in Scotland, preferred debts.

(7) In a case falling within both subsection (4) above (as a disposition of property as a result of which the property becomes subject to a market charge) and section 164(3) (as the provision of margin in relation to a market contract), section 164(4) applies with respect to the recovery of the amount or value of the margin and subsection (5) above does not apply.

176. Power to make provision about certain other charges

—(1) The Secretary of State may by regulations provide that the general law of insolvency has effect in relation to charges of such descriptions as may be specified in the regulations, and action taken in enforcing them, subject to such provisions as may be specified in the regulations.

(2) The regulations may specify any description of charge granted in favour of—

> (a) a body approved under section 170 (certain overseas exchanges and clearing houses),
>
> (b) a person included in the list maintained by the Bank of England for the purposes of section 171 (certain money market institutions),
>
> (c) the Bank of England,
>
> (d) an authorised person within the meaning of the [1986 c. 60.] Financial Services Act 1986, or
>
> (e) an international securities self-regulating organisation within the meaning of that Act,

for the purpose of securing debts or liabilities arising in connection with or as a result of the settlement of contracts or the transfer of assets, rights or interests on a financial market.

(3) The regulations may specify any description of charge granted for that purpose in favour of any other person in connection with exchange facilities or clearing services provided by a recognised investment exchange or recognised clearing house or by any such body, person, authority or organisation as is mentioned in subsection (2).

(4) Where a charge is granted partly for the purpose specified in subsection (2) and partly for other purposes, the power conferred by this section is exercisable in relation to the charge so far as it has effect for that purpose.

(5) The regulations may—

> (a) make the same or similar provision in relation to the charges to which they apply as is made by or under sections 174 and 175 in relation to market charges, or
>
> (b) apply any of those provisions with such exceptions, additions or adaptations as are specified in the regulations.(6) Before making regulations under this section relating to a descrip-

tion of charges defined by reference to their being granted—

(a) in favour of a person included in the list maintained by the Bank of England for the purposes of section 171, or in connection with exchange facilities or clearing services provided by a person included in that list, or

(b) in favour of the Bank of England, or in connection with settlement arrangements provided by the Bank,

the Secretary of State shall consult the Treasury and the Bank of England.

(7) Regulations under this section may provide that they apply or do not apply to a charge if or to the extent that it secures obligations of a specified description, is a charge over property of a specified description or contains provisions of a specified description.

Market property

177. Application of margin not affected by certain other interests

—(1) The following provisions have effect with respect to the application by a recognised investment exchange or recognised clearing house of property (other than land) held by the exchange or clearing house as margin in relation to a market contract.

(2) So far as necessary to enable the property to be applied in accordance with the rules of the exchange or clearing house, it may be so applied notwithstanding any prior equitable interest or right, or any right or remedy arising from a breach of fiduciary duty, unless the exchange or clearing house had notice of the interest, right or breach of duty at the time the property was provided as margin.

(3) No right or remedy arising subsequently to the property being provided as margin may be enforced so as to prevent or interfere with the application of the property by the exchange or clearing house in accordance with its rules.

(4) Where an exchange or clearing house has power by virtue of the above provisions to apply property notwithstanding an interest, right or remedy, a person to whom the exchange or clearing house disposes of the property in accordance with its rules takes free from that interest, right or remedy.

178. Priority of floating market charge over subsequent charges

—(1) The Secretary of State may by regulations provide that a market charge which is a floating charge has priority over a charge subsequently created or arising, including a fixed charge.

(2) The regulations may make different provision for cases defined, as regards the market charge or the subsequent charge, by reference to the description of charge, its terms, the circumstances in which it is created or arises, the nature of the charge, the person in favour of whom it is granted or arises or any other relevant factor.

179. Priority of market charge over unpaid vendor's lien

Where property subject to an unpaid vendor's lien becomes subject to a market charge, the charge has priority over the lien unless the chargee had actual notice of the lien at the time the property became subject to the charge.

180. Proceedings against market property by unsecured creditors

—(1) Where property (other than land) is held by a recognised investment exchange or recognised clearing house as margin in relation to market contracts or is subject to a market charge, no execution or other legal process for the enforcement of a judgment or order may be commenced or continued, and no distress may be levied, against the property by a person not seeking to enforce any interest in or security over the property, except with the consent of—

> (a) in the case of property provided as cover for margin, the investment exchange or clearing house in question, or

> (b) in the case of property subject to a market charge, the person in whose favour the charge was granted.

(2) Where consent is given the proceedings may be commenced or continued notwithstanding any provision of the [1986 c. 45.] Insolvency Act 1986 or the [1985 c. 66.] Bankruptcy (Scotland) Act 1985.

(3) Where by virtue of this section a person would not be entitled to enforce a judgment or order against any property, any injunction or other remedy granted with a view to facilitating the enforcement of any such judgment or order shall not extend to that property.

(4) In the application of this section to Scotland, the reference to execution being commenced or continued includes a reference to diligence being carried out or continued, and the reference to distress being levied shall be omitted.

181. Power to apply provisions to other cases

—(1) The power of the Secretary of State to make provision by regulations under—

> (a) section 170, 171 or 172 (power to extend provisions relating to market contracts), or

> (b) section 176 (power to extend provisions relating to market charges),

includes power to apply sections 177 to 180 to any description of property provided as cover for margin in relation to contracts in relation to which the power is exercised or, as the case may be, property subject to charges in relation to which the power is exercised.

(2) The regulations may provide that those sections apply with such exceptions, additions and adaptations as may be specified in the regulations.

Supplementary provisions

182. Powers of court in relation to certain proceedings begun before commencement

—(1) The powers conferred by this section are exercisable by the court where insolvency proceedings in respect of—

(a) a member of a recognised investment exchange or a recognised clearing house, or

(b) a person by whom a market charge has been granted,

are begun on or after 22nd December 1988 and before the commencement of this section.

That person is referred to in this section as "the relevant person".

(2) For the purposes of this section "insolvency proceedings" means proceedings under Part II, IV, V or IX of the [1986 c. 45.] Insolvency Act 1986 (administration, winding up and bankruptcy) or under the [1985 c. 66.] Bankruptcy (Scotland) Act 1985; and references in this section to the beginning of such proceedings are to—

(a) the presentation of a petition on which an administration order, winding-up order, bankruptcy order or award of sequestration is made, or

(b) the passing of a resolution for voluntary winding up.

(3) This section applies in relation to—

(a) in England and Wales, the administration of the insolvent estate of a deceased person, and

(b) in Scotland, the administration by a judicial factor appointed under section 11A of the [1889 c. 39.] Judicial Factors (Scotland) Act 1889 of the insolvent estate of a deceased person,

as it applies in relation to insolvency proceedings.

In such a case references to the beginning of the proceedings shall be construed as references to the death of the relevant person.

(4) The court may on an application made, within three months after the commencement of this section, by—

(a) a recognised investment exchange or recognised clearing house, or

(b) a person in whose favour a market charge has been granted,

make such order as it thinks fit for achieving, except so far as assets of the relevant person have been distributed before the making of the application, the same result as if the provisions of Schedule 22 had come into force on 22nd December 1988.

(5) The provisions of that Schedule ("the relevant provisions") reproduce the effect of certain provisions of this Part as they appeared in the Bill for this Act as introduced into the House of Lords and published on that date.

(6) The court may in particular—

>   (a) require the relevant person or a relevant office-holder—
>
>   > (i) to return property provided as cover for margin or which was subject to a market charge, or to pay to the applicant or any other person the proceeds of realisation of such property, or
>
>   > (ii) to pay to the applicant or any other person such amount as the court estimates would have been payable to that person if the relevant provisions had come into force on 22nd December 1988 and market contracts had been settled in accordance with the rules of the recognised investment exchange or recognised clearing house, or a proportion of that amount if the property of the relevant person or relevant office-holder is not sufficient to meet the amount in full;
>
>   (b) provide that contracts, rules and dispositions shall be treated as not having been void;
>
>   (c) modify the functions of a relevant office-holder, or the duties of the applicant or any other person, in relation to the insolvency proceedings, or indemnify any such person in respect of acts or omissions which would have been proper if the relevant provisions had been in force;
>
>   (d) provide that conduct which constituted an offence be treated as not having done so;
>
>   (e) dismiss proceedings which could not have been brought if the relevant provisions had come into force on 22nd December 1988, and reverse the effect of any order of a court which could not, or would not, have been made if those provisions had come into force on that date.

(7) An order under this section shall not be made against a relevant office-holder if the effect would be that his remuneration, costs and expenses could not be met.

183. Insolvency proceedings in other jurisdictions

—(1) The references to insolvency law in section 426 of the Insolvency [1986 c. 45.] Act 1986 (co-operation with courts exercising insolvency jurisdiction in other jurisdictions) include, in relation to a part of the United Kingdom, the provisions made by or under this Part and, in relation to a relevant country or territory within the meaning of that section, so much of the law of that country or territory as corresponds to any provisions made by or under this Part.

(2) A court shall not, in pursuance of that section or any other enactment or rule of law, recognise or give effect to—

> (a) any order of a court exercising jurisdiction in relation to insolvency law in a country or territory outside the United Kingdom, or

> (b) any act of a person appointed in such a country or territory to discharge any functions under insolvency law,

in so far as the making of the order or the doing of the act would be prohibited in the case of a court in the United Kingdom or a relevant office-holder by provisions made by or under this Part.

(3) Subsection (2) does not affect the recognition or enforcement of a judgment required to be recognised or enforced under or by virtue of the [1982 c. 27.] Civil Jurisdiction and Judgments Act 1982.

184. Indemnity for certain acts, &c

—(1) Where a relevant office-holder takes any action in relation to property of a defaulter which is liable to be dealt with in accordance with the default rules of a recognised investment exchange or recognised clearing house, and believes and has reasonable grounds for believing that he is entitled to take that action, he is not liable to any person in respect of any loss or damage resulting from his action except in so far as the loss or damage is caused by the office-holder's own negligence.

(2) Any failure by a recognised investment exchange or recognised clearing house to comply with its own rules in respect of any matter shall not prevent that matter being treated for the purposes of this Part as done in accordance with those rules so long as the failure does not substantially affect the rights of any person entitled to require compliance with the rules.

(3) No recognised investment exchange or recognised clearing house, nor any officer or servant or member of the governing body of a recognised investment exchange or recognised clearing house, shall be liable in damages for anything done or omitted in the discharge or purported discharge of any functions to which this subsection applies unless the act or omission is shown to have been in bad faith.

(4) The functions to which subsection (3) applies are the functions of the exchange or clearing house so far as relating to, or to matters arising out of—

> (a) its default rules, or

> (b) any obligations to which it is subject by virtue of this Part.

(5) No person exercising any functions by virtue of arrangements made pursuant to paragraph 5 or 12 of Schedule 21 (delegation of functions in connection with default procedures), nor any officer or servant of such a person, shall be liable in damages for anything done or omitted in the discharge or purported discharge of those functions unless the act or omission is shown to have been in bad faith.

185. Power to make further provision by regulations

—(1) The Secretary of State may by regulations make such further provision as appears to him necessary or expedient for the purposes of this Part.

(2) Provision may, in particular, be made—

    (a) for integrating the provisions of this Part with the general law of insolvency, and

    (b) for adapting the provisions of this Part in their application to overseas investment exchanges and clearing houses.

(3) Regulations under this section may add to, amend or repeal any of the provisions of this Part or provide that those provisions have effect subject to such additions, exceptions or adaptations as are specified in the regulations.

186. Supplementary provisions as to regulations

—(1) Regulations under this Part may make different provision for different cases and may contain such incidental, transitional and other supplementary provisions as appear to the Secretary of State to be necessary or expedient.

(2) Regulations under this Part shall be made by statutory instrument which shall be subject to annulment in pursuance of a resolution of either House of Parliament.

187. Construction of references to parties to market contracts

—(1) Where a person enters into market contracts in more than one capacity, the provisions of this Part apply (subject as follows) as if the contracts entered into in each different capacity were entered into by different persons.

(2) References in this Part to a market contract to which a person is a party include (subject as follows, and unless the context otherwise requires) contracts to which he is party as agent.

(3) The Secretary of State may by regulations—

    (a) modify or exclude the operation of subsections (1) and (2), and

    (b) make provision as to the circumstances in which a person is to be regarded for the purposes of those provisions as acting in different capacities.

188. Meaning of "default rules" and related expressions

—(1) In this Part "default rules" means rules of a recognised investment exchange or recognised clearing house which provide for the taking of action in the event of a person appearing to be unable, or likely to become unable, to meet his obligations in respect of one or more market contracts connected with the exchange or clearing house.

(2) References in this Part to a "defaulter" are to a person in respect of whom action has been taken by a recognised investment exchange or recognised clearing house under its default rules, whether by declaring him to be a defaulter or otherwise; and references in this Part to "default" shall be construed accordingly.

(3) In this Part "default proceedings" means proceedings taken by a recognised investment exchange or recognised clearing house under its default rules.

(4) If an exchange or clearing house takes action under its default rules in respect of a person, all subsequent proceedings under its rules for the purposes of or in connection with the settlement of market contracts to which the defaulter is a party shall be treated as done under its default rules.

189. Meaning of "relevant office-holder"

—(1) The following are relevant office-holders for the purposes of this Part—

(a) the official receiver,

(b) any person acting in relation to a company as its liquidator, provisional liquidator, administrator or administrative receiver,

(c) any person acting in relation to an individual (or, in Scotland, any debtor within the meaning of the [1985 c. 66.] Bankruptcy (Scotland) Act 1985) as his trustee in bankruptcy or interim receiver of his property or as permanent or interim trustee in the sequestration of his estate,

(d) any person acting as administrator of an insolvent estate of a deceased person.

(2) In subsection (1)(b) "company" means any company, society, association, partnership or other body which may be wound up under the [1986 c. 45.] Insolvency Act 1986.

190. Minor definitions

—(1) In this Part—

"administrative receiver" has the meaning given by section 251 of the Insolvency Act 1986;

"charge" means any form of security, including a mortgage and, in Scotland, a heritable security;

"clearing house" has the same meaning as in the [1986 c. 60.] Financial Services Act 1986;

"interim trustee" and "permanent trustee" have the same meaning as in the Bankruptcy (Scotland) Act 1985;

"investment" and "investment exchange" have the same meaning as in the Financial Services Act 1986;

"overseas", in relation to an investment exchange or clearing house, means having its head office outside the United Kingdom;

"recognised" means recognised under the Financial Services Act 1986;

"set-off", in relation to Scotland, includes compensation;

"The Stock Exchange" means The International Stock Exchange of the United Kingdom and the Republic of Ireland Limited;

"UK", in relation to an investment exchange or clearing house, means having its head office in the United Kingdom.

(2) References in this Part to settlement in relation to a market contract are to the discharge of the rights and liabilities of the parties to the contract, whether by performance, compromise or otherwise.

(3) In this Part the expressions "margin" and "cover for margin" have the same meaning.

(4) References in this Part to ensuring the performance of a transaction have the same meaning as in the [1986 c. 60.] Financial Services Act 1986.

(5) For the purposes of this Part a person shall be taken to have notice of a matter if he deliberately failed to make enquiries as to that matter in circumstances in which a reasonable and honest person would have done so.

This does not apply for the purposes of a provision requiring "actual notice".

(6) References in this Part to the law of insolvency include references to every provision made by or under the [1986 c. 45.] Insolvency Act 1986 or the [1985 c. 66.] Bankruptcy (Scotland) Act 1985; and in relation to a building society references to insolvency law or to any provision of the [1986 c. 45.] Insolvency Act 1986 are to that law or provision as modified by the [1986 c. 53.] Building Societies Act 1986.

(7) In relation to Scotland, references in this Part—

(a) to sequestration include references to the administration by a judicial factor of the insolvent estate of a deceased person, and

(b) to an interim or permanent trustee include references to a judicial factor on the insolvent estate of a deceased person,

unless the context otherwise requires.

191. Index of defined expressions

The following Table shows provisions defining or otherwise explaining expressions used in this Part (other than provisions defining or explaining an expression used only in the same section or paragraph)—

administrative receiver	section 190(1)
charge	section 190(1)
clearing house	section 190(1)
cover for margin	section 190(3)
default rules (and related expressions)	section 188
designated non-member	section 155(2)
ensuring the performance of a transaction	section 190(4)
insolvency law (and similar expressions)	section 190(6)
interim trustee	section 190(1) and (7)(b)
investment	section 190(1)
investment exchange	section 190(1)
margin	section 190(3)
market charge	section 173
market contract	section 155
notice	section 190(5)
overseas (in relation to an investment exchange or clearing house)	section 190(1)
party (in relation to a market contract)	section 187
permanent trustee	section 190(1) and (7)(b)
recognised	section 190(1)
relevant office-holder	section 189
sequestration	section 190(7)(a)
set off (in relation to Scotland)	section 190(1)
settlement and related expressions (in relation to a market contract)	section 190(2)
The Stock Exchange	section 190(1)
trustee, interim or permanent (in relation to Scotland)	section 190(7)(b)
UK (in relation to an investment exchange or clearing house)	section 190(1).

Part VIII: Amendments of the Financial Services Act 1986

192. Statements of principle

In Chapter V of Part I of the [1986 c. 60.] Financial Services Act 1986 (conduct of investment business), after section 47 insert—

"Statements of principle.

47A.—(1) The Secretary of State may issue statements of principle with respect to the conduct and financial standing expected of persons authorised to carry on investment business.

(2) The conduct expected may include compliance with a code or standard issued by another person, as for the time being in force, and may allow for the exercise of discretion by any person pursuant to any such code or standard.

(3) Failure to comply with a statement of principle under this section is a ground for the taking of disciplinary action or the exercise of powers of intervention, but it does not of itself give rise to any right of action by investors or other persons affected or affect the validity of any transaction.

(4) The disciplinary action which may be taken by virtue of subsection (3) is—

(a) the withdrawal or suspension of authorisation under section 28 or the termination or suspension of authorisation under section 33,

(b) the giving of a disqualification direction under section 59,

(c) the making of a public statement under section 60, or

(d) the application by the Secretary of State for an injunction, interdict or other order under section 61(1);

and the reference in that subsection to powers of intervention is to the powers conferred by Chapter VI of this Part.

(5) Where a statement of principle relates to compliance with a code or standard issued by another person, the statement of principle may provide—

(a) that failure to comply with the code or standard shall be a ground for the taking of disciplinary action, or the exercise of powers of intervention, only in such cases and to such extent as may be specified; and

(b) that no such action shall be taken, or any such power exercised, except at the request of the person by whom the code or standard in question was issued.

(6) The Secretary of State shall exercise his powers in such manner as appears to him appropriate to secure compliance with statements of principle under this section.

Modification or waiver of statements of principle in particular cases.

47B.—(1) The relevant regulatory authority may on the application of any person—

(a) modify a statement of principle issued under section 47A so as to adapt it to his circumstances or to any particular kind of business carried on by him, or

(b) dispense him from compliance with any such statement of principle, generally or in relation to any particular kind of business carried on by him.

(2) The powers conferred by this section shall not be exercised unless it appears to the relevant regulatory authority—

(a) that compliance with the statement of principle in question would be unduly burdensome for the applicant having regard to the benefit which compliance would confer on investors, and

(b) that the exercise of those powers will not result in any undue risk to investors.

(3) The powers conferred by this section may be exercised unconditionally or subject to conditions; and section 47A(3) applies in the case of failure to comply with a condition as in the case of failure to comply with a statement of principle.

(4) The relevant regulatory authority for the purposes of this section is—

(a) in the case of a member of a recognised self-regulating organisation or professional body, in relation to investment business in the carrying on of which he is subject to the rules of the organisation or body, that organisation or body;

(b) in any other case, or in relation to other investment business, the Secretary of State.

(5) The references in paragraph 4(1) of Schedule 2 and paragraph 4(2) of Schedule 3 (requirements for recognition of self-regulating organisations and professional bodies) to monitoring and enforcement of compliance with statements of principle include monitoring and enforcement of compliance with conditions imposed by the organisation or body under this section."

193. Restriction of right to bring action for contravention of rules, regulations, &c.

—(1) In Chapter V of Part I of the [1986 c. 60.] Financial Services Act 1986 (conduct of investment business), after section 62 (actions for damages) insert—

"Restriction of right of action.

62A.—(1) No action in respect of a contravention to which section 62 above applies shall lie at the suit of a person other than a private investor, except in such circumstances as may be specified by regulations made by the Secretary of State.

(2) The meaning of the expression "private investor" for the purposes of subsection (1) shall be defined by regulations made by the Secretary of State.

(3) Regulations under subsection (1) may make different provision with respect to different cases.

(4) The Secretary of State shall, before making any regulations affecting the right to bring an action in respect of a contravention of any rules or regulations made by a person other than himself, consult that person."

(2) In section 114(5) of the [1986 c. 60.] Financial Services Act 1986 (transfer of functions to designated agency: excluded functions), after paragraph (d) insert—

"(dd) section 62A;".

(3) In Schedule 11 to the Financial Services Act 1986 (friendly societies), after paragraph 22 insert—

"**22A.**—(1) No action in respect of a contravention to which paragraph 22(4) above applies shall lie at the suit of a person other than a private investor, except in such circumstances as may be specified by regulations made by the Registrar.

(2) The meaning of the expression "private investor" for the purposes of sub-paragraph (1) shall be defined by regulations made by the Registrar.

(3) Regulations under sub-paragraph (1) may make different provision with respect to different cases.

(4) The Registrar shall, before making any regulations affecting the right to bring an action in respect of a contravention of any rules or regulations made by a person other than himself, consult that person."

(4) In paragraph 28(5) of Schedule 11 to the Financial Services Act 1986 (transfer of Registrar's functions to transferee body), after "paragraphs 2 to 25" insert "(except paragraph 22A)".

194. Application of designated rules and regulations to members of self-regulating organisations

In Chapter V of Part I of the [1986 c. 60.] Financial Services Act 1986 (conduct of investment business), after section 63 insert—

"Application of designated rules and regulations to members of self-regulating organisations.

63A.—(1) The Secretary of State may in rules and regulations under—

(a) section 48 (conduct of business rules),

(b) section 49 (financial resources rules),

(c) section 55 (clients' money regulations), or

(d) section 56 (regulations as to unsolicited calls),

designate provisions which apply, to such extent as may be specified, to a member of a recognised self-regulating organisation in respect of investment business in the carrying on of which he is subject to the rules of the organisation.

(2) It may be provided that the designated rules or regulations have effect, generally or to such extent as may be specified, subject to the rules of the organisation.

(3) A member of a recognised self-regulating organisation who contravenes a rule or regulation applying to him by virtue of this section shall be treated as having contravened the rules of the organisation.

(4) It may be provided that, to such extent as may be specified, the designated rules or regulations may not be modified or waived (under section 63B below or section 50) in relation to a member of a recognised self-regulating organisation.

Where such provision is made any modification or waiver previously granted shall cease to have effect, subject to any transitional provision or saving contained in the rules or regulations.

(5) Except as mentioned in subsection (1), the rules and regulations referred to in that subsection do not apply to a member of a recognised self-regulating organisation in respect of investment business in the carrying on of which he is subject to the rules of the organisation.

Modification or waiver of designated rules and regulations.

63B.—(1) A recognised self-regulating organisation may on the application of a member of the organisation—

(a) modify a rule or regulation designated under section 63A so as to adapt it to his circumstances or to any particular kind of business carried on by him, or

(b) dispense him from compliance with any such rule or regulation, generally or in relation to any particular kind of business carried on by him.

(2) The powers conferred by this section shall not be exercised unless it appears to the organisation—

>(a) that compliance with the rule or regulation in question would be unduly burdensome for the applicant having regard to the benefit which compliance would confer on investors, and

>(b) that the exercise of those powers will not result in any undue risk to investors.

(3) The powers conferred by this section may be exercised unconditionally or subject to conditions; and section 63A(3) applies in the case of a contravention of a condition as in the case of contravention of a designated rule or regulation.

(4) The reference in paragraph 4(1) of Schedule 2 (requirements for recognition of self-regulating organisations) to monitoring and enforcement of compliance with rules and regulations includes monitoring and enforcement of compliance with conditions imposed by the organisation under this section."

195. Codes of practice

In Chapter V of Part I of the [1986 c. 60.] Financial Services Act 1986 (conduct of investment business), after the sections inserted by section 194 above, insert—

"Codes of practice.

63C.—(1) The Secretary of State may issue codes of practice with respect to any matters dealt with by statements of principle issued under section 47A or by rules or regulations made under any provision of this Chapter.

(2) In determining whether a person has failed to comply with a statement of principle—

>(a) a failure by him to comply with any relevant provision of a code of practice may be relied on as tending to establish failure to comply with the statement of principle, and

>(b) compliance by him with the relevant provisions of a code of practice may be relied on as tending to negative any such failure.

(3) A contravention of a code of practice with respect to a matter dealt with by rules or regulations shall not of itself give rise to any liability or invalidate any transaction; but in determining whether a person's conduct amounts to contravention of a rule or regulation—

>(a) contravention by him of any relevant provision of a code of practice may be relied on as tending to establish liability, and

>(b) compliance by him with the relevant provisions of a code of prac-

tice may be relied on as tending to negative liability.

(4) Where by virtue of section 63A (application of designated rules and regulations to members of self-regulating organisations) rules or regulations—

(a) do not apply, to any extent, to a member of a recognised self-regulating organisation, or

(b) apply, to any extent, subject to the rules of the organisation,

a code of practice with respect to a matter dealt with by the rules or regulations may contain provision limiting its application to a corresponding extent."

196. Relations with other regulatory authorities

In Part I of the Financial Services Act 1986 (regulation of investment business), after section 128 insert—

"Chapter XV

Relations with other Regulatory Authorities

"Relevance of other controls.

128A. In determining—

(a) in relation to a self-regulating organisation, whether the requirements of Schedule 2 are met, or

(b) in relation to a professional body, whether the requirements of Schedule 3 are met,

the Secretary of State shall take into account the effect of any other controls to which members of the organisation or body are subject.

"Relevance of information given and action taken by other regulatory authorities.

128B.—(1) The following provisions apply in the case of—

(a) a person whose principal place of business is in a country or territory outside the United Kingdom, or

(b) a person whose principal business is other than investment business;

and in relation to such a person "the relevant regulatory authority" means the appropriate regulatory authority in that country or territory or, as the case may be, in relation to his principal business.

(2) The Secretary of State may regard himself as satisfied with respect to any matter relevant for the purposes of this Part if—

    (a) the relevant regulatory authority informs him that it is satisfied with respect to that matter, and

    (b) he is satisfied as to the nature and scope of the supervision exercised by that authority.

(3) In making any decision with respect to the exercise of his powers under this Part in relation to any such person, the Secretary of State may take into account whether the relevant regulatory authority has exercised, or proposes to exercise, its powers in relation to that person.

(4) The Secretary of State may enter into such arrangements with other regulatory authorities as he thinks fit for the purposes of this section.

(5) Where any functions under this Part have been transferred to a designated agency, nothing in this section shall be construed as affecting the responsibility of the Secretary of State for the discharge of Community obligations or other international obligations of the United Kingdom.

"Enforcement in support of overseas regulatory authority.

128C.—(1) The Secretary of State may exercise his disciplinary powers or powers of intervention at the request of, or for the purpose of assisting, an overseas regulatory authority.

(2) The disciplinary powers of the Secretary of State means his powers—

    (a) to withdraw or suspend authorisation under section 28 or to terminate or suspend authorisation under section 33,

    (b) to give a disqualification direction under section 59,

    (c) to make a public statement under section 60, or

    (d) to apply for an injunction, interdict or other order under section 61(1);

and the reference to his powers of intervention is to the powers conferred by Chapter VI of this Part.

(3) An "overseas regulatory authority" means an authority in a country or territory outside the United Kingdom which exercises—

    (a) any function corresponding to—

        (i) a function of the Secretary of State under this Act, the Insurance Companies Act 1982 or the [1985 c. 6.]

Companies Act 1985,

(ii) a function under this Act of a designated agency, transferee body or competent authority, or

(iii) a function of the Bank of England under the Banking Act 1987, or

(b) any functions in connection with the investigation of, or the enforcement of rules (whether or not having the force of law) relating to, conduct of the kind prohibited by the Company Securities (Insider Dealing) Act 1985, or

(c) any function prescribed for the purposes of this subsection, being a function which in the opinion of the Secretary of State relates to companies or financial services.

(4) In deciding whether to exercise those powers the Secretary of State may take into account, in particular—

(a) whether corresponding assistance would be given in that country or territory to an authority exercising regulatory functions in the United Kingdom;

(b) whether the case concerns the breach of a law, or other requirement, which has no close parallel in the United Kingdom or involves the assertion of a jurisdiction not recognised by the United Kingdom;

(c) the seriousness of the case and its importance to persons in the United Kingdom;

(d) whether it is otherwise appropriate in the public interest to give the assistance sought.

(5) The Secretary of State may decline to exercise those powers unless the overseas regulatory authority undertakes to make such contribution towards the cost of their exercise as the Secretary of State considers appropriate.

(6) The reference in subsection (3)(c) to financial services includes, in particular, investment business, insurance and banking.

197. Construction of references to incurring civil liability

—(1) In section 150(6) of the [1986 c. 60.] Financial Services Act 1986 (exclusion of liability in respect of false or misleading listing particulars), at the end insert—

"The reference above to a person incurring liability includes a reference to any other person being entitled as against that person to be granted any civil remedy or to rescind or repudiate any agreement."

(2) In section 154(5) of the Financial Services Act 1986 (exclusion of civil liability in respect of advertisements or other information in connection with listing application), at the end insert—

"The reference above to a person incurring civil liability includes a reference to any other person being entitled as against that person to be granted any civil remedy or to rescind or repudiate any agreement."

198. Offers of unlisted securities

—(1) In Part V of the Financial Services Act 1986 (offers of unlisted securities), after section 160 insert—

"Exemptions. **160A.**—(1) The Secretary of State may by order exempt from sections 159 and 160 when issued in such circumstances as may be specified in the order—

(a) advertisements appearing to him to have a private character, whether by reason of a connection between the person issuing them and those to whom they are addressed or otherwise;

(b) advertisements appearing to him to deal with investments only incidentally;

(c) advertisements issued to persons appearing to him to be sufficiently expert to understand any risks involved;

(d) such other classes of advertisements as he thinks fit.

(2) The Secretary of State may by order exempt from sections 159 and 160 an advertisement issued in whatever circumstances which relates to securities appearing to him to be of a kind that can be expected normally to be bought or dealt in only by persons sufficiently expert to understand any risks involved.

(3) An order under subsection (1) or (2) may require a person who by virtue of the order is authorised to issue an advertisement to comply with such requirements as are specified in the order.

(4) An order made by virtue of subsection (1)(a), (b) or (c) or subsection (2) shall be subject to annulment in pursuance of a resolution of either House of Parliament; and no order shall be made by virtue of subsection (1)(d) unless a draft of it has been laid before and approved by a resolution of each House of Parliament."

that above.

(3) In section 159, in subsection (1) omit the words from the beginning to "section 161 below," and after subsection (2) insert—

"(3) Subsection (1) above has effect subject to section 160A (exemptions) and section 161 (exceptions).".

(4) In section 160, in subsection (1) omit the words from the beginning to "section 161 below," and for subsections (6) to (9) substitute—

"(6) Subsection (1) above has effect subject to section 160A (exemptions) and section 161 (exceptions).".

(5) In section 171, in subsection (1)(b) and subsection (3) for "section 160(6) or (7)" substitute "section 160A".

199. Offers of securities by private companies and old public companies

In Part V of the Financial Services Act 1986 (offers of unlisted securities), in section 170 (advertisements by private companies and old public companies), for subsections (2) to (4) substitute—

"(2) The Secretary of State may by order exempt from subsection (1) when issued in such circumstances as may be specified in the order—

(a) advertisements appearing to him to have a private character, whether by reason of a connection between the person issuing them and those to whom they are addressed or otherwise;

(b) advertisements appearing to him to deal with investments only incidentally;

(c) advertisements issued to persons appearing to him to be sufficiently expert to understand any risks involved;

(d) such other classes of advertisements as he thinks fit.

(3) The Secretary of State may by order exempt from subsection (1) an advertisement issued in whatever circumstances which relates to securities appearing to him to be of a kind that can be expected normally to be bought or dealt in only by persons sufficiently expert to understand any risks involved.

(4) An order under subsection (2) or (3) may require a person who by virtue of the order is authorised to issue an advertisement to comply with such requirements as are specified in the order.

(4A) An order made by virtue of subsection (2)(a), (b) or (c) or subsection (3) shall be subject to annulment in pursuance of a resolution of either House of Parliament; and no order shall be made by virtue of subsection (2)(d) unless a draft of it has been laid before and approved by a resolution of each House of Parliament." .

200. Jurisdiction of High Court and Court of Session

—(1) In the [1986 c. 60.] Financial Services Act 1986, for section 188 (jurisdiction as respects actions concerning designated agency, &c.), substitute—

"Jurisdiction of High Court and Court of Session.

188.—(1) Proceedings arising out of any act or omission (or proposed act or omission) of—

(a) a recognised self-regulating organisation,

(b) a designated agency,

(c) a transferee body, or

(d) the competent authority,

in the discharge or purported discharge of any of its functions under this Act may be brought in the High Court or the Court of Session.

(2) The jurisdiction conferred by subsection (1) is in addition to any other jurisdiction exercisable by those courts."

(2) In Schedule 5 to the [1982 c. 27.] Civil Jurisdiction and Judgments Act 1982 (proceedings excluded from general provisions as to allocation of jurisdiction within the United Kingdom), for paragraph 10 substitute—

"Financial Services Act 1986

10. Proceedings such as are mentioned in section 188 of the Financial Services Act 1986.

201. Directions to secure compliance with international obligations

In the Financial Services Act 1986, for section 192 (international obligations) substitute—

"International obligations.

192.—(1) If it appears to the Secretary of State—

(a) that any action proposed to be taken by an authority or body to which this section applies would be incompatible with Community obligations or any other international obligations of the United Kingdom, or

(b) that any action which that authority or body has power to take is required for the purpose of implementing any such obligation,

he may direct the authority or body not to take or, as the case may be, to take the action in question.

(2) The authorities and bodies to which this section applies are the following—

(a) a recognised self-regulating organisation,

(b) a recognised investment exchange (other than an overseas investment exchange),

(c) a recognised clearing house (other than an overseas clearing house),

(d) a designated agency,

(e) a transferee body,

(f) a competent authority.

(3) This section also applies to an approved exchange within the meaning of Part V of this Act in respect of any action which it proposes to take or has power to take in respect of rules applying to a prospectus by virtue of a direction under section 162(3) above.

(4) A direction under this section may include such supplementary or incidental requirements as the Secretary of State thinks necessary or expedient.

(5) Where the function of making or revoking a recognition order in respect of an authority or body to which this section applies is exercisable by a designated agency, any direction in respect of that authority or body shall be a direction requiring the agency to give the authority or body such a direction as is specified in the direction given by the Secretary of State.

(6) A direction under this section is enforceable, on the application of the person who gave it, by injunction or, in Scotland, by an order under section 45 of the Court of Session Act 1988."

202. Offers of short-dated debentures

In section 195 of the [1986 c. 60.] Financial Services Act 1986 (circumstances in which certain offers of debentures not treated as offers to the public), for "repaid within less than one year of the date of issue" substitute "repaid within five years of the date of issue".

203. Standard of protection for investors

—(1) In Schedule 2 to the Financial Services Act 1986 (requirements for recognition of self-regulating organisations), in paragraph 3 (safeguards for investors) for sub-paragraphs (1) and (2) substitute—

"(1) The organisation must have rules governing the carrying on of investment business by its members which, together with the statements of principle, rules, regulations and codes of practice to which its members are subject under Chapter V of Part I of this Act, are such as to afford an adequate level of protection for investors.

(2) In determining in any case whether an adequate level of protection is afforded for investors of any description, regard shall be had to the nature of the investment business carried on by members of the organisation, the kinds of investors involved and the effectiveness of the organisation's arrangements for enforcing compliance." .

(2) In Schedule 3 to the Financial Services Act 1986 (requirements for recognition of professional bodies), for paragraph 3 (safeguards for investors) substitute—

"**3.**—(1) The body must have rules regulating the carrying on of investment business by persons certified by it which, together with the statements of principle, rules, regulations and codes of practice to which those persons are subject under Chapter V of Part I of this Act, afford an adequate level of protection for investors.

(2) In determining in any case whether an adequate level of protection is afforded for investors of any description, regard shall be had to the nature of the investment business carried on by persons certified by the body, the kinds of investors involved and the effectiveness of the body's arrangements for enforcing compliance."

(3) The order bringing this section into force may provide that, for a transitional period, a self-regulating organisation or professional body may elect whether to comply with the new requirement having effect by virtue of subsection (1) or (2) above or with the requirement which it replaces.

The Secretary of State may by order specify when the transitional period is to end.

204. Costs of compliance

—(1) In Schedule 2 to the [1986 c. 60.] Financial Services Act 1986 (requirements for recognition of self-regulating organisations), after paragraph 3 insert

"Taking account of costs of compliance

3A. The organisation must have satisfactory arrangements for taking account, in framing its rules, of the cost to those to whom the rules would apply of complying with those rules and any other controls to which they are subject.

and in Schedule 3 to that Act (requirements for recognition of professional body), after paragraph 3 insert—

"Taking account of costs of compliance

3A. The body must have satisfactory arrangements for taking account, in framing its rules, of the cost to those to whom the rules would apply of complying with those rules and any other controls to which they are subject.

(2) The additional requirements having effect by virtue of subsection (1) do not affect the status of a self-regulating organisation or professional body recognised before the commencement of that subsection; but if the Secretary of State is of the opinion that any of those requirements is not met in the case of such an organisation or body, he shall within one month of commencement give notice to the organisation or body stating his opinion.

(3) Where the Secretary of State gives such a notice, he shall not—

(a) take action to revoke the recognition of such an organisation or body on the ground that any of the additional requirements is not met, unless he considers it essential to do so in the interests of investors, or

(b) apply on any such ground for a compliance order under section 12 of the Financial Services Act 1986,

until after the end of the period of six months beginning with the date on which the notice was given.

(4) In Schedule 7 to the Financial Services Act 1986 (qualifications of designated agency), after paragraph 2 insert—

"Taking account of costs of compliance

2A.—(1) The agency must have satisfactory arrangements for taking account, in framing any provisions which it proposes to make in the exercise of its legislative functions, of the cost to those to whom the provisions would apply of complying with those provisions and any other controls to which they are subject.

(2) In this paragraph "legislative functions" means the functions of issuing or making statements of principle, rules, regulations or codes of practice."

(5) The additional requirement having effect by virtue of subsection (4) above does not affect the status of a designated agency to which functions have been transferred before the commencement of that subsection; but if the Secretary of State is of the opinion the requirement is not met in the case of such an agency, he shall within one month of commencement give notice to the agency stating his opinion.

(6) Where the Secretary of State gives such a notice, he shall not take action under section 115(2) of the [1986 c. 60.] Financial Services Act 1986 to resume any functions exercisable by such an agency on the ground that the additional requirement is not met until after the end of the period of six months beginning with the date on which the notice was given.

(7) References in this section to a recognised self-regulating organisation include a recognised self-regulating organisation for friendly societies and references to a designated agency include a transferee body (within the meaning of that Act).

In relation to such an organisation or body—

> (a) references to the Secretary of State shall be construed as references to the Registrar (within the meaning of Schedule 11 to the Financial Services Act 1986), and

> (b) the reference to section 12 of that Act shall be construed as a reference to paragraph 6 of that Schedule.

205. Requirements for recognition of investment exchange

—(1) In Schedule 4 to the Financial Services Act 1986 (requirements for recognition of investment exchange), after paragraph 5 insert—

> *"Supplementary*
>
> **6.**—(1) The provisions of this Schedule relate to an exchange only so far as it provides facilities for the carrying on of investment business; and nothing in this Schedule shall be construed as requiring an exchange to limit dealings on the exchange to dealings in investments.
>
> (2) The references in this Schedule, and elsewhere in this Act, to ensuring the performance of transactions on an exchange are to providing satisfactory procedures (including default procedures) for the settlement of transactions on the exchange."

(2) The above amendment shall be deemed always to have had effect.

(3) In section 207(1) of the Financial Services Act 1986 (interpretation), at the appropriate place insert—

> """ensure" and "ensuring", in relation to the performance of transactions on an investment exchange, have the meaning given in paragraph 6 of Schedule 4 to this Act;"".

206. Consequential amendments and delegation of functions on commencement

—(1) The Financial Services Act 1986 has effect with the amendments specified in Schedule 23 which are consequential on the amendments made by sections 192, 194 and 195.

(2) If immediately before the commencement of any provision of this Part which amends Part I of

the Financial Services Act 1986—

> (a) a designated agency is exercising by virtue of a delegation order under section 114 of that Act any functions of the Secretary of State under that Part, and
>
> (b) no draft order is lying before Parliament resuming any of those functions,

the order bringing that provision into force may make, in relation to any functions conferred on the Secretary of State by the amendment, any such provision as may be made by an order under that section.

(3) If immediately before the commencement of any provision of Schedule 23 which amends Part III of the Financial Services Act 1986—

> (a) a transferee body (within the meaning of that Act) is exercising by virtue of a transfer order under paragraph 28 of Schedule 11 to that Act any functions of the Registrar under that Part, and
>
> (b) no draft order is lying before Parliament resuming any of those functions,

the order bringing that provision into force may make, in relation to any functions conferred on the Registrar by the amendment, any such provision as may be made by an order under that paragraph.

(4) References in the Financial Services Act 1986 to a delegation order made under section 114 of that Act or to a transfer order made under paragraph 28 of Schedule 11 to that Act include an order made containing any such provision as is authorised by subsection (2) or (3).

Part IX: Transfer of Securities

207.   Transfer of Securities

—(1) The Secretary of State may make provision by regulations for enabling title to securities to be evidenced and transferred without a written instrument.

In this section—

> (a) "securities" means shares, stock, debentures, debenture stock, loan stock, bonds, units of a collective investment scheme within the meaning of the Financial Services Act 1986 and other securities of any description;
>
> (b) references to title to securities include any legal or equitable interest in securities; and

    (c) references to a transfer of title include a transfer by way of security.

(2) The regulations may make provision—

    (a) for procedures for recording and transferring title to securities, and

    (b) for the regulation of those procedures and the persons responsible for or involved in their operation.

(3) The regulations shall contain such safeguards as appear to the Secretary of State appropriate for the protection of investors and for ensuring that competition is not restricted, distorted or prevented.

(4) The regulations may for the purpose of enabling or facilitating the operation of the new procedures make provision with respect to the rights and obligations of persons in relation to securities dealt with under the procedures.

But the regulations shall be framed so as to secure that the rights and obligations in relation to securities dealt with under the new procedures correspond, so far as practicable, with those which would arise apart from any regulations under this section.

(5) The regulations may include such supplementary, incidental and transitional provisions as appear to the Secretary of State to be necessary or expedient.

In particular, provision may be made for the purpose of giving effect to—

    (a) the transmission of title to securities by operation of law;

    (b) any restriction on the transfer of title to securities arising by virtue of the provisions of any enactment or instrument, court order or agreement;

    (c) any power conferred by any such provision on a person to deal with securities on behalf of the person entitled.

(6) The regulations may make provision with respect to the persons responsible for the operation of the new procedures—

    (a) as to the consequences of their insolvency or incapacity, or

    (b) as to the transfer from them to other persons of their functions in relation to the new procedures.

(7) The regulations may for the purposes mentioned above—

    (a) modify or exclude any provision of any enactment or instrument, or any rule of law;

    (b) apply, with such modifications as may be appropriate, the provisions of any enactment or instrument (including provisions creating criminal offences);

(c) require the payment of fees, or enable persons to require the payment of fees, of such amounts as may be specified in the regulations or determined in accordance with them;

(d) empower the Secretary of State to delegate to any person willing and able to discharge them any functions of his under the regulations.

(8) The regulations may make different provision for different cases.

(9) Regulations under this section shall be made by statutory instrument; and no such regulations shall be made unless a draft of the instrument has been laid before and approved by resolution of each House of Parliament.

Part X: Miscellaneous and General Provisions

Miscellaneous

208.   Summary proceedings in Scotland for offences in connection with disqualification of directors

In section 21 of the [1986 c .46.] Company Directors Disqualification Act 1986 (application of provisions of the [1986 c. 45.] Insolvency Act 1986), after subsection (3) add—

"(4) For the purposes of summary proceedings in Scotland, section 431 of that Act applies to summary proceedings for an offence under section 11 or 13 of this Act as it applies to summary proceedings for an offence under Parts I to VII of that Act." .

209.   Prosecutions in connection with insider dealing

In section 8 of the [1985 c. 8.] Company Securities (Insider Dealing) Act 1985 (punishment of contraventions), in subsection (2) (institution of proceedings in England and Wales), for "by the Secretary of State or by, or with the consent of, the Director of Public Prosecutions" substitute "by, or with the consent of, the Secretary of State or the Director of Public Prosecutions".

210.   Restriction of duty to supply statements of premium income

—(1) Schedule 3 to the [1975 c. 75.] Policyholders Protection Act 1975 (provisions with respect to levies on authorised insurance companies) is amended as follows.

(2) For paragraph 4 (statements of premium income to be sent to Secretary of State) substitute—

"**4.**—(1) The Secretary of State may by notice in writing require an authorised insurance company to send him a statement of—

(a) any income of the company for the year preceding that in which the notice is received by the company which is income liable to the general business levy, and

(b) any income of the company for that year which is income liable to the long term business levy.

(2) An authorised insurance company which receives a notice under this paragraph shall send the statement required by the notice to the Secretary of State within three months of receiving the notice.

(3) Where an authorised insurance company is required under this paragraph to send a statement to the Secretary of State in respect of income of both descriptions mentioned in sub-paragraph (1)(a) and (b) above it shall send a separate statement in respect of income of each description."

(3) In paragraph 5(3) (application of provisions of the [1982 c. 50.] Insurance Companies Act 1982 to failure to meet obligation imposed by paragraph 4) for "the obligation imposed on an insurance company by paragraph 4" substitute "an obligation imposed on an insurance company under paragraph 4".

(4) In paragraph 6 (declaration and enforcement of levies) omit sub-paragraph (4) (provision about notices).

(5) After paragraph 7 insert—

"*Notices under paragraphs 4 and 6*

8. A notice under paragraph 4 or 6 above may be sent by post, and a letter containing such a notice shall be deemed to be properly addressed if it is addressed to the insurance company to which it is sent at its last known place of business in the United Kingdom.

211. Building societies: miscellaneous amendments

—(1) In section 104 of the [1986 c. 53.] Building Societies Act 1986 (power to assimilate law relating to building societies and law relating to companies), in subsection (2) (relevant provisions of that Act), omit the word "and" before paragraph (d) and after that paragraph add—

"; and

(e) section 110 (provisions exempting officers and auditors from liability)." .

(2) In Schedule 15 to the Building Societies Act 1986 (application of companies winding-up legislation)—

    (a) in paragraph 1(a) (provisions of [1986 c. 45.] Insolvency Act 1986 applied) for "and XII" substitute ", XII and XIII";

    (b) in paragraph 3(2)(b) (adaptations: references to be omitted), omit ", a shadow director".

(3) In the [1986 c. 46.] Company Directors Disqualification Act 1986, after section 22 insert—

"Application of Act to building societies.

22A.—(1) This Act applies to building societies as it applies to companies.

(2) References in this Act to a company, or to a director or an officer of a company include, respectively, references to a building society within the meaning of the Building Societies Act 1986 or to a director or officer, within the meaning of that Act, of a building society.

(3) In relation to a building society the definition of "shadow director" in section 22(5) applies with the substitution of "building society" for "company".

(4) In the application of Schedule 1 to the directors of a building society, references to provisions of the Insolvency Act or the Companies Act include references to the corresponding provisions of the Building Societies Act 1986."

General Provisions

212. Repeals

The enactments mentioned in Schedule 24 are repealed to the extent specified there.

213. Provisions extending to Northern Ireland

—(1) The provisions of this Act extend to Northern Ireland so far as they amend, or provide for the amendment of, an enactment which so extends.

(2) So far as any provision of this Act amends the [1985 c. 6.] Companies Act 1985 or the [1986 c. 45.] Insolvency Act 1986, its application to companies registered or incorporated in Northern Ireland is subject to section 745(1) of the [1985 c. 6.] Companies Act 1985 or section 441(2) of the Insolvency Act 1986, as the case may be.

(3) In Part III (investigations and powers to obtain information), sections 82 to 91, (powers exercisable to assist overseas regulatory authorities) extend to Northern Ireland.

(4) Part VI (mergers and related matters) extends to Northern Ireland.

(5) In Part VII (financial markets and insolvency) the following provisions extend to Northern Ireland—

    (a) sections 154 and 155 (introductory provisions and definition of "market contract"),

    (b) section 156 and Schedule 21 (additional requirements for recognition of investment exchange or clearing house),

    (c) sections 157, 160, 162, and 166 to 169 (provisions relating to recognised investment exchanges and clearing houses),

    (d) sections 170 to 172 (power to extend provisions to other financial markets),

    (e) section 184 (indemnity for certain acts), and

    (f) sections 185 to 191 (supplementary provisions).

(6) Part VIII (amendments of [1986 c. 60.] Financial Services Act 1986) extends to Northern Ireland.

(7) Part IX (transfer of securities) extends to Northern Ireland.

Subject to any Order made after the passing of this Act by virtue of section 3(1)(a) of the [1973 c. 36.] Northern Ireland Constitution Act 1973, the transfer of securities shall not be a transferred matter for the purposes of that Act but shall for the purposes of section 3(2) be treated as specified in Schedule 3 to that Act.

(8) In Part X (miscellaneous and general provisions), this section and sections 214 to 216 (general provisions) extend to Northern Ireland.

(9) Except as mentioned above, the provisions of this Act do not extend to Northern Ireland.

214. Making of corresponding provision for Northern Ireland

—(1) An Order in Council under paragraph 1(1)(b) of Schedule 1 to the [1974 c. 28.] Northern Ireland Act 1974 (legislation for Northern Ireland in the interim period) which contains a statement that it is only made for purposes corresponding to the purposes of provisions of this Act to which this section applies—

    (a) shall not be subject to paragraph 1(4) and (5) of that Schedule (affirmative resolution of both Houses of Parliament), but

    (b) shall be subject to annulment in pursuance of a resolution of either House of Parliament.

(2) The provisions of this Act to which this section applies are—

(a) Parts I to V, and

(b) Part VII, except sections 156, 157, 169 and Schedule 21.

215. Commencement and transitional provisions

—(1) The following provisions of this Act come into force on Royal Assent—

(a) in Part V (amendments of company law), section 141 (application to declare dissolution of company void);

(b) in Part VI (mergers)—

(i) sections 147 to 150, and

(ii) paragraphs 2 to 12, 14 to 16, 18 to 20, 22 to 25 of Schedule 20, and section 153 so far as relating to those paragraphs;

(c) in Part VIII (amendments of the [1986 c. 60.] Financial Services Act 1986), section 202 (offers of short-dated debentures);

(d) in Part X (miscellaneous and general provisions), the repeals made by Schedule 24 in sections 71, 74, 88 and 89 of, and Schedule 9 to, the [1973 c. 41.] Fair Trading Act 1973, and section 212 so far as relating to those repeals.

(2) The other provisions of this Act come into force on such day as the Secretary of State may appoint by order made by statutory instrument; and different days may be appointed for different provisions and different purposes.

(3) An order bringing into force any provision may contain such transitional provisions and savings as appear to the Secretary of State to be necessary or expedient.

(4) The Secretary of State may also by order under this section amend any enactment which refers to the commencement of a provision brought into force by the order so as to substitute a reference to the actual date on which it comes into force.

216. Short title

This Act may be cited as the Companies Act 1989.